4WD Tracks of the High Country

a touring guide to australia's alpine region

Boiling Billy Publications
www.boilingbilly.com.au

4WD Tracks of the High Country
is published by
Boiling Billy Publications
Locked Bag 1
Wyndham NSW 2550
Ph/Fax: 02/6494 2727
E-mail: info@boilingbilly.com.au
Web: www.boilingbilly.com.au

designed and typeset in-house by
Boiling Billy Publications

printed in Australia for the publisher by
Southwood Press Pty Ltd
76-82 Chapel St, Marrickville, NSW, 2204

This First Edition August 2001
Reprinted with minor amendments 2003

ISBN 1 876296 15 1

If you come across any shortcomings in this book please write and let us know so we can update in subsequent editions.

Cover photographs:

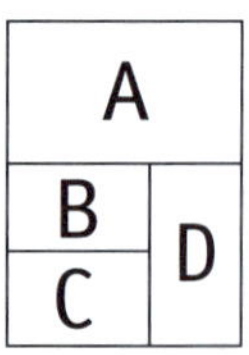

A: Mt Wellington Track near the summit
B: Dimmick Lookout on Howitt Road
C: Craig's Hut on Clear Hills
D: Snow gum on Davies Plain

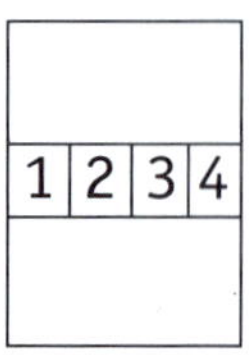

1: Summer wildflowers on Mt Stirling
2: Camping at Horseyard Flat on the Moroka River
3: Davies Plain Hut
4: Looking towards the western fall of the Main Range from Geehi

CONTENTS

THE HIGH COUNTRY

FOUR-WHEEL DRIVE TREKS IN THE VICTORIAN HIGH COUNTRY

FOUR-WHEEL DRIVE TREKS IN THE NEW SOUTH WALES HIGH COUNTRY

ABOUT THE AUTHORS

Craig Lewis and Cathy Savage established Boiling Billy Publications in 1995 with the aim to produce accurate and up-to-date guidebooks for people who love exploring the wild and remote places of Australia. Both have, along with their teenage son Ryan and red kelpie Kelly, travelled extensively throughout Australia on writing assignments and have experienced the very best that is on offer across this vast country.

Apart from this comprehensive and exciting new book on Australia's High Country, they have also researched and written numerous newspaper and magazine travel articles. This new title is their ninth guidebook on four-wheel drive touring. They have also compiled a very successful series of camping guides that will soon encompass all states of Australia.

When not on the road travelling they throw down their swag on their secluded New South Wales Far South Coast property at the foothills of the Great Dividing Range, inland from the seaside village of Bermagui.

Their website is at www.boilingbilly.com.au

INTRODUCTION

The Australian High Country, which comprises both the Victorian and New South Wales Alpine Areas offers some of the best four-wheel drive touring in Australia. In this detailed guide we have assembled twenty of the best touring destinations in this region, taking in the area's renowned features—delightful mountain scenery, wonderful camping and fishing opportunities as well as the High Country's unique history and folklore.

The opportunity to research and compile this book allowed us the chance to revisit many of the well known and much touted destinations in the Alps—places we had been keen to return to for a number of years. The fabled Wonnangatta Valley was a 'must see', the much photographed Craig's Hut on Clear Hills and the picturesque Talbotville area tucked away beside the Crooked River were some of the areas we had longed to revisit—and we were not disappointed. Other places that seemed appealing where merely names on maps—new places that we were eager to explore and uncover their history.

Whilst compiling this book our main focus was to introduce four-wheel drivers to some of the vast touring opportunities that exist throughout the High Country. This is by no means a complete collection of all the possible treks scattered throughout the High Country—we will include more High Country treks in future editions of this guide.

Please remember that the emphasis on four-wheel drive touring is to have fun, and as such, the majority of the treks detailed will provide enjoyable, and at times, challenging four-wheel driving for both individuals and families wishing to explore this great area. If tackled with care and with regards to the weather conditions, the treks in this guide can be confidently undertaken by competent drivers travelling in high clearance four-wheel drive vehicles carrying suitable recovery gear.

Although you may have the urge to jump in feet first and see everything in a day, take your time and enjoy the journey. Remember – half the fun of any four-wheel drive trip is not the final destination, but in the journey itself! If you are new to four-wheel driving then try out one or two of the easier trips first. As your skills increase you can move onto some of the more challenging treks.

You will find the treks in this guide have been arranged in a 'hub' type formation, with a number of treks radiating from a town or village in a particular area. We designed the guide this way so on your visits to the High Country you can fully explore each area by following treks from the hub. It is possible to use each hub as a base for accommodation (if you choose not to camp), fuel and supplies.

In addition to the hub formation, a number of the treks can be linked together, providing a 'Grand Tour' of the High Country. By stringing these treks together it is possible to travel from either Mansfield or Licola in Victoria to the outskirts of Canberra, or vice versa, using four-wheel drive tracks and gravel roads while traversing only a small section of bitumen.

And finally...we hope that you too enjoy the treks in this book. We had a heap of fun, along with the odd adventure or two, while exploring Australia's magical High Country.

Puen Buen, New South Wales, 2001

HOW TO USE THIS GUIDE

The twenty treks in this book have been designed in a user-friendly step by step format for adventurers wishing to get 'off the beaten track' and explore the best of the Australian High Country.

To help make it easier to plan your adventure each trek has a **fast facts box** that contains the essential information you need to know about each trek. Use this as a quick reference when planning your trip and remember, always contact the land manager listed to check on track conditions before you leave home. Each trek also has detailed information on the **degree of difficulty** of the route, **permit requirements and restrictions, areas available for camping** and a listing of **recommended maps** that are essential for you to take with you.

In addition, each trek is accompanied by a '**mud map**'. These sketch maps provide a convenient overview of the route traversed on each trek and contain only those features required for orientation of the route. It is highly recommended (we consider essential) that the mud maps in this book be used in conjunction with the appropriate cartographic maps that are listed in the recommended maps section of each trek. Having a detailed map of the area you are travelling through gives a greater understanding of the terrain as well as peace of mind in knowing where you are at any given time.

Trek Standard

The trek standard or ratings are intended as a guide only and will vary depending on the driver's experience, vehicle type, weather conditions and track maintenance. Generally, we base our ratings on the route being traversed during dry weather, the driver having only limited four-wheel drive experience or having completed a four-wheel drive driver training course and is travelling in a standard high clearance four-wheel drive vehicle such as a Toyota Landcruiser, Nissan Patrol or similar.

However, we recommend for travelling the treks in this guide that as a minimum you fit *all terrain* or better still, *mud terrain* type tyres. The *highway terrain* type tyres may not provide adequate enough traction on the numerous steep and muddy track surfaces that are often encountered in the High Country. We highly recommend any of the Cooper range of 4WD tyres.

Also, on all your four-wheel drive treks a basic vehicle recovery kit consisting of a snatch strap with bow shackles, axe and a shovel should always be carried.

We do not recommend towing trailers on the treks detailed in this guide.

Below is a description of the degree of difficulty and trek ratings that are used throughout this guide.

Easy — The route notes traverse maintained gravel or formed dirt roads and tracks. Water crossings (if any) are mostly bridges and/or concrete causeways. Generally 2WD or high range 4WD in wet weather. Ideal for first timers.

Easy/Medium — A mix of gravel and formed natural earth roads/tracks in good to fair condition with shallow water crossings. High range 4WD required in wet weather.

Medium — Natural earth surface with some rough sections. Some moderate to steep grades encountered. Water crossings may require care at high water. Some low range 4WD.

Medium/Hard — Natural earth surface with rough sections. Steep grades where careful wheel placement is required. Water crossings will require care. Moderate use of low range 4WD.

Hard — Natural earth surface with numerous rough sections. Deep mud/water holes and/or erosion/wash-aways and/or rock ledges. Steep grades where careful wheel placement is required. Water crossings will require care. Repeated use of low range 4WD. Best tackled by experienced drivers.

Route Notes Legend

The **route notes** provide specific directions for following the trek, as well as highlighting points of interest along the route.

Outward Reading

▼ 38.5 (0.7)
SP Tunnel Bend on left. A 50m walk leads to tunnel through hill. Notes CSA.

▲ *90.9 (1.1)*
Tunnel Bend on left. CSA.

Return Reading

Route note readings in this guide are presented with the outward readings indicated by the arrow pointing downwards ▼ and text in standard type and the return readings having the arrow pointing from the bottom of the page to the top ▲ with the text in *italics*. The first reading ie. 38.5 is the accumulated kilometres travelled from the beginning of the trek. The reading in brackets ie. (0.7) is the intermediate distance between the previous reading and the current reading.

Please Note: Due to the rolling variation of wheels and tyres from vehicle to vehicle you may find some route note readings don't correspond with your vehicle's trip meter. You will obtain the most accuracy from the notes by resetting your trip meter at each intermediate reading. By doing this any variations in distance will not be compounded over the whole trek.

It is highly recommended that these route notes be used as a guide in conjunction with the recommended maps.

Route Note Abbreviations

Below is a listing of abbreviations for instructions used in the route notes.

TL	Turn Left	CSA	Continue Straight Ahead
TR	Turn Right	PSA	Proceed Straight Ahead
KL	Keep Left	SP	Signpost
KR	Keep Right	SO	Straight On
VL	Veer Left	LAF	Leave As Found
VR	Veer Right		

Map Legend

Camp Site	Picnic Area	Toilets	Caravan Access/Park
Scenic Point	Electric/Gas BBQ	Walking Trails	Information
Drinking Water	Store	Fuel	Hotel
Fishing	Seasonal Closure Gate		

MAPS AND GPS

Maps and Guides

We cannot stress enough the importance of carrying appropriate maps with you on your travels throughout the High Country. Not only will this give you piece of mind in being able to plot your location while travelling, but will also aid you if for some reason you come across a track that is impassable or encounter a vehicle problem or a medical emergency. You can then consult your maps and locate the most direct route to gain assistance.

There are a number of excellent maps that cover the High Country ranging from those that provide an overview of the entire region such as *Hema Maps High Country - Victoria* through to area specific maps such as those produced by *Brookes Bush Maps - Victoria*, *Paoletti Maps* and *Rooftop Mapping Services*. These specialist maps are produced in differing scales and show similar features to topographic maps but often show additional visitor information such as camp sites, walking tracks, lookouts etc.

The High Country is also completely covered by topographic maps from Vicmap, LPI (NSW) and Auslig. Vicmap and LPI topos are produced in 1:25 000 scale for the majority of the alpine region as well as in 1:50 000 scale. Auslig produces maps in 1:100 000 scale for the whole of the High Country.

The Country Fire Authority produces the *North-East Rural Directory-Regions 23 and 24*—a book of 1:100 000 scale topographic maps covering the north-east Victorian High Country. Contact the CFA Wangaratta office on 03/5721 4122 for details.

Each trek in this guide has a listing of recommended maps that we advise you carry with you on your trip. All of these maps are available from specialist map retailers (see *Useful Contacts* at the back of this guide) and at selected stockists in and around the High Country region.

There are some very informative guidebooks available dealing with both the natural and cultural aspects of the High Country. It is highly recommended that you obtain at least one guidebook to the plants and animals of this region to take with you on your travels (See *Further Reading* on page 191).

Global Positioning System (GPS)

The Global Positioning System (GPS) is a satellite based navigation system widely used for navigation, positioning, surveying and associated applications. A GPS unit establishes its position by calculating the distance from four or more of the 24 satellites that orbit the earth. GPS readings are accessible 24 hours a day from anywhere in the world in all types of weather. The accuracy of GPS receivers, provided the correct datum is used, is usually within 30 metres and often within 10 metres. Garmin manufacture a range of GPS receivers and are highly recommended for their accuracy and ease of use.

There are a number of excellent publications available dealing with navigation, map reading and using GPS and these are worthwhile seeking out to gain further knowledge in these areas.

Notes for GPS Users

The GPS *waypoints* (Latitude and Longitude) listed in the route notes in this guide can be utilised by those with GPS units and/or topographic maps as an additional means of navigating each trek.

All the GPS waypoints in the route notes were acquired during field research using a Garmin GPS II Plus and have been taken using WGS 84 map datum. This is usually the default datum on most GPS units, however it is best to check your unit. By using the nominated map datum a greater degree of accuracy between the waypoints in the route notes and field position may be obtained.

In addition to the GPS waypoints, UTM (*Universal Transverse Mercator*) readings are also given. These readings are as Eastings and Northings and are used to provide grid references on topographic maps.

It is essential that a compass is also included as part of your navigation kit.

VEHICLE PREPARATION AND EQUIPMENT

On any trip to the High Country, whether it be a leisurely day trip, weekend adventure or multi day expedition there are always a number of basic preparations you should undertake before venturing off on your trip. In addition, there is some basic equipment you should always carry in your vehicle. Remember, the longer and more remote your journey, the higher the level of preparation.

From our experience, the items listed below should be considered as a minimum for safe and enjoyable four-wheel drive touring.

Before you leave home always check your vehicle's:

- Oil levels
- Coolant levels
- Tyre pressures

On any four-wheel drive trip always carry in your vehicle:

- Basic recovery gear (snatch strap, bow shackles, axe, shovel, gloves)
- Basic tool kit (sockets, spanners, pliers, screwdrivers, hammer, etc)
- Workshop manual for your make and model of vehicle
- Winch (hand operated or power)
- 10 litres of water
- First aid kit
- Engine Oil
- Drive belts
- Jumper leads
- Top and bottom radiator hoses
- Heater hoses
- Compass
- Cigarette lighter and fire lighters
- Fuel filter
- WD40 or similar
- Torch and/or 12 volt fluoro light
- Electrical tape
- Poly-tarp
- Tyre pressure gauge
- Fire extinguisher
- Appropriate maps
- Spare fuses
- Air compressor
- Drag chain
- Some emergency food and drink in case of delays

In addition to the above you could also consider:

- UHF radio
- Chainsaw
- GPS
- Power jack (Bull Bag)
- Jack plate (wooden jack base)
- Puncture repair kit and tyre changing equipment

Below is how we have our 1998 Hilux 3.0 litre diesel dual cab setup for 4WD touring.

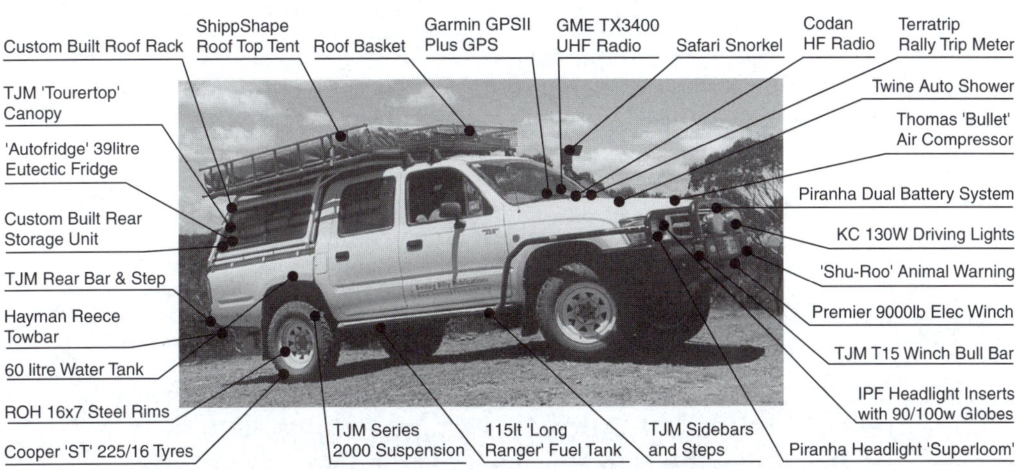

4WD 2R

LOOKING AFTER THE HIGH COUNTRY

Heading off into the High Country on a four-wheel drive and camping holiday whether for a day, or a week comes with a certain level of responsibility. When you are out and about exploring and four-wheel drive touring it's important to be environmentally conscious.

As well as preparing your vehicle and equipment before heading into the High Country we advise you to always check with the land managers, local council or police listed in the fast facts box at the beginning of each chapter on current road and access conditions. This is best done a couple of days or so before your planned departure date so any changes can be incorporated into your itinerary.

If there has been an extended period of wet weather then plan your escape for another time. Remember to stay on formed tracks or if the track is wet use an alternative route if possible. Many of the routes detailed in this guide may become impassable and dangerous during these times. Obey road signs and respect stock and private property. Be well prepared in case of a break down or hold-up from wet weather by always carrying some extra food and water. Please, let common sense prevail. We can all do our bit looking after the High Country by treading lightly on public and private land.

If you are new to four-wheel driving a four-wheel drive driver training course is a good way to gain the skills needed to traverse the routes detailed in this guide, as well as familiarise yourself with the capabilities of your vehicle. There are a number of professional driver training companies that run very comprehensive courses and we recommend any one of these to you. Most four-wheel drive clubs also operate a driver training program.

Minimal Impact 4WD Touring

- *Stay on the track* - only drive on roads open to the public and never 'bush bash'. Please respect private property and the landowner's instructions.
- *Obey track closures* - if a road or track is closed it should not be used.
- *Drive Softly* - avoid tracks when they are wet and muddy. By minimising track damage you can also help reduce erosion and costly road repairs.
- *Use an alternative route* - bypass wet areas or wait until they dry out. This is one good reason why maps are essential items to take on your travels.
- *Avoid wheel spin* - wheel ruts become channels that cause erosion.
- *Creek crossings* - use existing entry and exit points if there are no culverts or bridges. Always check the water depth first and check for hidden obstacles such as large rocks and logs.
- *Winching* - if you need to winch use a tree trunk protector or ground anchors. Always carry a range of recovery gear on your trips.

THE HIGH COUNTRY

Snow gum on Mt St Bernard

VISITING THE HIGH COUNTRY

Australia's alpine region, which in broad terms is considered to be the part of the Great Dividing Range that stretches from north of Melbourne to the outskirts of Canberra, is the result of huge uplifts of the earth's surface that occurred between 50-60 million years ago. However, eons of rain, wind, snow and ice have had a marked effect on this once massive mountain range, having weathered this ancient landscape to world standards as 'vertically challenged'.

Although low in altitude—in fact, the country's highest peak, Mt Kosciuszko, which stands at 2228 metres is around one quarter the height of Mt Everest—Australia's alpine region is a place of extremes.

When to Visit

The majority of summertime visitors to the High Country visit over the December/January holiday break, at Easter and if prepared for cooler weather, the June Long Weekend. At these times popular destinations such as the Howqua Hills, Wonnangatta Valley and Davies Plain are buzzing with people.

To experience the High Country without the crowds it is best to plan your visit outside these peak holiday periods such as early to mid December, February/March and the weeks following Easter. Our preferred time to visit is during late February and March when the often erratic High Country weather pattern seems to be at its most stable with clear blue skies and warm, sunny days with mild nights.

Seasonal Track Closures

Most of the treks detailed in this guide are subject to **seasonal closures** which are generally in place in Victoria from the Thursday after the Queen's Birthday Long Weekend in June to the weekend following the Melbourne Cup in November. These restrictions can, and often are extended in some areas due to unstable track conditions from winter snow and rain, the need for track clearing and maintenance etc.

In New South Wales similar restrictions apply and these too can vary from time to time.

To check on seasonal track closures contact the land managers listed in the *Further Information* section of eack trek or for closures in Victoria visit the Treadlightly Victoria website at **www.treadvic.org.au** or the Parks Victoria website at **www.parkweb.vic.gov.au**

Climate

The temperatures in the more elevated areas of the High Country can be up to 10°C or more lower than those in the foothills and valleys below—year round. So when the valley's are baking in temperatures into the high 30°s during Australia's long hot summers those fortunate enough to be up in the High Country at these times will find the temperatures much more pleasant.

This aside, the weather in the High Country is extremely changeable and visitors should be prepared for all seasons in one day. The alpine region's unpredictable weather pattern is the result of the High Country acting as a barrier to the prevailing weather, forcing moisture bearing clouds to rise and in doing so drop their cargo as rain, sleet, mist or snow—depending on the temperature. It's not uncommon to have a sudden blast of blizzard-like conditions with driving rain, icy gale-force winds and even snow falls effecting parts of the High Country during the middle of summer!

Fire Danger Periods

Although the temperatures in the High Country are generally milder than the lowlands, this does not exclude the area from the potential threat of bushfires. Over the last decade bushfires have razed large areas of Victoria's alpine region, with a savage fire burning a large part of the Wellington River/ Moroka Road area in recent times.

When planning a visit to the High Country over the summer bushfire danger period always keep a check on fire danger information for days of total fire ban. Even on days of high fire danger it is more prudent to use a gas/fuel stove for cooking rather than have an open fire—especially when it's windy.

Camping in the High Country

There are literally hundreds of delightful camp sites scattered throughout the High Country where you can pitch your tent or roll out a swag. Some sites are best suited for an overnight stay whilst others can be best appreciated as a base camp while exploring a particular region of the mountains.

Camp sites fall into two categories—established areas with facilities and bush camp sites. Established camp sites throughout the High Country usually, but not always, have basic facilities such as fireplaces and pit toilets and occasionally picnic tables. Bush camp sites are usually void of any facilities so you will need to be fully prepared.

No special camping equipment is needed for sojourns to the High Country as long as your current gear, or new gear if you're setting up, is waterproof and reliable. Always take along a gas or liquid fuel stove for cooking during wet weather so as not to be inconvenienced when a cooking fire is impracticable. Be sure to pack some warm clothes, especially for night when even summertime temperatures can drop dramatically. Wet weather gear is also recommended.

For a complete guide to camp sites along with facilities and activities throughout the High Country see *Camping Guide to Victoria* and *Camping Guide to New South Wales*, published by Boiling Billy Publications.

Walking in the High Country

Bushwalking is a popular activity throughout the High Country with numerous marked walking trails ranging from short easy strolls taking around thirty minutes to multi week expeditions crisscrossing the alpine region. Many of the areas visited in this guide give access to these walking tracks which often radiate from camping and picnic areas and lookouts. Details of these walks along with relevant brochures are given in the appropriate chapter.

For the more adventurous there are three major long distance walking tracks snaking their way through the Alps.

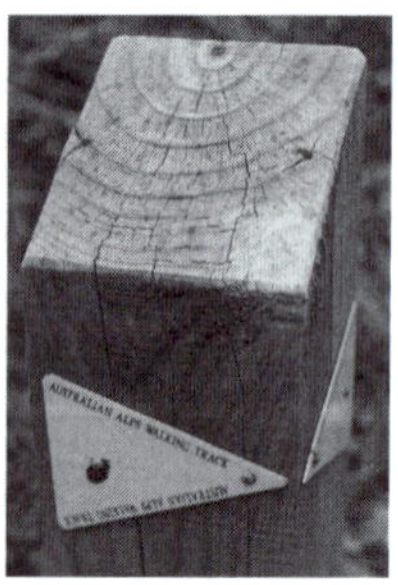

Australian Alps Walking Track — runs from Walhalla in Victoria to just outside Canberra in New South Wales. This 680km walking track takes in the highest peaks of the Alps, covering a variety of terrain from lofty mountains to snow plains to delightful river valleys. The track can be walked in sections ranging from day walks to week long adventures.

The Bicentennial National Trail — this 5300km route stretches from Cooktown in Queensland to Healesville in Victoria. Mainly used by horse riders, the trail is increasing in popularity with walkers and mountain bikers. A set of 12 guidebooks cover the entire trail with guides 11 and 12 detailing the High Country.

McMillans Walking Track — named in recognition of explorer Angus McMillan who cut bridle tracks to join a number of remote gold mining areas throughout the High Country. The present day route commences at Omeo, then onto the Dargo River before crossing Dargo High Plains and descending to Talbotville. The route concludes at Woods Point. The walk is about 200km and takes around two weeks to walk its entire length. It can also be walked in stages.

Fishing in the High Country

The High Country is a fisherfolks paradise with many of the lakes, rivers and streams in the Alps holding stocks of both rainbow and brown trout.

Both New South Wales and Victoria have regulations regarding trout fishing. There is a 'closed' season over the winter months effecting rivers and streams and this usually extends from just after the Queen's Birthday long weekend to the long weekend in October each year. Bag limits also apply.

In addition, anglers over 16 years of age may require a recreational fishing permit and these are widely available from retailers throughout the High Country. Further information on permits and regulations is available from each state's fisheries department.

HIGH COUNTRY VEGETATION

Although you will come across numerous species of animals while visiting the High Country, it is the area's unique vegetation that is more readily noticable. There are roughly 1400 different plant types growing in Australia's High Country, with a number of these native to this area. Although some plant types grow at varying altitudes, most can be grouped into identifiable communities which are found in their favoured aspect and altitude.

Below is a brief description of each of the various vegetation zones found throughout the alps:

Lowland Forests — found up to around 800 metres above sea level. Much of this area has been cleared for agricultural uses since European settlement with mostly remnant forest sections remaining. Tree types that characterise this area include red gums, box and stringy-barks in the more open areas with manna, or ribbon gums, mountain swamp gums, peppermints and silver wattle growing in the more moist sites near rivers. You'll find a good example of this vegetation zone along the Wellington River between Licola and the Wellington River Camping Area.

Wet and Dry Mountain Forests — higher up the slopes to around 1500 metres above sea level where rainfall is higher and evaporation is lower you find tall, open forests of mixed eucalypts that are taller and more dense, and which grow closer together than in the Lowland Forests. Here grows blue gums, peppermints and manna gums and in certain areas towering brown barrel. The understorey usually consists of ferns and small trees. At the higher end of this zone and just below the Subalpine Zone grows the magnificent alpine ash, or woolly butt. Usually growing in pure stands of like size trees, the prized alpine ash is the tallest eucalypt of the High Country. Mountain ash, another massive eucalypt, can be found growing in Victorian wet mountain forests just below the alpine ash zone. These types of forest are found throughout much of the High Country with good examples around the Howqua Hills/ The Bluff area.

Subalpine Zone — the dominant tree type of this zone is the snow gum. These are the only trees that will tolerate temperatures at this altitude where snow may cover the ground for up to four months of the year. The understorey plants of this zone are low growing shrubs, herbs and grasses. Examples of this zone are around Davies High Plain and Mt St Bernard.

Alpine Zone — in general terms the Alpine Zone is the area that exists above the treeline and is usually where the mean summer temperature is about 10°C. This zone is often snow covered for four months of the year or longer and is characterised by heath land, grassland and herb fields with bare, rocky pavements such as found on the summits of Mt Stirling and Mt Wellington.

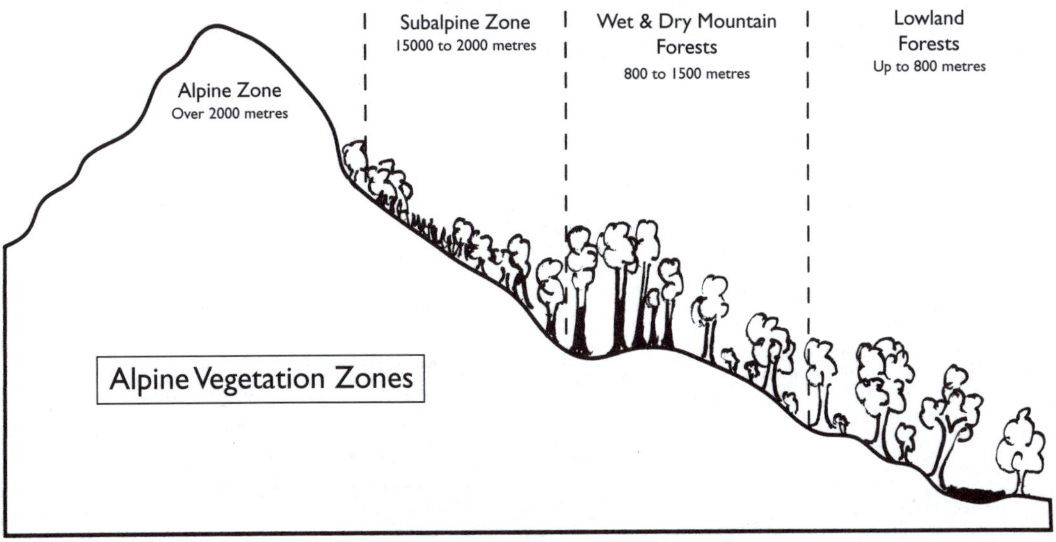

ABORIGINAL OCCUPATION

For thousands of years Aboriginal people travelled hundreds of kilometres to meet in the High Country each summer. Tribes from the south-west slopes and as far as the coast and South Gippsland would come to the High Country to partake in tribal and intertribal gatherings. At these gatherings they would trade items such as possum skin rugs, ochre and greenstone, have corroborees and initiations, exchange stories and songs, have marriages and settle arguments.

During their stay at their 'summer camps' the aborigines feasted on bogong moths that were found in abundance in the rock crevasses in the higher peaks. These moths, which were easily collected were roasted in a fire, the wings removed and eaten. As a food bogong moths are high in protien and fat and are said to taste like walnut.

The demise of Aboriginal High Country culture started in the late 1820s when Europeans started moving into the High Country, bringing with them disease and guns, that within 25 years had wiped out whole tribes. By 1914 the aboriginal tribes that had gathered in the High Country for 200 generations were extinct.

EUROPEAN DISCOVERY AND EXPLORATION

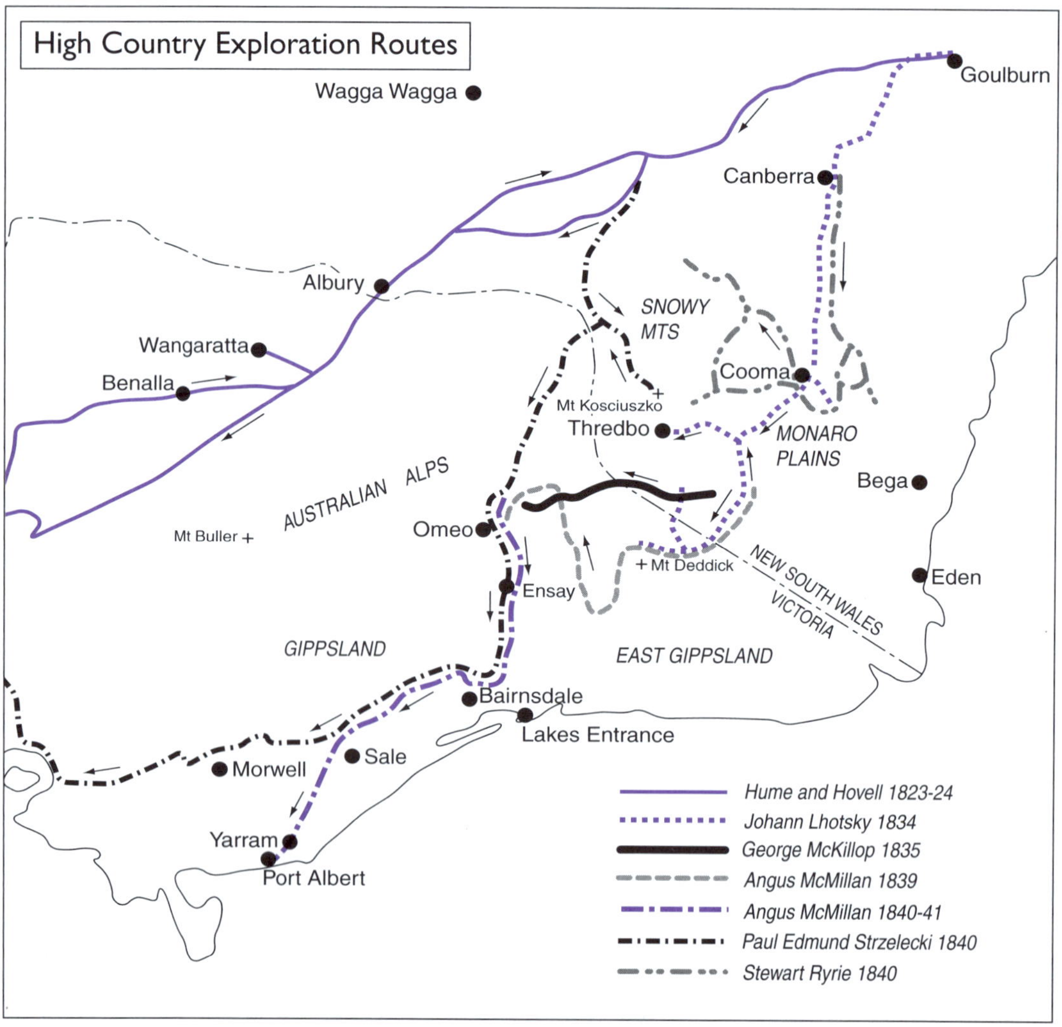

Hume and Hovell Expedition 1824-25

Hamilton Hume and William Hinton Hovell were two of the first Europeans to see the Snowy Mountains during their 1824-25 expedition.

By the 1820s the population of the NSW colony had been steadily growing. The Goulburn Plains was the furthest settlement had penetrated to the south and the question of what lay between here and Bass Strait was one that the new Governor, Sir Thomas Brisbane wanted an answer to.

William Hovell

After discussions with property owner and successful trader, Alexander Berry, it was decided that an expedition with a skilled bushman as leader be sent out to discover the area. Berry, having previously used Hamilton Hume's expertise to find new land suggested Hume as the leader of the expedition. Hume then put forward a proposal for an exploring party to travel from Lake George to Bass Strait along with detailed information of supplies, equipment and animals required for the journey. However, Governor Brisbane lost interest in the project. The Surveyor General John Oxley also felt this expedition would be a waste of money and time.

Hume, after this set back, decided he would proceed with the expedition at his own expense. At about this time William Hovell heard of the expedition and wanted to be involved. Hovell made contact with Alexander Berry who then introduced the two men. Although they were from different worlds, their enthusiasm for exploring made them oblivious of the other's differences.

On October 2, 1824 the party gathered at Hume's father's property at Appin and set out in the afternoon of Sunday October 3, 1824. With Hume and Hovell were six convicts; Claude Bossawa, Henry Angel and James Fitzpatrick who were assigned to Hume, and Samuel Bollard and Ben Smith assigned to Hovell. Hume's uncle sent a convict Thomas Boyd, who was allocated to Hovell.

After crossing the Nepean River the party travelled 123 miles (198km) to reach the furthest point of settlement on October 13 near Goulburn. From this point their journey was to be of exploration. They finally reached the Murrumbidgee River on October 19, however as the river was quite high they had to wait for the water to drop. By October 22 there had been no drop in the river level so a decision was made to cross by making one of their carts into a punt.

Hamilton Hume

Once across the Murrumbidgee River the party were caught in mountainous country. By November 1 the daytime temperature was beginning to rise and the party had started to stop in the middle of the day to rest. By now the mountain ranges were forcing the party to travel further west and on November 6 they arrived at the site of present day Tumbarumba.

Two days later, on November 8 the party sighted a magnificent mountain range. Some of the peaks were covered in snow and as the sun shone on the mountains it gave them a brilliant appearance. By reckoning, the mountains would have been the western faces of Mount Townsend, Mount Carruthers, Sentinel Peak and part of Mount Twynam. They referred to these mountains as the South Australian Alps, thinking that these would be the same mountain ranges that Major Ovens and Captain Currie had seen during their 1823 expedition into the Monaro district.

On November 16, at the site of today's Albury, the group unexpectedly came across a river which Hovell recorded as Humes River. It was only six years later, in 1930, that the river's name was changed by Sturt to the Murray River after Sir George Murray, Secretary for the colonies.

The party crossed this river near today's Hume Weir, then continued in a south-westerly direction, crossing the Mitta Mitta and Kiewa Rivers in the following days.

On November 24 they crossed the Ovens River, which they named after Major John Ovens and on the 25th saw a buffalo shaped, snow capped mountain which was aptly named Mount Buffalo. By this time the exhausted party were on short rations as most of their pork had spoiled and their kangaroo dogs, which were in bad condition, were unable to catch any game.

The next few days proved to be extremely frustrating for the party, battling thick bush and ranges with broken stones. Finally by December 14 the country improved and they eventually reached the coastline on December 16, thinking they were at Western Port. Actually, they were at Corio Bay on Port Phillip. This error was due to Hovell's incorrect calculations from the very beginning of the expedition, each incorrect calculation compounding on the next. Although Hovell had calculated the latitude correctly for Corio Bay, he gave the longitude at a position that was more than 80km from where they stood.

After resting for two days the group began their return trip on December 18, arriving back at Hume's home on January 18, 1825—sixteen weeks after beginning their journey.

In later years Hume served under Charles Sturt on his 1828-29 Darling River expedition. After this he retired from exploring and moved to the Yass district with his wife where he became an influential landowner. Hamilton Hume died at Cooma cottage in 1873 and is buried in the Yass Cemetery.

William Hovell returned to his Narellan property before moving to Goulburn where he was appointed Commissioner for Crown Lands in 1847. He died in Sydney on November 9, 1875 and is buried in the old St Saviours Cemetery at Goulburn.

Johann Lhotsky 1834

At the age of 34, Dr Johann Lhotsky decided that he would penetrate the heart of the Australian Alps. Although a trained botanist and physician, Lhotsky was also an amateur explorer.

In early January 1834, Lhotsky left Sydney with four servants along with a horse and cart that carried special paper for drying specimens and insect needles. Lhotsky, not being aware of the rural conditions he would be travelling through assumed there would be an abundance of food and water available from English style inns along the way. He was to learn his mistake early, as the so-called Great South Road on Mitchell's maps ended at Liverpool and there were no public houses between Marulan and Goulburn. Lhotsky was fortunate that the 'lower classes' in huts and houses along the way welcomed his small party and provided them with provisions.

The party reached Robert Campbell's station 'Duntroon' on January 29. Campbell was one of the first settlers in the Canberra region and Lhotsky was able to present letters of introduction and to make preparation for his mountain journey.

Lhotsky's party left Duntroon on February 4 to head south to the Monaro Plains. What lay beyond was virtually unknown territory.

After resting a few days beside the Murrumbidgee River, Lhotsky and his men had a steady climb to reach the site of today's Cooma on February 16. From here they continued south-west and on February 24 reached the site of where Delegate now stands. The next day Lhotsky came upon a river of icy water flowing swiftly southwards towards the sea which we now know as the Snowy River. This discovery was later disputed.

The expeditions furthest point was reached on March 4 near the site of today's Thredbo Village. It was here that the explorer wrote: "The waterpots were covered with ice an inch thick. It was impossible to go farther." He did however see to the south-south-west, from the highest point, an extremely large plain that the natives called Omeo. Lhotsky tried to reach the plain by retracing his steps to the Snowy River, which he reached on March 9. The party then veered west to encounter Mount Deddick. However, the river here was too wide to cross. Fatigued, Lhotsky was forced to return to Sydney, taking with him a cart full of mineral specimens, dried plants, insects and animal skins.

On his return to Sydney Lhotsky's discoveries were ignored by government officials, including the Surveyor General Major Thomas Mitchell. Lhotsky was also unable to gain a scientific position with the government and he did not receive any sort of remuneration for his expedition. Lhotsky moved to Hobart in 1836.

Lhotsky was later followed by McMillan and Strzelecki to the alpine region and to this date there is still conjecture as to who was the first to climb Mount Kosciuszko. Did Lhotsky climb it before Strzelecki or not?

Angus McMillan's 1839 and 1864 Expeditions

Angus McMillan

The eventual discovery of a route through the rugged Gippsland ranges to the southern coastline was achieved by 29 year old Scot, Angus McMillan after he persuaded his employers, Currawong Station owners Captain Lachlan Macalister and James McFarlane, to let him search for new grazing land.

McMillan set off from Currawong Station on the Monaro Plains on May 28, 1839 with only a pocket compass and an old chart done by Matthew Flinders for navigation. Accompanying McMillan was an aboriginal guide Jimmy Gibber, who had been given directions from his tribal elders. It took the pair two days to reach the Snowy River after which large hills slowed their pace and the weather started to become much colder.

On the afternoon of June 4 after climbing a steep hill, they were rewarded with the splendid view of low country to the south and the shimmer of the sea. From his vantage point McMillan searched for a break in the timber which Jimmy's tribe said would lead to good grazing land. McMillan was jubilant and had visions of what the future for the land would be. His landmark was Mount McLeod, from which he envisioned the start of his next journey and from where he could make a dash for the sea. After making careful notations of his bearings McMillan and Jimmy headed north-east towards Omeo.

They arrived at McFarlane's Omeo run on June 11 where they rested for two days before returning to Currawong Station.

In August 1839 McMillan once again set out from Currawong Station, this time for Omeo. With McMillan were Matthew Macalister, nephew of Lachlan, Alan Cameron, a fellow Scot whom Macalister brought out to assist with his enterprises, and three prisoners. From Omeo the party continued south-east to the present site of Ensay where they established a station for Macalister and built a hut. The group then returned to Currawong Station to gather stock for the new station.

After driving cattle from Currawong to the new station at Ensay in early December, McMillan, along with Matthew Macalister, Alan Cameron and a prisoner Edward Bath, headed off again on December 20 looking for new pasture. However, the party returned to Ensay on Christmas Day after one of the pack horses suffered bad injuries after rolling down a hill and hitting a tree.

McMillan, along with an expanded party left Macalister's Ensay property on January 11, 1840 and headed in a south-south-west direction. This time McMillan was not taking any risk and therefore laid down the rules for the journey. Each person was given specific daily jobs and there were strict instructions as to night watches, levels of noise and daily time schedules. Accompanying him were Matthew Macalister, Alan Cameron, Edward Bath and two aborigines, Cobone Johnny—reputed King of the Omeo tribe and a young boy they nicknamed Friday.

On January 16 the party arrived at the shores of a great lake which fed to the ocean. McMillan named it Victoria after her Majesty. The party then continued to the north-west and discovered rich country that McMillan exclaimed as being well adapted for sheep and cultivation. They also came across the sites of where Maffra and Sale now stand and discovered and named the Avon, Nicholson, Mitchell, Perry, Macalister and Thomson Rivers along with Mount Wellington and the Macarthur Plains.

After numerous encounters with aborigines and with supplies running low the party turned back, reaching the site of Bruthen on January 25 and after a further seven days, to the base camp at Ensay.

When McMillan returned to Currawong Station with news of the party's discovery, Lachlan Macalister was loath to spread the news for fear of others taking up this fertile new land. However, McMillan's discovery was not kept secret for long. In May 1840 Strzelecki's party arrived in Melbourne after covering some of the same ground as McMillan, prompting people to move to Gippsland.

In March 1844 McMillan took up 16 000 acres of land at Bushy Park near Stratford.

In 1864, thirteen years after gold was first discovered the government decided to assist the industry by building a network of tracks to help with the transport of supplies and equipment, and more importantly the delivery of gold to Melbourne, as gold had become a considerable part of the economy. Baron Ferdinand von Mueller, who at the time was the Director of Botanical Gardens in Melbourne, recommended McMillan as the party leader to cut these tracks through the alpine regions.

McMillan, who was having financial problems at the time, was ecstatic that he was finally being recognised by the government for his skills. The pay from this job would assist with his farming.

Accompanied by two qualified surveyors, Short and Jones and two working hands, Cotton and Berry, McMillan and his party purchased horses, supplies and equipment in Stratford and employed additional men, including some aborigines.

With gold strikes having been made on the Crooked River and with an expected rush to follow, McMillan and his party set out to make a road to the river, starting work in March 1864. The party was separated into three groups. Work commenced at seven o'clock and finished at six thirty every day, except Sundays when McMillan insisted that everyone rest. The men spent their days cutting and hacking away at the bush along the steep and rocky tracks clearing for the roads to be cut in.

In early April McMillan's health began deteriorating due to the hard physical work and on April 9 he made a quick trip home to visit his wife and children. His wife urged him to relinquish his leadership, however he refused and returned to his party on Monday April 11.

During McMillan's absence some of the men had found a rich quartz reef and on his return the majority of them had downed tools and left to prospect their discovery. This left McMillan with only five men and having to hire an extra eight men.

The group reached the Macalister River on May 6 and by May 18 they had cleared and marked the road to Jordan. The physical effort cutting the road to Jordan had left McMillan very weak and unable to continue with the party. He stayed in camp with one of the aborigines caring for him. The party continued the work and progressed through the summer of 1864 and the autumn of 1865, although very slowly. McMillan had rejoined the party in the spring on 1864, however made regular trips home when possible.

On May 18, 1865 McMillan was cutting a road from Dargo towards Iguana Creek accompanied by a native who helped carry equipment and cook. On this day his packhorse lost its footing on some loose rocks and rolled over carrying McMillan down a steep incline. Even though his injuries were serious and he was quite shaken, McMillan, with the help of the native boy remounted his horse and they made way for Gilleo's Shanty at Iguana Creek.

On their arrival at the shanty McMillan was almost unconscious. The bar patrons ran to his aid and caught him as he fell from his horse and carried him to a bed. Whilst they were forcing some brandy down his throat, another went off to Sale to get a doctor. However, by the time the doctor arrived at the shanty McMillan was dead, having only survived for a few hours after arriving there.

The news of Angus McMillan's death travelled fast and men from Bairnsdale, Sale, Stratford, Port Albert and further afield gathered at the Club Hotel in Sale for his funeral.

By the end of 1865 some 222 miles (357km) of tracks, well defined with blazed trees, had been cut by McMillan's party from Omeo over the Dargo and Cobungra High Plains and towards Harrietville, Mount Useful and the Wellington and Moroka Rivers.

Paul Edmund de Strzelecki 1840

Polish born Strzelecki arrived in New South Wales in 1839 at the age of 42 after spending many years travelling throughout England and America. In the four short years he spent in Australia, Strzelecki became a legend in our history. His charisma was such that we was credited for discovering Gippsland in 1840, when in fact the area had actually been discovered by McMillan in 1839.

Paul Edmund Strzelecki

Strzelecki, along with James Macarthur began their journey in search of good grazing land in 1840 by heading south down the Murray Valley to the foothills of the Alps where they set up camp at the foot of what they believed to be the highest peak on the range. This was Mount Townsend. Both men climbed the peak, however, by using a clinometer, Strezlecki found that one of the peaks was in fact about 15 metres higher than the one they were on.

A few days later on March 15, Strzelecki set off to climb Australia's highest peak. After struggling through snow to reach the summit of the 2228 metre peak, Strzelecki named Australia's highest mountain after Polish patriot, Tadeusz Kosciuszko.

From the Alps they continued south-west to the Omeo Plains and then onto Ensay where they replenished their supplies. Although Strzelecki claimed that the country was 'untrodden by white man', they were in fact following a route pioneered by McMillan in 1839.

The party arrived in the four year old settlement of Melbourne on May 28, 1840. Strzelecki named the newly discovered area Gippsland, in honour of the then governor. His reports of rich fertile land soon saw settlers flocking to the new region with its lush grazing lands.

Strzelecki spent a few weeks in Melbourne before continuing onto Tasmania, from where he returned to Sydney. Strzelecki returned to England in late 1842. He died in London in October 1873, aged 76.

Alfred Howitt

Alfred William Howitt was born in England in 1830 and arrived in Australia at the age of 22 and made his way to the Victorian goldfields. Before long Howitt had become an accomplished bushman, explorer and exhibited potential as a great leader.

Alfred Howitt

In June 1861, Howitt set out from Melbourne as leader of a search party to find Burke, Wills and King, and to try to solve the riddle of the missing men. Howitt found the sole survivor of the Burke and Wills Expedition, John King living with aborigines at Cooper Creek and after feeding King and aiding his recovery, he led Howitt to Wills' shallow grave. Here Howitt recovered to expeditions journals, giving us an insight into the tragic story of Burke and Wills.

Howitt was appointed Police Magistrate and Goldfields Warden in 1863, a post he held until 1889. Howitt based himself in Omeo, Bairnsdale and Sale, travelling extensively throughout the region where he was credited with the official discovery of gold in Crooked River in 1860 when he was in charge of a government prospecting party. Having spent most of his life in Gippsland, he called the area 'my country'.

Howitt was also a distinguished explorer and scientist specialising in botany, geology and anthropology. He made many important botanical and geological observations throughout his travels in the Gippsland and alpine regions, spending over 20 years gathering information on the tribal customs and social organisations, language and mythology of the remaining aboriginals in the Gippsland area.

Alfred William Howitt died in March 1908. He was described as 'a man of simple and noble character, whose one aim was a ceaseless and tireless search for truth'.

Other High Country Explorers

Royal Navy Captain, Mark Currie is thought to have been the first white man to venture onto the northern approaches to the Australian Alps when he crossed Limestone Plain (present day Canberra) in June 1823. Squatters soon followed after hearing of Currie's reports of the extensive grazing lands of the Monaro Plains.

A group of early settlers—George McKillop, George Livingstone, James Pendergast and James MacFarlane, all who had settled on the Monaro, set out in 1835 to find a route from the Monaro Plains to the southern Gippsland coast. After numerous attempts to find a gap through the mountains to the plains that Lhotsky spoke of, the party took a more easterly route and in doing so they came across the Snowy River. From here they followed the Australian Alps before arriving at the extensive Omeo Plains, which they named Strathdownie. Here they established a large station of some 60 000 acres of fine grazing land.

Others to explore this region during the mid 1800s were mostly squatters in search of new grazing country. In 1837 Edward Buckly had pushed beyond Omeo to reach the Ensay area and in 1838 Edward Bayliss discovered good pasture at Buchan. These small runs had already been established by the time Angus McMillan began his explorations into Gippsland.

From the Monaro region graziers pushed into the northern Alps and in 1839 Terrance Murray of Yarralumla pioneered a route across the Brindabella Mountains and up onto the high plains of what is now the northern section of Kosciuszko National Park. Here he established an outstation for summer grazing which was to eventually become the Long Plain lease.

Stewart Ryrie explored the headwaters of the Murrumbidgee and Snowy Rivers in 1840.

On the western side of the Alps graziers moved into the mountains in search of summer pastures to run their stock. John Mitchell first visited the area in 1843. Stockmen James Brown, John Wells, George Gray and others pioneered routes in the Bogong Plains area and eventually established Cobungra Station in 1851. Brown and Wells made popular the route over Mt Hotham to the Ovens Valley which was used by miners heading to the Omeo fields. The two stockmen also named many of the prominent natural features on the Bogong High Plains.

During the 1850s, Government Botanist Dr Ferdinand von Mueller visited the Alps on a number of separate occasions, naming Mt Hotham as well as travelling through the upper reaches of the Goulburn River. He also collected botanical specimens on his journeys to the High Country.

It was from the 1860s through to the 1880s that much of the High Country was opened up by cattlemen and prospectors searching for riches. Even Victoria's gentleman bushranger, John Payne—alias Bogong Jack has been credited with pioneering routes across the Bogong High Plains.

4WD TREKS IN THE VICTORIAN HIGH COUNTRY

Crossing the Dargo River at Collins Flat

KEY MAP I - VICTORIA

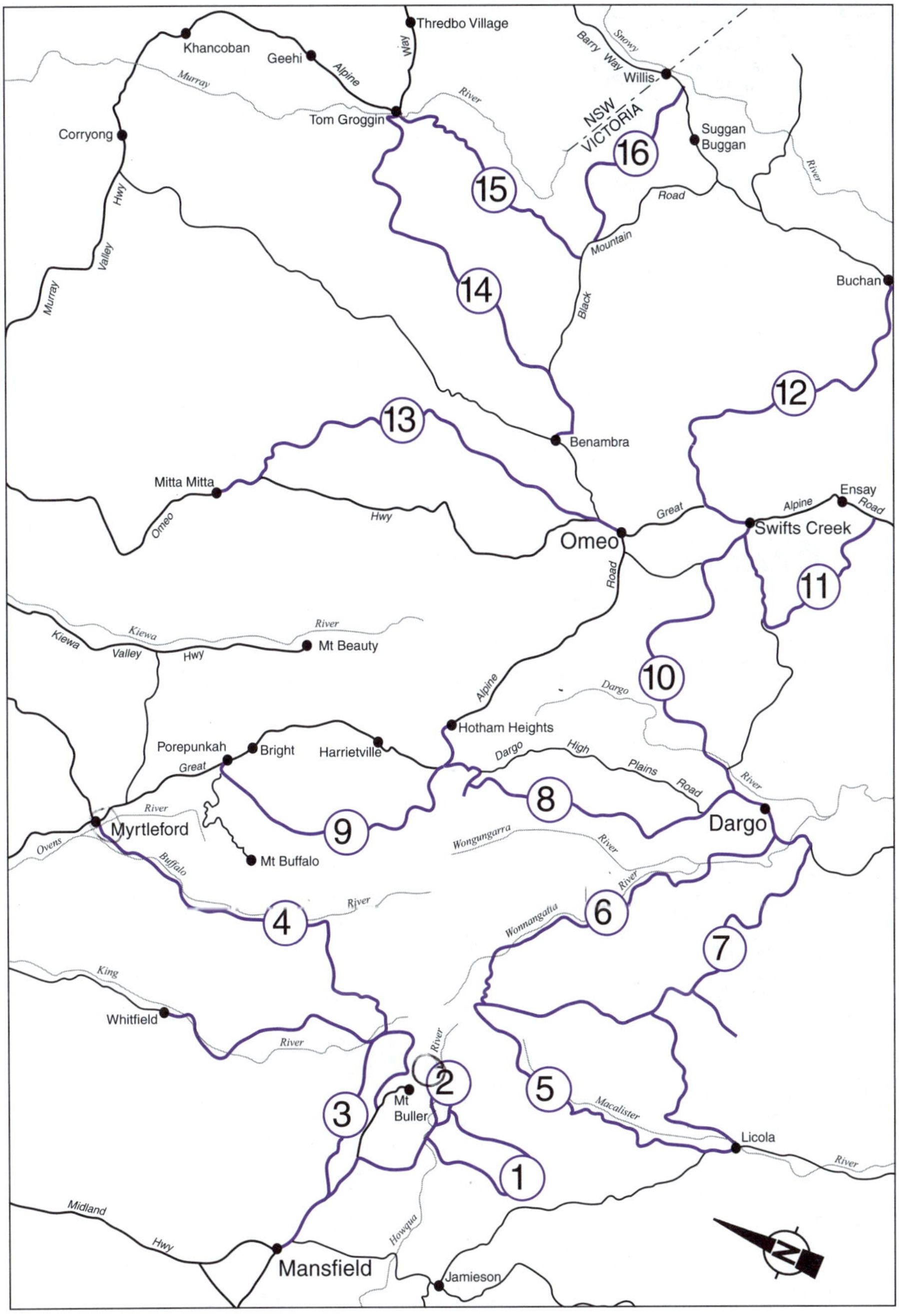

1. Howqua - Mitchell's Trek
2. The Bluff and Beyond
3. Craig's Hut and Mt Stirling
4. The Cobbler Plateau
5. Butcher Country
6. Wonnangatta Valley
7. Moroka Magic
8. The Crooked River
9. The Buckland Valley
10. Swifts Creek to Dargo
11. The Haunted Stream
12. Camp Oven Gap
13. Wombat Amble
14. Mount Pinnibar
15. Davies Plain
16. The Playgrounds

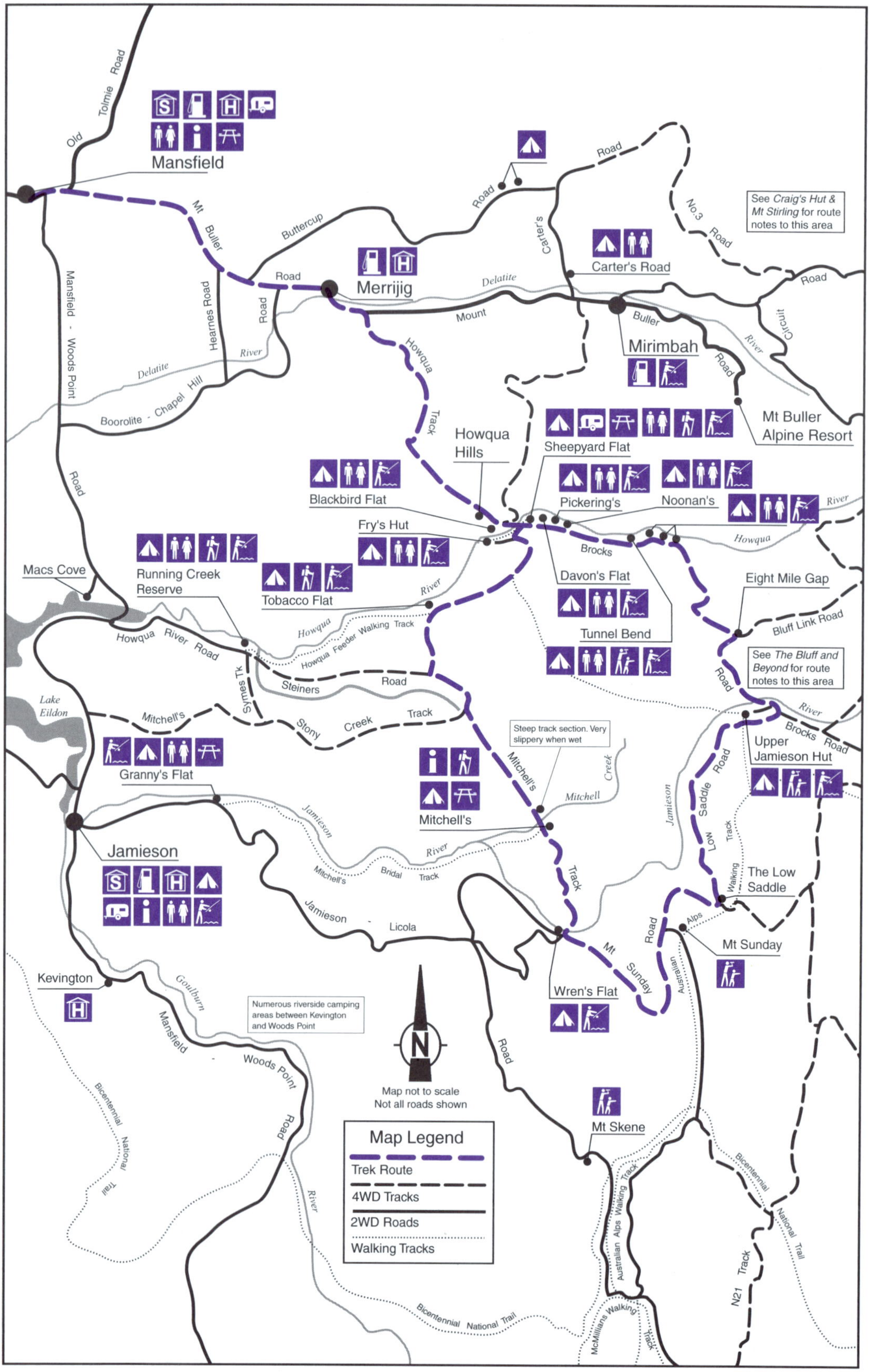
Old Tolmie Road
Mansfield
Mt Buller Road
Buttercup Road
Merrijig
Mansfield - Woods Point Road
Hearnes Road
Road
Delatite River
Boorolite - Chapel Hill
Howqua Track
Mount Buller Road
Carter's Road
No.3 Road
Circuit Road
See Craig's Hut & Mt Stirling for route notes to this area
Carter's Road
Mirimbah
Mt Buller Alpine Resort
Howqua Hills
Sheepyard Flat
Blackbird Flat
Pickering's
Noonan's
Fry's Hut
Brocks
Davon's Flat
Running Creek Reserve
Tobacco Flat
Tunnel Bend
Eight Mile Gap
Bluff Link Road
See The Bluff and Beyond for route notes to this area
Macs Cove
Howqua River Road
Howqua Feeder Walking Track
Steiners Road
Symes Tk
Lake Eildon
Mitchell's
Stony Creek Track
Howqua River
Brocks Road
Upper Jamieson Hut
Steep track section. Very slippery when wet
Mitchell's Track
Mitchell Creek
Granny's Flat
Mitchell's
Jamieson River
Low Saddle Road
Low Saddle Walking Track
The Low Saddle
Jamieson
Mitchell's Bridal Track
Jamieson - Licola Road
Mt Sunday
Alps
Australian
Wren's Flat
Mt Sunday
Kevington
Goulburn River
Numerous riverside camping areas between Kevington and Woods Point
Mansfield - Woods Point Road
Road
Map not to scale
Not all roads shown
Mt Skene
Map Legend
Trek Route
4WD Tracks
2WD Roads
Walking Tracks
Bicentennial National Trail
Australian Alps Walking Track
McMillans Walking Track
N21 Track

TREK ONE

HOWQUA - MITCHELL'S TREK

THE HOWQUA HILLS and Mitchell's Flat areas first came to the attention of European settlers in the 1840s when they were taken up for grazing. Prior to this aborigines used the area as a trade route across The Great Dividing Range. Quarries in the area provided stone for tools and weapons.

However, it was the discovery of alluvial gold in the 1860s and subsequent finds of reef gold a decade later that brought major changes to this once tranquil valley. Mining companies were formed and in 1888 the township of Howqua was proclaimed—boasting a butcher, baker, post office, blacksmith and several boarding houses along with Lovick's Hotel. The town was sited on the opposite bank to Fry's Flat.

Unlike other short-lived high country mining ventures, the Howqua Hills rush lasted about thirty years until mining finally ceased in 1905.

Things to Do and See

At Howqua Hills Historic Area, along with the many excellent camp sites on the banks of the Howqua River, there are a number of walking tracks ranging from the easy 1½ hour return Howqua Hills Historic Walk from Sheepyard Flat to Fry's Flat to the more demanding walks to Upper Jamieson Hut via Eagles Peaks or Lickhole Creek Walking Tracks. For the more adventurous and well equipped a multi day walk is possible from Running Creek Camping Area along most of the length of the Howqua River to the summit of Mt Howitt.

View the tunnel cut by prospectors to feed water to the water race for the Great Rand Goldmine at Tunnel Bend and visit Upper Jamieson Hut which was one of the many huts in the area built by the legendary Fred Fry.

fast facts

Mansfield to Sheepyard Flat via The Low Saddle and Mitchell's Flat

Trek distance: 130km

Standard: Medium (Dry weather only)

Fuel and supplies: Mansfield & Merrijig

Trek highlights: Sheepyard Flat, Tunnel Bend, Mitchell's Historic Site, Upper Jamieson and Fry's Huts

Track conditions:
Parks Vic/DNRE Mansfield
Ph 03/5733 0120

Need help?: RACV Mansfield (4WD Recovery) Ph 03/5775 2256

At Mitchell's Flat you can soak up the isolation of this former remote farm and take a short walk downstream on Mitchell's Creek to a small gorge with moss covered boulders. A longer 24km walk following the old Mitchell's Bridle Trail is also possible from Mitchell's Flat (*see Further Information*).

At Fry's Flat look over the hut that Fred Fry lived in (no overnight camping permitted in the hut) and try to picture the surrounding area as it was during the gold mining years of the 1870s.

Access

We commence this jaunt at Mansfield where the route then makes its way to Sheepyard Flat in the Howqua Hills Historic Area. Sheepyard Flat is situated 40km south east of Mansfield and is easily accessed by the signposted Howqua Track from the Mt Buller Road just east of Merrijig.

The Trek

Beginning at Mansfield, the route notes head towards Mt Buller before turning into the signposted Howqua Track at Merrijig then onto Howqua Hills Historic Area and the delightful camping and picnic areas at Sheepyard Flat. From the camping area at Sheepyard Flat the route follows the Howqua River along Brocks Road, passing a number of delightful riverside camp sites until you reach Tunnel Bend. Park your vehicle near the signposted walking track and make your way down the steps to the river where the water diversion tunnel constructed by gold miners in 1884 can be seen.

From Tunnel Bend, Brocks Road now climbs to Eight Mile Gap where the route continues along Brocks Road until its junction with Low Saddle Road. A short distance before Low Saddle Road a hard to see track leaves Brocks Road on the right and drops down to cross the Jamieson River before coming to Upper Jamieson Hut. It is well worth the short detour to enjoy the hut and its surrounds.

Continuing on Low Saddle Road the route winds upwards to The Low Saddle and passes Mt Sunday before arriving at Wren's Flat on the banks of the Jamieson River.

From Wren's Flat the trek follows Mitchell's Track to Mitchell's Flat—the site of a one time isolated farm and homestead and now a pleasant camping area. If you wish to explore this area further you can walk downstream on Mitchell's Creek to Mitchell's Gorge.

Leaving Mitchell's Flat our route climbs steeply out of the valley to a now disused slate mine. This section can be very hard going in the wet with its greasy red clay track surface. Continue past the slate mine to the junction of Steiners Road and the Mitchell's - Howqua Hills Track where we turn into the Howqua Hills Track, dropping down to Wares Flat and Tobacco Flat before coming to the short detour to Fry's Flat—named after the now legendary bushman Fred Fry, who lived in the Howqua Hills area for most of his life.

At Fry's Flat you'll find a slab hut beside the Howqua River where Fred Fry lived. You cannot stay in the hut, which is for day visitors only, however there are many excellent camp sites on the banks of the Howqua River at Fry's Flat.

From Fry's Flat it is only a short drive to Sheepyard Flat.

Standard

This trek is given a medium rating. There is a steep climb out of Mitchell's Flat which would be particularly difficult in the wet and the descent from Steiners Road to Wares Flat on Howqua Track has some moderately steep sections, although the track surface is generally good.

The access track to Upper Jamieson Hut crosses the Jamieson River which may become impassable after recent heavy rain.

Camping

At Howqua Hills Historic Area there is excellent camping with toilets, picnic tables, fireplaces and water from the river available at Sheepyard Flat, Davon's Flat, Pickering's Flat, Noonan's Flat and Tunnel Bend. Additional camp sites along the Howqua River are at Six Mile Flat and Eight Mile Flat.

Camping is also possible at Upper Jamieson Hut and in the hut's vicinity.

A number of camp sites exist at Wren's Flat beside the Jamieson River. Facilities here are limited.

Good camping is available at Mitchell's Flat. Here you will find a number of large, open grassy areas, some with picnic tables and fireplaces. There is also a pit toilet.

Bush camping is possible at Tobacco Flat (please do not trespass on private property) and excellent camp sites are located near the conclusion of the trek at Fry's Flat—a large grassy river flat on the banks of the Howqua River.

Permits/Restrictions

Seasonal road closures apply to this trek and are usually in force from after the Queen's Birthday Long Weekend to just after the Melbourne Cup in November.

Recommended Maps/Guides

We recommend the Brookes Bush Maps, Victoria *Watersheds of the King, Howqua and Jamieson Rivers* and *Map of the Macalister River Watershed*. In addition, the Brookes Bush Maps, Victoria *Lower Howqua Track* shows the section of the trek from Wren's Flat to Sheepyard Flat.

The *Mansfield - Mt Howitt Adventure Map* and the *Jamieson - Licola Adventure Map* by Rooftop Mapping Services details the route and is suitable for this trek.

Topographic maps for this trek are *Mansfield* in the 1:100 000 series and *Skene North* and *Buller South* 1:25 000 series.

Hema Maps *High Country - Victoria* map also shows the trek route as does the CFA *North East Rural Directory - Regions 23 and 24* (maps 368, 369, 409, 408).

Further Information

Parks Victoria and Dept of Natural Resources and Environment
33 Highett Street, Mansfield VIC 3722 Ph 03/5733 0120 Fax 03/5775 1063

Mansfield Visitor Information Centre
Mansfield Railway Station, Maroondah Highway, Mansfield Ph 03/5775 1464

Brochures - Parks Victoria: *Howqua Hills Visitor Guide*
Mansfield Country 4WD Discovery Tracks *Tour 4: Mitchells' Flat*
DNRE Forest Notes: *Mitchell's Bridle Trail (& Jamieson Quicksilver Mine)*

HISTORY

Mitchell's Flat

In the late 1860s alluvial gold was found in what is now known as Mitchell's Creek by Robert Wren and Thomas Larken. The pair 'worked' the area for about two years after their initial find before selling the claim to Fred Mitchell, who in the true spirit of never letting an opportunity pass by, named the creek Mitchell's, after himself. The river flats which are known as Mitchell's Flat was used by Fred Mitchell to store mining equipment.

Mitchell prospected his claim up until 1881 when the reality of finding more payable gold had faded, he leased 1000 acres (404 hectares) of Mitchell's Flat to William Hoskins of Jamieson. The Hoskins family set about clearing the land, building fences, stockyards and sheds as well as a homestead. Like most farms, they also planted an orchard of fruit trees and in the high country tradition, an avenue of English trees.

Even though the farm was in an isolated location, the Hoskins had a well deserved reputation for their hospitality and many social events were held at the homestead, some lasting 3-4 days.

The Hoskins terminated the Mitchell's lease in 1926 and moved back to Jamieson. Today, little remains of the Hoskins' efforts of eking out a living from their remote farm except for a few charred remains of the homestead that was destroyed by fire in 1989.

Mitchell's Flat is now part of the Alpine National Park.

Fred Fry - Howqua Hills' Legendary Bushman

"A man must be the possessor of many rare qualities if he can live alone in comparative isolation for a great part of his life and yet enjoy the love and respect of a circle of friends in every walk of life numbering far above the ordinary."

So read Fred Fry's obituary in the Mansfield Courier after his death from a long illness in 1971.

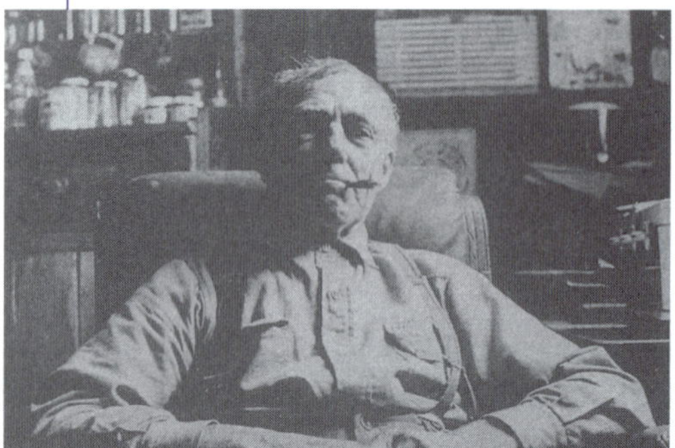

ABOVE: *Fred Fry*

Fred lived for most of his life in the Mansfield - Howqua Hills area and was well known for his skills as a bushman. His workmanship as a bush carpenter is carried on by way of the many huts he built in the region. An excellent axeman, Fred cut and split all the timber for his hut as well as the other huts he built which include Gardiner's Hut, Ritchie's Hut, Upper Jamieson Hut and Schuster's.

Fred Fry was born in 1895 in Mansfield, the youngest son of George and Mary Ann Fry. As a young man during the gold rush years Fred carried supplies to the goldfields along the Woods Point run until modern modes of transport took over. After this he worked as a stockman on Wonnangatta Station before moving into the home of his Uncle Jim on the Howqua River. This house was supposedly the original mine manager's house, dating to the mining heyday of Howqua Hills of the late 1800s. Fred lived here by himself for a while until his older brother Steve joined him. When the old house finally succumb to white ants around 1940 Fred built himself a hut out of split timber, which still stands today on the picturesque Fry's Flat on the banks of the Howqua River.

ABOVE: *Upper Jamieson Hut*

When the Howqua Hills area came to the attention of loggers, Fred spent a number of years helping the Forests Commission open up the Howqua Hills area by clearing tracks throughout the mountain areas he knew so well. He also worked for the Lands Department packing in salt to kill weeds. At other times he helped pack in and guide adventurous anglers and bushwalkers who wanted to fish and explore the waters of the Howqua.

Fred, along with his brother Steve also spent time prospecting around the Howqua Hills area in the hope of 'striking it rich', however that magic 'strike' seemed to have eluded them.

BELOW: *Fry's Hut beside the Howqua River*

In the 1950 novel, 'Far Country' which was written by Neville Shute when he spent some time living in a hut on the Howqua, the character Billy Slim is said to have been loosely based on Fred Fry.

Always welcoming to those who visited the Howqua, Fred's door was said to be always open and the billy on the boil. With Fred's passing came the closing of another chapter in the Howqua Hills Story—the legendary hermit of Howqua Hills.

ROUTE NOTES

Trek commences in front of the BP Service Station just outside Mansfield on the Mansfield-Mt Buller Road.

▼ 0.0 (0.0)
Zero trip meter on the Mansfield-Mt Buller Road at the BP Service Station. PSA in a south-east direction towards Mt Buller.
▲ *129.4 (16.9)*
BP Service Station on your right. CSA into Mansfield.
GPS S:37 03.624 E:146 05.880
UTM Zone 55 0419812E 5898046N

▼ 16.9 (16.9)
Merrijig. Club Hunt Hotel on right. CSA towards Mt Buller.
▲ *112.5 (2.1)*
Club Hunt Hotel on left. CSA towards Mansfield.

▼ 19.0 (2.1)
Road junction. TR. SP Sheepyard Flat. This is SP Howqua Track.
▲ *110.4 (7.6)*
Road junction. Notes TL. SP 2 Merrijig 21 Mansfield. TR for SP Mt Buller 27.
GPS S:37 06.720 E:146 16.766
UTM Zone 55 0435979E 5892458N

▼ 26.6 (7.6)
SP Mt Timbertop Walking Track on left. CSA.
▲ *102.8 (8.9)*
SP Mt Timbertop Walking Track on right. CSA.

▼ 35.5 (8.9)
Track junction. SP Doughtys Rd on left. SP Blackbird Flat Camping Area on right. Notes CSA across bridge over Howqua River.
▲ *93.9 (0.2)*
SP Blackbird Flat on left. SP Doughtys Rd on right. CSA.

▼ 35.7 (0.2)
SP Sheepyard Flat Camping Area on left and right. Track on right leads 2.4km to Frys Hut and Fry's Flat Camping Area. Notes CSA.
▲ *93.7 (0.4)*
Sheepyard Flat Camping Area. CSA across bridge over Howqua River.
GPS S:37 11.631 E:146 20.788
UTM Zone 55 0441955E 5883165N

▼ 36.1 (0.4)
SP Davons Flat Camping Area on left. CSA.
▲ *93.3 (0.6)*
Davons Flat Camping Area on right. CSA.

▼ 36.7 (0.6)
SP Pickerings Flat Camping Area on left. CSA.
▲ *92.7 (0.7)*
Pickerings Flat Camping Area on right. CSA.

▼ 37.4 (0.7)
SP Noonans Flat Camping Area on left. CSA.
▲ *92.0 (0.4)*
Noonans Flat Camping Area on right. CSA.

▼ 37.8 (0.4)
SP Tunnel Bend Flat Camping Area on left. CSA.
▲ *91.6 (0.7)*
Tunnel Bend Flat Camping Area on right. CSA.

▼ 38.5 (0.7)
SP Tunnel Bend on left. A 50m walk leads to tunnel through hill. Notes CSA.
▲ *90.9 (1.1)*
Tunnel Bend on left. CSA.

▼ 39.6 (1.1)
Track on left. KR uphill.
▲ *89.8 (4.1)*
Track on right. CSA.

▼ 43.7 (4.1)
SP Six Mile Flat Camping Area on left. CSA.
▲ *85.7 (1.9)*
Six Mile Flat Camping Area on right. CSA.

▼ 45.6 (1.9)
SP 7 Mile Flat Camping Area on left. CSA.
▲ *83.8 (1.3)*
7 Mile Flat Camping Area on right. CSA.

▼ 46.9 (1.3)
SP Eight Mile Flat Camping Area on left. CSA.
▲ *82.5 (8.0)*
Eight Mile Flat Camping Area on right. CSA.

TOYOTA

▼ 54.9 (8.0)
Road junction. This is SP Eight Mile Gap. TR. SP Brocks Rd. Road SO SP Bluff Link Rd.
▲ *74.5 (6.8)*
Road junction. TL. SP Brocks Road. SP Sheepyard Ft.
GPS S:37 13.931 E:146 26.618
UTM Zone 55 0450651E 5879212N

▼ 61.7 (6.8)
Track junction. KL on main track. Track on right leads 800m to Upper Jamieson Hut beside Jamieson River.
▲ *67.7 (1.0)*
Track on left. KR on main track.
GPS S:37 15.529 E:146 27.358
UTM Zone 55 0451759E 5876284N

▼ 62.7 (1.0)
Track on right leads to possible bush camp site. Notes CSA.
▲ *66.7 (0.2)*
Track on left. CSA.

▼ 62.9 (0.2)
Road junction. VR. SP Low Saddle Rd. Road on left SP Brocks Rd.
▲ *66.5 (0.1)*
Road junction. CSA. Road on right SP Brocks Rd.
GPS S:37 15.562 E:146 28.023
UTM Zone 55 0452737E 5876223N

▼ 63.0 (0.1)
Bridge. CSA on main track uphill. Track on left leads to bush camp sites.
▲ *66.4 (5.5)*
Track on right leads to camp sites. CSA over bridge.

▼ 68.5 (5.5)
Bridge.
▲ *60.9 (7.1)*
Bridge.

▼ 75.6 (7.1)
Minor track on right. CSA.
▲ *53.8 (3.7)*
Minor track on left. CSA.

▼ 79.3 (3.7)
Minor track on right. KL.
▲ *50.1 (1.6)*
Minor track on left. CSA.

OPPOSITE: *Camp site at Mitchell's Flat.*

▼ 80.9 (1.6)
SP The Low Saddle. CSA 50m to track junction and KR uphill. Track on left SP Heyfield.
▲ *48.5 (5.8)*
Track junction. KL and continue to SP The Low Saddle. Track on right SP Heyfield.
GPS S:37 20.001 E:146 26.552
UTM Zone 55 0450617E 5867999N

▼ 86.7 (5.8)
Track on left leads to Mt Sunday. CSA.
▲ *42.7 (11.0)*
Track on right. CSA.

▼ 97.7 (11.0)
Track on right. CSA.
▲ *31.7 (2.1)*
Track on left. CSA.

▼ 99.8 (2.1)
Track on right. KL.
▲ *29.6 (0.3)*
Track on left. CSA.

▼ 100.1 (0.3)
Tracks on right. CSA on main track.
▲ *29.3 (0.7)*
Tracks on left. CSA on main track.

▼ 100.8 (0.7)
Track junction. CSA. SP Mitchells Ck. Track on left leads 400m to Wrens Flat bush camp sites.
▲ *28.6 (0.2)*
Track junction. KL uphill SP Mt Sunday Rd.
GPS S:37 20.609 E:146 22.403
UTM Zone 55 0444497E 5866838N

▼ 101.0 (0.2)
Seasonal closure gate. CSA over bridge.
▲ *28.4 (0.1)*
Bridge. CSA through seasonal closure gate.

▼ 101.1 (0.1)
Y junction. KR uphill. Track on left leads to bush camp sites by river.
▲ *28.3 (0.4)*
Track on right. CSA.

▼ 101.5 (0.4)
Y junction. KL on main track. Track on right SP Management Vehicles Only.
▲ *27.9 (1.8)*
Track on left. CSA on main track.

▼ 103.3 (1.8)
Track on right. CSA.
▲ *26.1 (0.4)*
Track on left. KR.

▼ 103.7 (0.4)
Track on right SP Management Vehicles Only. CSA.
▲ *25.7 (1.5)*
Track on left. CSA.

▼ 105.2 (1.5)
Track on right SP Management Vehicles Only. CSA.
▲ *24.2 (0.7)*
Track on left. CSA.

▼ 105.9 (0.7)
Enter SP Alpine National Park. CSA.
▲ *23.5 (2.1)*
Leave Alpine National Park. CSA.

▼ 108.0 (2.1)
Enter SP Mitchells.
▲ *21.4 (1.2)*
Leave SP Mitchells.

▼ 109.2 (1.2)
Cross roads. Parks Vic information board on right. Notes CSA. Track on right leads 400m to the Old Mitchell Homestead ruins and small camp site beside Mitchells Creek. Track on left leads 500m to bush camp sites beside Mitchells Creek.
▲ *20.2 (0.1)*
Cross roads. Information board on left. CSA uphill.
GPS S:37 18.140 E:146 21.509
UTM Zone 55 0443147E 5871381N

▼ 109.3 (0.1)
Cross Mitchells Creek. Track climbs steeply from here.
▲ *20.1 (1.6)*
Cross Mitchells Creek.

▼ 110.9 (1.6)
Leave Alpine National Park.
▲ *18.5 (3.0)*
Enter Alpine National Park. Steep decline from here.

▼ 113.9 (3.0)
Seasonal closure gate.
▲ *15.5 (0.7)*
Seasonal closure gate.

▼ 114.6 (0.7)
Track on right. CSA.
▲ *14.8 (0.2)*
Track on left. CSA.

▼ 114.8 (0.2)
Slate mine.
▲ *14.6 (0.1)*
Slate mine.
GPS S:37 16.107 E:146 19.829
UTM Zone 55 0440640E 5875136N

▼ 114.9 (0.1)
Track on right. CSA.
▲ *14.5 (0.3)*
Track on left. CSA.

▼ 115.2 (0.3)
Track on left. CSA.
▲ *14.2 (0.9)*
Track on right. CSA.

▼ 116.1 (0.9)
Track on right. CSA.
▲ *13.3 (3.5)*
Track on left. CSA.

▼ 119.6 (3.5)
Track junction. TR. SP Frys and Sheepyard Flat.
▲ *9.8 (3.2)*
Track junction. TL. This is SP Alpine National Park.
GPS S:37 14.560 E:146 18.621
UTM Zone 55 0438831E 5877986N

▼ 122.8 (3.2)
Small creek crossing. This is Wares Flat. CSA uphill.
▲ *6.6 (0.6)*
Small creek crossing. This is Wares Flat. CSA uphill.

▼ 123.4 (0.6)
Track junction. KR. Track on left to camp sites.
▲ *6.0 (0.1)*
Track junction. TL uphill. Track on right to camp sites.

▼ 123.5 (0.1)
Creek crossing. Cross creek and TR. SP Frys & Sheepyard Flat. Track on left to SP Tobacco Flat and camping areas.

▲ *5.9 (1.2)*
Track junction. TL over creek. Track on right to Tobacco Flat.
GPS S:37 13.037 E:146 18.959
UTM Zone 55 0439317E 5880756N

▼ 124.7 (1.2)
Track on left. CSA.
▲ *4.7 (0.4)*
Track on right. KL.

▼ 125.1 (0.4)
Track on right. KL.
▲ *4.3 (0.2)*
Track on left. CSA.

▼ 125.3 (0.2)
Track on left. CSA.
▲ *4.1 (0.5)*
Track on right. CSA.

▼ 125.8 (0.5)
Track on left. CSA.
▲ *3.6 (0.4)*
Track on right. KL downhill.

▼ 126.2 (0.4)
Seasonal closure gate.
▲ *3.2 (0.2)*
Seasonal closure gate.

▼ 126.4 (0.2)
Track on right SP Lickhole Crk Trk. CSA.
▲ *3.0 (1.0)*
SP Lickhole Crk Trk on left. CSA.

▼ 127.4 (1.0)
Track junction. KR. Track on left leads 400m to Fry's Flat and camping.
▲ *2.0 (2.0)*
Track junction. TL uphill. SP Tobacco Flat 4 x 4 Only. Track on right to Fry's Flat.
GPS S:37 11.849 E:146 20.002
UTM Zone 55 0440841E 5883007N

▼ 129.4 (2.0)
Sheepyard Flat.
▲ *0.0 (0.0)*
Zero trip meter at Sheepyard Flat Camping Area. Proceed through camping area uphill to Fry's Hut Camping Area.
GPS S:37 11.631 E:146 20.788
UTM Zone 55 0441955E 5883165N

ABOVE: *There are many excellent camp sites to be found at Sheepyard Flat.*

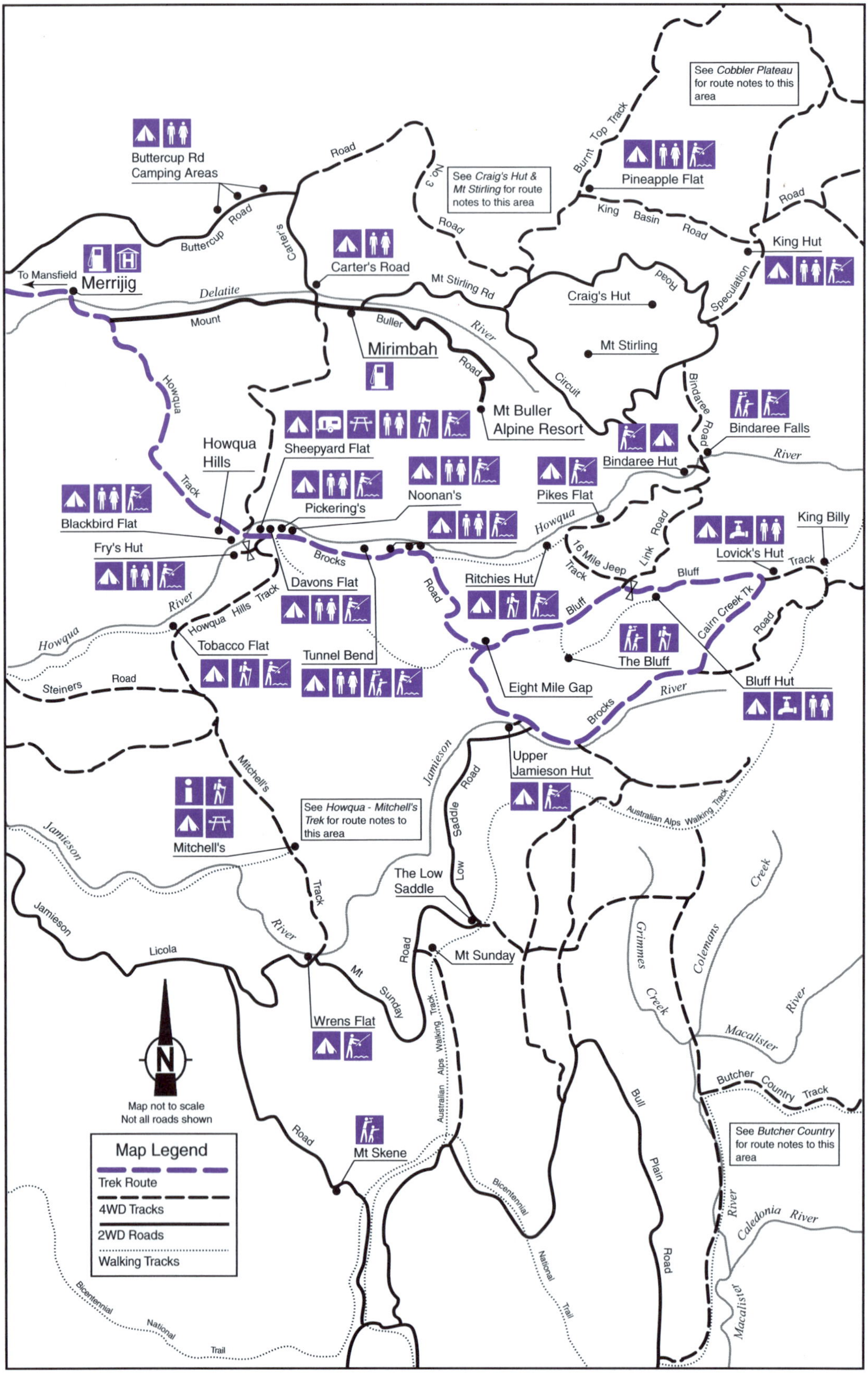
See Cobbler Plateau for route notes to this area
Burnt Top Track
Pineapple Flat
Buttercup Rd Camping Areas
Road
No. 3
See Craig's Hut & Mt Stirling for route notes to this area
King Basin Road
Road
King Hut
Road
Buttercup Road
Carter's
Carter's Road
Road
To Mansfield
Merrijig
Delatite
Mt Stirling Rd
Craig's Hut
Speculation
Mount
Buller
River
Mirimbah
Mt Stirling
Road
Circuit
Bindaree Road
Bindaree Falls
Howqua
Mt Buller Alpine Resort
Howqua Hills
Sheepyard Flat
Bindaree Hut
River
Noonan's
Pikes Flat
Track
Pickering's
Blackbird Flat
Howqua
Road
King Billy
Lovick's Hut
Link
16 Mile Jeep Track
Track
Fry's Hut
Brocks
Davons Flat
Bluff
Ritchies Hut
River
Howqua Hills Track
Road
Bluff
Cairn Creek Tk
Road
Howqua
Tobacco Flat
Tunnel Bend
The Bluff
Steiners Road
Eight Mile Gap
River
Bluff Hut
Brocks
Jamieson
Mitchell's
Upper Jamieson Hut
Road
See Howqua - Mitchell's Trek for route notes to this area
Australian Alps Walking Track
Jamieson
Saddle
Mitchell's
The Low Saddle
Low
Track
Creek
Grimmes
Jamieson
River
Colemans
Licola
Road
Mt Sunday
Creek
Mt
Sunday
River
Track
Macalister
Wrens Flat
Walking
Alps
Australian
Bull
Butcher Country Track
Map not to scale
Not all roads shown
See Butcher Country for route notes to this area
Road
Mt Skene
Plain
Map Legend
Trek Route
4WD Tracks
2WD Roads
Walking Tracks
Bicentennial
River
Caledonia River
National
Road
Trail
Bicentennial
National
Trail
Macalister

TREK TWO

THE BLUFF & BEYOND

THIS TREK IS AN IDEAL introduction to some of the many varied touring opportunities that are available in the Howqua Hills and The Bluff area.

Things to Do and See

On this trek we visit Howqua Hills Historic Area as well as Bluff and Lovick's Huts—two historic cattlemen's huts that are scattered throughout the mountains.

For those of you who would like a bird's-eye view of the mountains then a walk to The Bluff (3½ hrs return) is possible from Bluff Hut. Features of this walk are Mt Eadley Stoney and the alpine herb fields of The Bluff.

Access

Mansfield is the start point for this trek.

There are good all weather bitumen roads linking Mansfield via the Maroondah Highway from Melbourne (180km) and the Midland Highway from Benalla.

The Trek

From Mansfield head towards Merrijig on the Mt Buller Road, turning into the signposted Howqua Track 1½km past Merrijig. From Merrijig it's 16km along the Howqua Track to Howqua Hills Historic Area and the delightful camping areas such as Sheepyard Flat. Part way along Howqua Track a walking trail leads 1½km from Timbertop Saddle to the summit of Mt Timbertop.

From Howqua Hills continue along Brocks Road, passing numerous camping areas beside the Howqua River until the route notes reach Eight Mile Gap.

At Eight Mile Gap the trek swings into Bluff Link Road, with Brocks Road continuing on to the right. Follow Bluff Link Road to Refrigerator Gap where the imposing bulk of The Bluff towers above you. From Refrigerator Gap a walking track leads to The Bluff, however you can also walk to The Bluff from Bluff Hut.

fast facts

Mansfield to Eight Mile Gap via Howqua Hills and Bluff Hut

Trek distance: 102km

Standard: Easy (Dry weather only)

Fuel and supplies: Mansfield & Merrijig

Trek highlights: Howqua Hills, The Bluff and Bluff and Lovick's Huts

Track conditions:
Parks Vic/DNRE Mansfield
Ph 03/5733 0120

Need help?: RACV Mansfield (4WD Recovery) Ph 03/5775 2256

Just under 5km past Refrigerator Gap the trek notes turn into Bluff 4x4 Track and a short distance later you arrive at Bluff Hut, owned by the Stoney family. Camping is possible in the vicinity of the hut and an 8½km (3½hrs return) walking track to the summit of The Bluff commences from here.

Leaving Bluff Hut the route continues on Bluff 4x4 Track, over Mt Lovick to Lovick's Hut, another of the area's cattlemen's huts. It is possible to continue on past Lovick's Hut via King Billy Track (which is usually very rough and slow going), however we retrace our route a short distance from Lovick's Hut to Cairn Creek Track, which is then followed to its intersection with Brocks Road.

Once at the junction of Cairn Creek Track and Brocks Road you can choose to follow the route notes which conclude at Eight Mile Gap, or alternatively pick up Trek 1 - *Howqua Hills and Mitchell's Trek* at Low Saddle Road or take Brocks Road to Howitt Road on Howitt Plain where you can join with Trek 5 - *Butcher Country* or Trek 6 - *Wonnangatta Valley*.

Standard

Generally easy under normal conditions. The route detailed is an ideal introduction to the alpine areas around Mansfield and can be completed easily as a day trip. A camp at Howqua Hills Historic Area would provide a good base for this trek.

We recommend this as a dry weather only trek and is best avoided during times of wet weather.

Camping

You can set up camp at one of the many excellent camping areas beside the Howqua River at Howqua Hills. As already mentioned, this would make a good base from which to explore this trek.

Camping is also available in the vicinity of Bluff Hut (it is advisable to bring water) and in the surrounds of Lovick's Hut. Pit toilets are available at both sites.

In addition, a number of possible bush camp sites are detailed in the route notes.

Permits/Restrictions

This trek is restricted by seasonal road closures which are usually in force from after the Queen's Birthday Long Weekend to just after the Melbourne Cup in November.

Recommended Maps/Guides

The Brookes Bush Maps, Victoria *Watersheds of the King, Howqua and Jamieson Rivers* and the *Mansfield - Mt Howitt Adventure Map* by Rooftop Mapping Services are the best maps for this trek. The *Jamieson - Licola Adventure Map* and the *Bush Huts Around Mansfield Map* by Rooftop Mapping Services also covers this route.

Hema Maps *High Country - Victoria* map and the CFA *North East Rural Directory - Regions 23 and 24* (maps 368, 369, 409,408) also show the trek route.

Topographic maps for this trek are the *Mansfield* and *Howitt* 1:100 000 series.

Further Information

Parks Victoria and Dept of Natural Resources and Environment
33 Highett Street, Mansfield VIC 3722 Ph 03/5733 0120 Fax 03/5775 1063

Mansfield Visitor Information Centre
Mansfield Railway Station, Maroondah Highway, Mansfield Ph 03/5775 1464

Brochures - Parks Victoria: *Alpine National Park - valleys and bluffs around Mansfield and Whitfield.*
Mansfield Country 4WD Discovery Tracks *Tour 3: The Bluff*

High Country Huts and Homesteads

Moroka Hut

Coolamine Homestead

Charlie's Plain Hut

The numerous mountain cattlemen's huts and homesteads scattered throughout the High Country provide lasting, if not fragile reminders to the isolation and hardships often endured by the early pioneers who pushed into the alps. Often situated in remote locations, these buildings provided shelter for stockmen during their musterings on the High Country runs, which at times could last for weeks. At some locations, such as the Wonnangatta Valley and Coolamine these first buildings were latter extended to provide permanent accommodation.

The earliest of these shelters were usually constructed of locally available materials such as round logs or split slabs for the walls and bark or split shingle roofs. Mostly stringybark or ironbark trees were used if they were available. These trees were favoured because the bark peeled easily and in large sheets, providing good roofing material. Alpine ash, which was easily worked, was also used as was snow gum. However, as these structures fell into decay or were destroyed by fire they were often replaced by the more durable, if not as aesthetically pleasing symbol of Australian bush architecture—corrugated iron.

Many huts had common features, these being a main room with a large fireplace that was used for cooking and for heating in the cooler weather. Often there was a large cast iron kettle hanging in the fireplace to provide a ready supply of hot water. Beside the hearth was a table and sometimes a few chairs constructed out of bush timber or whatever was available. The remaining area was taken up with roughly built beds, often made from hessian bags and bush poles. Where possible huts were built close to a water source such as a soak or stream.

In all there are roughly 230 huts still standing in the Victorian and New South Wales High Country. Not all are cattlemen's huts as such; some were constructed by prospectors who scoured the mountains in search of gold, while others were built by skiing enthusiasts or by the hydro-electric authorities.

A number of the huts visited on treks in this book are available for public use. Please remember if you intend bunking down overnight in a hut (which should never be relied upon except in an emergency) then there is a simple hut etiquette that should always be followed: unlocked huts are for use by all so be prepared to make room for others, never leave a fire unattended and always extinguish it properly before leaving, leave the hut tidier than you found it and always replace any firewood that you use.

Geehi Hut

Guys Hut

Dogmans Hut

ROUTE NOTES

TREK 2

Trek commences in front of the BP Service Station just outside Mansfield on the Mansfield-Mt Buller Road.

▼ 0.0 (0.0)
Zero trip meter on the Mansfield-Mt Buller Road with the BP Service Station on your left. PSA in a south-east direction towards Mt Buller.
▲ *102.3 (16.9)*
BP Service Station on your right. CSA into Mansfield.
GPS S:37 03.624 E:146 05.880
UTM Zone 55 0419812E 5898046N

▼ 16.9 (16.9)
Merrijig. Club Hunt Hotel on right. CSA towards Mt Buller.
▲ *85.4 (2.1)*
Club Hunt Hotel on left. CSA towards Mansfield.

▼ 19.0 (2.1)
Road junction. TR. SP Sheepyard Flat. This is SP Howqua Track.
▲ *83.3 (7.6)*
Road junction. Notes TL. SP 2 Merrijig 21 Mansfield. TR for SP Mt Buller 27.
GPS S:37 06.720 E:146 16.766
UTM Zone 55 0435979E 5892458N

▼ 26.6 (7.6)
SP Mt Timbertop Walking Track on left. CSA.
▲ *75.7 (8.9)*
SP Mt Timbertop Walking Track on right. CSA.

▼ 35.5 (8.9)
Track junction. SP Doughtys Rd on left. Blackbird Flat Camping Area on right. Notes CSA across bridge over Howqua River.
▲ *66.8 (0.2)*
SP Blackbird Flat on left. SP Doughtys Rd on right. CSA.

▼ 35.7 (0.2)
SP Sheepyard Flat Camping Area on left and right. Track on right leads 2.4km to Frys Hut and Fry's Flat Camping Area. Notes CSA.
▲ *66.6 (0.4)*
Sheepyard Flat Camping Area. CSA across bridge over Howqua River.
GPS S:37 11.631 E:146 20.788
UTM Zone 55 0441955E 5883165N

▼ 36.1 (0.4)
SP Davons Flat Camping Area on left. CSA.
▲ *66.2 (0.6)*
Davons Flat Camping Area on right. CSA.

▼ 36.7 (0.6)
SP Pickerings Flat Camping Area on left. CSA.
▲ *65.6 (0.7)*
Pickerings Flat Camping Area on right. CSA.

▼ 37.4 (0.7)
SP Noonans Flat Camping Area on left. CSA.
▲ *64.9 (0.4)*
Noonans Flat Camping Area on right. CSA.

▼ 37.8 (0.4)
SP Tunnel Bend Flat Camping Area on left. CSA.
▲ *64.5 (0.7)*
Tunnel Bend Flat Camping Area on right. CSA.

▼ 38.5 (0.7)
SP Tunnel Bend on left. A 50m walk leads to tunnel through hill. Notes CSA.
▲ *63.8 (1.1)*
Tunnel Bend on left. CSA.

▼ 39.6 (1.1)
Track on left. KR uphill.
▲ *62.7 (4.1)*
Track on right. CSA.

▼ 43.7 (4.1)
SP Six Mile Flat Camping Area on left. CSA.
▲ *58.6 (1.9)*
Six Mile Flat Camping Area on right. CSA.

▼ 45.6 (1.9)
SP 7 Mile Flat Camping Area on left. CSA.
▲ *56.7 (1.3)*
7 Mile Flat Camping Area on right. CSA.

▼ 46.9 (1.3)
SP Eight Mile Flat Camping Area on left. CSA.
▲ *55.4 (8.0)*
Eight Mile Flat Camping Area on right. CSA.

▼ 54.9 (8.0)
Road junction. This is SP Eight Mile Gap. CSA. SP Bluff Link Rd. Road on right SP Brocks Rd.

▲ *47.4 (1.3)*
Road junction. This is SP Eight Mile Gap. CSA. SP Brocks Road. SP Sheepyard Ft. Road on left SP Brocks Rd.

GPS S:37 13.934 E:146 26.623
UTM Zone 55 0450655E 5879219N

▼ 56.2 (1.3)
Minor track on right. CSA. Good views across to The Bluff.

▲ *46.1 (3.4)*
Minor track on left. KR uphill.

▼ 59.6 (3.4)
Track on right. CSA.

▲ *42.7 (1.1)*
Track on left. CSA.

▼ 60.7 (1.1)
Car park on right for The Bluff Walk. This is Refrigerator Gap. Notes CSA.

▲ *41.6 (4.5)*
Car park on left. CSA.

▼ 65.2 (4.5)
Track junction. TR. SP Bluff Hut 4x4 Only.

▲ *37.1 (2.2)*
Track junction. TL.

GPS S:37 12.668 E:146 30.543
UTM Zone 55 0456433E 5881590N

▼ 67.4 (2.2)
Bluff Hut and camping area on right. Walk to The Bluff from hut is 8.5km – 3½ hours return. Notes CSA.

▲ *34.9 (0.8)*
Bluff Hut on left. CSA.

GPS S:37 12.960 E:146 31.441
UTM Zone 55 0457774E 5881060N

▼ 68.2 (0.8)
Possible bush camp sites in this vicinity.

▲ *34.1 (5.5)*
Possible bush camp sites in this vicinity.

▼ 73.7 (5.5)
Track junction. VR. SP Cairn Ck Tk. Track on left leads 300m to Lovick's Hut and camping area.

ABOVE: *The Bluff Track with The Bluff in the background.*

▲ *28.6 (0.4)*
Track junction. CSA uphill. Track on right leads 300m to Lovick's Hut.

GPS S:37 12.558 E:146 34.623
UTM Zone 55 0462471E 5881822N

▼ 74.1 (0.4)
T junction. TR.

▲ *28.2 (10.5)*
Track junction. TL uphill.

▼ 84.6 (10.5)
Cross Jamieson River.

▲ *17.7 (0.1)*
Cross Jamieson River.

▼ 84.7 (0.1)
Road junction. TR. SP Brocks Rd. *NB:* TL onto Brocks Road to Howitt Rd to meet Trek 5 - Butcher Country Trek and Trek 6 - Wonnangatta Valley.

▲ *17.6 (6.1)*
Road junction. TL. SP Cairn Ck Tk.

GPS S:37 14.699 E:146 32.684
UTM Zone 55 0459623E 5877848N

▼ 90.8 (6.1)
Bridge.
▲ *11.5 (0.2)*
Bridge.

▼ 91.0 (0.2)
Track junction. CSA. SP Sheepyard Flat.
▲ *11.3 (0.8)*
Track junction. KL. SP King Billy 1 & 2.

▼ 91.8 (0.8)
Bridge.
▲ *10.5 (1.8)*
Bridge.

▼ 93.6 (1.8)
Track on right. KL.
▲ *8.7 (0.8)*
Track on left. CSA.

▼ 94.4 (0.8)
Track junction. CSA. Track on left SP Low Saddle Rd. *NB:* TL into Low Saddle Rd is the 62.9km reading of Trek 1 - Howqua - Mitchells Trek.
▲ *7.9 (1.2)*
Track junction. KL. SP Brocks Rd. Track on right SP Low Saddle Rd.
GPS S:37 15.554 E:146 28.029
UTM Zone 55 0452751E 5876232N

▼ 95.6 (1.2)
Track junction. KR. Track on left leads to Upper Jamieson Hut.
▲ *6.7 (1.0)*
Track on right. KL.

▼ 96.6 (1.0)
Bridge.
▲ *5.7 (5.7)*
Bridge.

▼ 102.3 (5.7)
SP Eight Mile Gap. TL along SP Brocks Rd to Sheepyard Flat and Mansfield.
▲ *0.0 (0.0)*
Zero trip meter at SP Eight Mile Gap. TL. SP Brocks Rd. Road SO SP Bluff Link Rd.
GPS S:37 13.934 E:146 26.623
UTM Zone 55 0450655E 5879219N

ABOVE: *Lovick's Hut.*

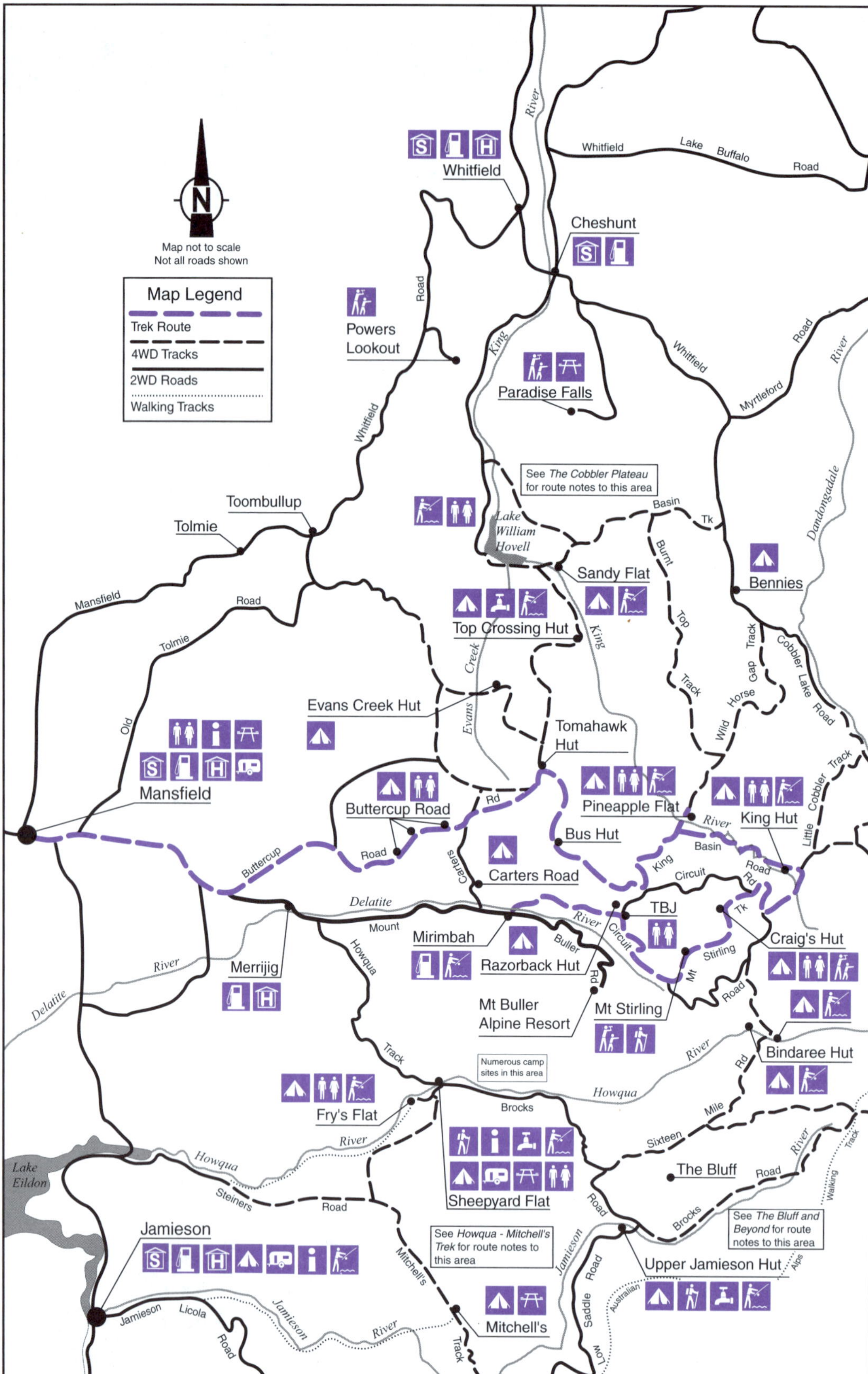
Map not to scale
Not all roads shown
Map Legend
Trek Route
4WD Tracks
2WD Roads
Walking Tracks
Whitfield
Cheshunt
Whitfield Lake Buffalo Road
River
King
Powers Lookout
Road
Whitfield
Paradise Falls
Whitfield
Myrtleford
Road
River
Dandongadale
See The Cobbler Plateau for route notes to this area
Basin
Tk
Burnt
Top
Track
Lake William Hovell
Sandy Flat
Bennies
Toombullup
Tolmie
Mansfield
Road
Tolmie
Old
Top Crossing Hut
King
Creek
Evans
Evans Creek Hut
Tomahawk Hut
Wild Horse Gap Track
Cobbler Lake Road
Little Cobbler Track
Mansfield
Buttercup Road
Rd
Pineapple Flat
River
King Hut
Bus Hut
Basin
Road
Buttercup
Road
Carters
Carters Road
King
Circuit
Rd
Tk
Delatite
Mount
River
TBJ
Circuit
Buller
Mirimbah
Howqua
Razorback Hut
Rd
Stirling
Mt
Road
Craig's Hut
River
Merrijig
Delatite
Mt Buller Alpine Resort
Mt Stirling
Track
Numerous camp sites in this area
River
Howqua
Rd
Bindaree Hut
Fry's Flat
Brocks
Mile
Sixteen
River
Howqua
Lake Eildon
The Bluff
Road
River
Walking
Track
Steiners
Road
Sheepyard Flat
Road
Brocks
See The Bluff and Beyond for route notes to this area
Jamieson
See Howqua - Mitchell's Trek for route notes to this area
Mitchell's
Jamieson
Upper Jamieson Hut
Alps
Road
Saddle
Australian
Jamieson
Licola
Road
Jamieson
River
Mitchell's
Track
Low

TREK THREE

CRAIG'S HUT & MT STIRLING

THE HIGH COUNTRY AREA to the east of Mansfield is without doubt one of the most popular and highly visited areas in the Victorian Alps—and not without good reason. Here you will find some of the best four-wheel drive journeys on offer along with stunning mountain scenery, delightful camping and history galore.

Another plus for this area is that it is easily accessible, making a weekend getaway to the High Country a possibility for those with limited time at their disposal.

Things to Do and See

The two main points of interest on this trek are the drive to the summit of Mt Stirling with its stunning 360° views, and a visit to Craig's Hut—made famous in the movie 'The Man From Snowy River' which was filmed in 1983.

Mount Stirling, at 1747m is one of Victoria's notable peaks and is covered by snow for up to four months a year. In winter it is a popular cross-country skiing destination and in summer attracts bushwalkers, mountain bikers and four-wheel drive tourers.

This trek takes you to within 100m of the summit and the short, relatively easy walk from the parking area will reveal one of the best scenic vistas in the Victorian Alps with views across to Mt Buller and The Bluff in the south, Mt Cobbler in the north and Mt Howitt and Howitt Plains to the east.

For the keen fisherfolk there is good fishing for trout in all of the rivers and streams, including the King and Delatite Rivers.

Access

This trek commences at the regional centre of Mansfield with good all weather bitumen road access via the Maroondah Highway from Melbourne (180km) and the Midland Highway from Benalla.

fast facts

Mansfield to Mirimbah via Craig's Hut and Mt Stirling

Trek distance: 110km

Standard: Medium/Hard (Dry weather only)

Fuel and supplies: Mansfield & Merrijig

Trek highlights: King River, Craig's Hut and Mt Stirling

Track conditions:
Parks Vic/DNRE Mansfield
Ph 03/5733 0120

Need help?: RACV Mansfield (4WD Recovery) Ph 03/5775 2256

The Trek

Leaving Mansfield, the trek heads out along Buttercup Road to Carters Road and onto Tomahawk Hut. From here the route climbs Razorback Spur, passing The Pinnacle to join with Circuit Road near Razorback Hut.

The route then follows King Basin Road to Pineapple Flat then onto King Hut, passing a number of camp sites along the way.

From King Hut the route turns into Speculation Road to join again with Circuit Road before traversing Clear Hills Trail to Craig's Hut with its stunning views across The Clear Hills towards Mt Cobbler.

After enjoying Craig's Hut the trek climbs past The Monument and onto the summit of Mt Stirling via the steep and shaly Mt Stirling Track.

Leaving Mt Stirling it is a steep and bumpy descent to Howqua Gap where the route once again joins with Circuit Road for the run down to Telephone Box Junction before concluding on the Mount Buller Road at Mirimbah.

Standard

This trek is given a medium/hard rating due to the rough climb and descent of Mt Stirling. Sections of Mt Stirling Track from the summit to Howqua Gap and also to Craig's Hut at times can be quite eroded, requiring careful wheel placement.

There are a number of crossings of the King River along King Basin Road as well as the access to Pineapple Flat and recent heavy rain may make this section impassable.

This is a dry weather only trek and is best avoided during times of rain.

Camping

There are a number of camping areas with facilities along Buttercup Road that are suitable for an overnight stop. Camping is also possible in the vicinities of Tomahawk Hut and Bus Hut as well as Razorback Hut. There is a toilet at Razorback Hut.

Excellent camping is available at Pineapple Flat on the King River. Facilities include a pit toilet and water from the river.

There are a number of bush camp sites beside the King River on King Basin Road and a large, grassy camping area in the vicinity of King River Hut. Facilities here include a pit toilet and horse yards. Water is available from the river.

You can camp amongst the snow gums near Craig's Hut, however this is a popular spot and if you wish to have a camp fire it is wise to bring some wood with you. Facilities here include a pit toilet and picnic tables.

Permits/Restrictions

Seasonal road closures apply to this trek and are usually in force from after the Queen's Birthday Long Weekend to just after the Melbourne Cup in November. The Mount Stirling Summit Track is closed from the 1st May until the end of October.

Recommended Maps/Guides

The best maps for this trek are the Brookes Bush Maps, Victoria *Watersheds of the King, Howqua and Jamieson Rivers* and the *Mansfield - Mt Howitt Adventure Map* or the *Bush Huts Around Mansfield Map* by Rooftop Mapping Services.

Hema Maps *High Country - Victoria* map and the CFA *North East Rural Directory - Regions 23 and 24* (maps 367, 368, 369) also show the trek route.

Topographic maps for this trek are the *Mansfield* and *Howitt* 1:100 000 series.

Further Information

Parks Victoria and Dept of Natural Resources and Environment
33 Highett Street, Mansfield VIC 3722   Ph 03/5733 0120   Fax 03/5775 1063

Mansfield Visitor Information Centre
Mansfield Railway Station, Maroondah Highway, Mansfield   Ph 03/5775 1464

Brochures - Mansfield Country 4WD Discovery Tracks *Tour 1: Craig's Hut*
Mansfield Country 4WD Discovery Tracks *Tour 2: Mount Stirling*
DNRE Forest Notes: *Circuit Road - Mt Stirling*

OPPOSITE: *On a clear day there are stunning 360° panoramas from the summit of Mt Stirling.*

ROUTE NOTES

Trek commences in front of the BP Service Station just outside Mansfield on the Mansfield-Mt Buller Road.

▼ 0.0 (0.0)
Zero trip meter on the Mansfield-Mt Buller Road. BP Service Station on your left. PSA towards Mt Buller.
▲ *109.9 (13.0)*
BP Service Station on your right. CSA to Mansfield.
GPS S:37 03.624 E:146 05.880
UTM Zone 55 0419812E 5898046N

▼ 13.0 (13.0)
TL. SP Buttercup Rd.
▲ *96.9 (3.9)*
Road junction. This is the Mansfield-Mt Buller Road. Notes TR SP Mansfield 14. TL for SP 32 Mt Buller.

▼ 16.9 (3.9)
Road junction. CSA. Road on right SP Purcell Ln.
▲ *93.0 (0.7)*
SP Purcell Ln on left. CSA.

▼ 17.6 (0.7)
Cross roads. CSA. SP Buttercup Rd.
▲ *92.3 (2.6)*
Cross roads. CSA.

▼ 20.2 (2.6)
Road junction. CSA. Road on left SP Greenways Rd.
▲ *89.7 (2.0)*
SP Greenways Rd on right. CSA.

▼ 22.2 (2.0)
Natural causeway. Enter Buttercup Reserve.
▲ *87.7 (0.4)*
Natural causeway.
GPS S:37 05.078 E:146 18.181
UTM Zone 55 0438055E 5895508N

▼ 22.6 (0.4)
Cross creek.
▲ *87.3 (1.5)*
Cross creek.

▼ 24.1 (1.5)
SP Camp site 1 on left. Notes CSA. Camp sites 2, 3 and 4 are on the left between here and the next reading.
▲ *85.8 (4.1)*
SP Camp site 1 on right. CSA.

▼ 28.2 (4.1)
SP Camp site No 5 on left. This is the last camp site. CSA.
▲ *81.7 (0.7)*
SP Camp site No 5 on right. CSA. Camp sites 4, 3 and 2 are on the right between here and the next reading.
GPS S:37 03.945 E:146 21.334
UTM Zone 55 0442720E 5897639N

▼ 28.9 (0.7)
T junction. TL. SP Carters Rd.
▲ *81.0 (0.3)*
Road junction. TL. SP Buttercup Road.
GPS S:37 03.982 E:146 21.811
UTM Zone 55 0443417E 5897581N

▼ 29.2 (0.3)
Track on left. CSA.
▲ *80.7 (2.2)*
Track on right. CSA.

▼ 31.4 (2.2)
Track junction. KL. Track on right SP Plain Ck Tk.
▲ *78.5 (1.9)*
Track on left SP Plain Ck Tk. CSA.

▼ 33.3 (1.9)
Track on left. CSA.
▲ *76.6 (1.5)*
Track on right. CSA.

▼ 34.8 (1.5)
Y junction. KR. SP No 3 Road and pass through area of recent logging. CSA on the main track. Track on left SP Tomohawk Spur Tk leads 500m to Tomahawk Hut.
▲ *75.1 (2.1)*
Track on left SP Tomohawk Spur Tk. CSA.
GPS S:37 02.616 E:146 24.621
UTM Zone 55 0447566E 5900127N

▼ 36.9 (2.1)
Seasonal closure gate.

▲ *73.0 (2.6)*
Seasonal closure gate. Before next reading you will pass through area of recent logging, CSA on the main track.

▼ 39.5 (2.6)
Track junction. Excellent views on right from here. Notes CSA. Track on left SP Westons Tk 4x4 only.
▲ *70.4 (1.1)*
SP Westons Tk on right. CSA.
GPS S:37 03.355 E:146 25.468
UTM Zone 55 0448828E 5898769N

▼ 40.6 (1.1)
Track junction. CSA. SP Telephone Box 10.2km. SP King Saddle 8.2km. Track on right leads to Refuge Hut.
▲ *69.3 (2.7)*
Track on left to Refuge Hut. CSA. SP Mt No 3 1.1km.

▼ 43.3 (2.7)
Track junction. CSA. Road on right SP No Through Road.
▲ *66.6 (0.3)*
SP No Through Road on left. CSA.

▼ 43.6 (0.3)
Track junction. CSA. Track on left SP Mine Creek Tk.
▲ *66.3 (1.4)*
SP Mine Creek Tk on right. KL.

▼ 45.0 (1.4)
Bus Hut on left. CSA.
▲ *64.9 (3.3)*
Bus Hut on right. CSA.

▼ 48.3 (3.3)
T junction. TL. SP Circuit Rd. SP Craigs Hut. Track on right leads to Mt Stirling.
NB: Track to Razorback Hut and camping area is just on the right when turning to Mt Stirling.
▲ *61.6 (2.2)*
Track junction. TR. SP No 3 Rd. Track on left to Mt Stirling.
GPS S:37 05.990 E:146 27.928
UTM Zone 55 0452498E 5893913N

▼ 50.5 (2.2)
Track junction. Sharp TL. SP King Basin Rd. SP Pineapple Flat.
▲ *59.4 (5.0)*
Track junction. TR uphill. This is Circuit Rd.
GPS S:37 06.022 E:146 28.700
UTM Zone 55 0453652E 5893867N

▼ 55.5 (5.0)
Track on left. KR.
▲ *54.4 (1.0)*
Track on right. KL uphill.

▼ 56.5 (1.0)
Track on left. CSA.
▲ *53.4 (2.3)*
Track on right. CSA.

THINGS TO SEE AND DO

Craig's Hut and 'The Man From Snowy River' Movie

The hut pictured on the left, known as Craig's Hut, was part of the set of 'The Man From Snowy River' movie and the home of the movie's main character Jim Craig, played by Tom Burlinson. The movie, based loosely on the poem of the same name by 'Banjo' Paterson was shot in and around the Clear Hills area in 1983.

Originally constructed for the movie, the hut comprised only of a shell—the walls as shown in the photograph opposite, the verandah and roof. The scenes taken inside the hut where shot in a studio.

After completion of filming the hut was left to deteriorate until it was rebuilt in1993. Perched in a magnificent setting on The Clear Hills and ringed by snow gums, the hut looks out across to Mt Cobbler and is now one of the more popular visitor attractions in the area.

▼ 58.8 (2.3)
Track junction. CSA. Track on left SP Westons Tk 4x4 Only.
▲ *51.1 (1.2)*
SP Westons Tk on right. KL.

▼ 60.0 (1.2)
Track junction. CSA. Track on right SP Black Landing Tk 4x4 Only.
▲ *49.9 (0.8)*
SP Black Landing Tk on left. CSA.

▼ 60.8 (0.8)
Track junction. Notes VR. SP King Basin Rd. Track on left SP Pineapple Flat leads 700m to Pineapple Flat Camping Area - a pleasant site across the King River in the Alpine National Park.
▲ *49.1 (2.9)*
Track on right SP Pineapple Flat. Notes CSA.
GPS S:37 04.162 E:146 29.814
UTM Zone 55 0455276E 5897312N

▼ 63.7 (2.9)
Minor track on right. KL.
▲ *46.2 (1.3)*
Minor track on left. CSA.

▼ 65.0 (1.3)
Tracks on left lead to camp sites by river. Notes CSA.
▲ *44.9 (2.0)*
Tracks on right. CSA.

▼ 67.0 (2.0)
Track on left leads to camp site by river. Notes CSA.
▲ *42.9 (1.3)*
Track on right. CSA.

▼ 68.3 (1.3)
Cross King River and enter SP Alpine National Park.
▲ *41.6 (0.4)*
Cross King River.
GPS S:37 04.809 E:146 33.564
UTM Zone 55 0460833E 5896140N

▼ 68.7 (0.4)
Cross King River. Bush camp sites on left over river.
▲ *41.2 (0.5)*
Bush camp site on right. CSA and cross King River.

▼ 69.2 (0.5)
Cross river.
▲ *40.7 (0.3)*
Cross river.

▼ 69.5 (0.3)
Cross river.
▲ *40.4 (0.4)*
Cross river.

▼ 69.9 (0.4)
Cross river.
▲ *40.0 (0.1)*
Cross river.

▼ 70.0 (0.1)
King Hut on right. Camping in this vicinity. Notes CSA.
▲ *39.9 (0.1)*
King Hut on left. CSA.
GPS S:37 05.298 E:146 34.336
UTM Zone 55 0461986E 5895245N

▼ 70.1 (0.1)
Track junction. KL.
▲ *39.8 (0.8)*
Track on left. CSA.

▼ 70.9 (0.8)
Track junction. TR and cross bridge. SP Speculation Rd. Road SO has gate.
▲ *39.0 (2.3)*
Track junction. TL. SP King Hut.

▼ 73.2 (2.3)
Bridge. Small camp site on left prior to bridge.
▲ *36.7 (1.0)*
Bridge.

▼ 74.2 (1.0)
Minor track on left. KR.
▲ *35.7 (2.7)*
Minor track on right. KL.

▼ 76.9 (2.7)
T junction. TR. SP Circuit Rd.
▲ *33.0 (2.4)*
Track junction. TL. SP Speculation Rd. SP King Hut.
GPS S:37 06.855 E:146 33.079
UTM Zone 55 0460142E 5892362N

▼ 79.3 (2.4)
Track on right. This is Peter's Corner. KL uphill.

▲ *30.6 (3.6)*
Track on left. KR downhill.

▼ 82.9 (3.6)
Track junction. TL. SP Craig's Hut 4x4 Access Only.
▲ *27.0 (2.2)*
T junction. TR. This is Circuit Road.

▼ 85.1 (2.2)
Track junction. Notes CSA. Track on right leads to car park and Craig's Hut.
▲ *24.8 (1.2)*
Track junction. Notes KR downhill. Track on left leads to car park and Craig's Hut.
GPS S:37 06.566 E:146 31.939
UTM Zone 55 0458446E 5892885N

▼ 86.3 (1.2)
Track junction. CSA. SP Clear Hills Trail. Track on left SP Monument Track.
▲ *23.6 (2.9)*
Track junction. CSA. SP Clear Hills Trail. Track on right SP Monument Track.
GPS S:37 06.901 E:146 31.450
UTM Zone 55 0457726E 5892262N

▼ 89.2 (2.9)
Track junction. TL uphill. Track SO SP Stirling Trail leads 90m to GGS Hut.
▲ *20.7 (0.5)*
T junction. TR. Track on left SP Stirling Trail.

▼ 89.7 (0.5)
Mt Stirling Summit Walking Trail on right. 100m walk to trig and excellent 360° views.
▲ *20.2 (3.9)*
Mt Stirling Summit Walking Trail on left.
GPS S:37 07.678 E:146 29.926
UTM Zone 55 0455476E 5890814N

▼ 93.6 (3.9)
Howqua Gap Hut on right. CSA.
▲ *16.3 (0.1)*
Howqua Gap Hut on left. CSA.

▼ 93.7 (0.1)
Road junction. This is Howqua Gap. TR. This is Circuit Road.
▲ *16.2 (7.1)*
Howqua Gap. TL. SP Howqua Gap Trail.
GPS S:37 08.665 E:146 29.407
UTM Zone 55 0454716E 5888983N

ABOVE: *Mt Stirling Track near Mt Stirling summit.*

▼ 100.8 (7.1)
Telephone Box Junction. Mt Stirling Resort. CSA through Winter Barrier Gates. Road on right SP King Saddle 2km.
▲ *9.1 (9.1)*
Telephone Box Junction. Mt Stirling Resort. Notes VR uphill. SP Howqua Gap 7km. Road SO SP King Saddle.
GPS S:37 06.796 E:146 27.806
UTM Zone 55 0452323E 5892416N

▼ 109.9 (9.1)
Mirimbah. Road junction. TL for SP 14 Mt Buller. TR for SP Mansfield 32.
▲ *0.0 (0.0)*
Zero trip meter at Mirimbah at road junction to SP Mt Stirling. PSA to Mt Stirling. This junction is 32km from Mansfield and 14km from Mt Buller on the C320 Road.
GPS S:37 06.608 E:146 23.892
UTM Zone 55 0446533E 5892743N

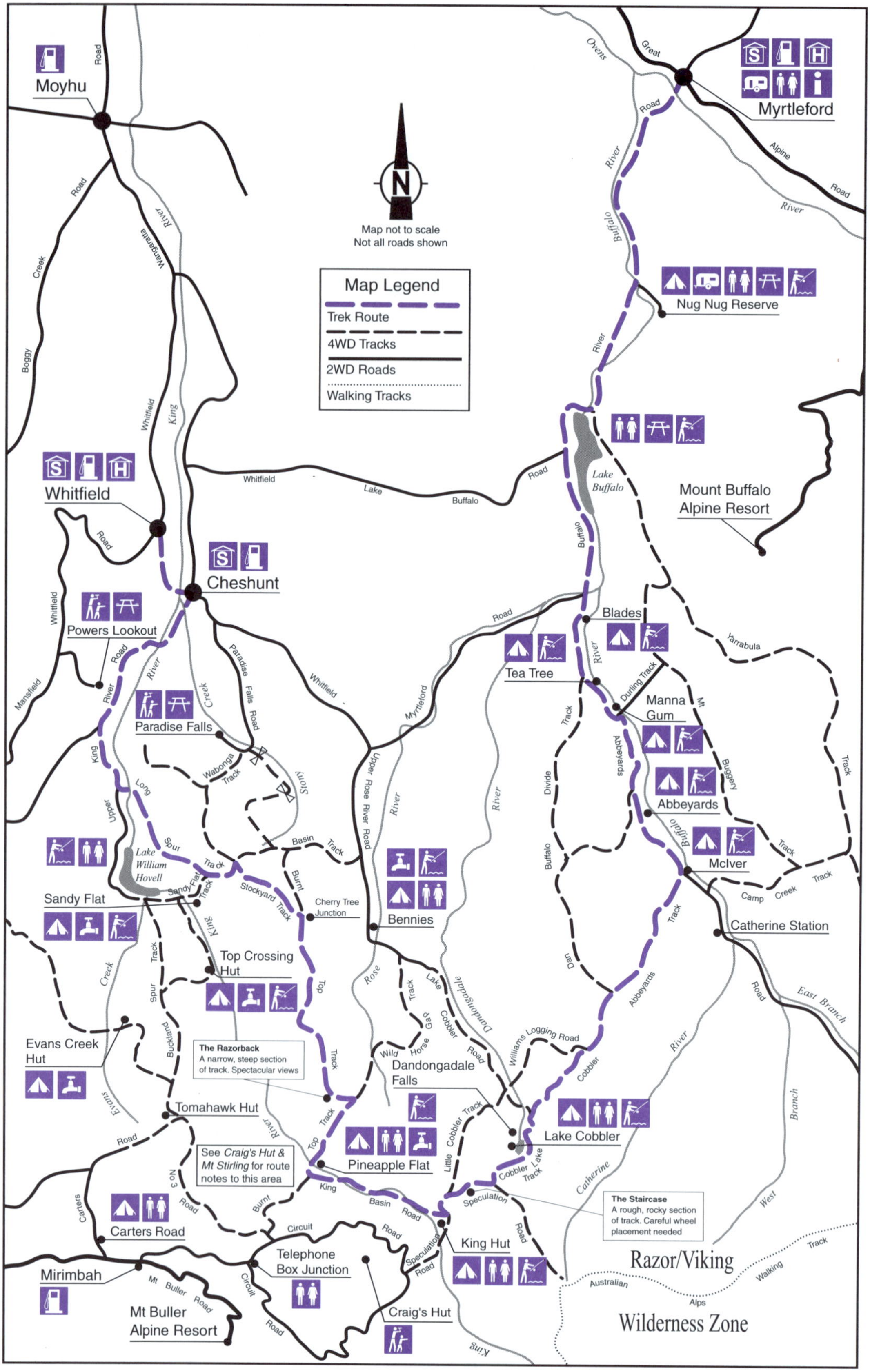

Map not to scale
Not all roads shown
Map Legend
Trek Route
4WD Tracks
2WD Roads
Walking Tracks
Moyhu
Myrtleford
Nug Nug Reserve
Whitfield
Cheshunt
Lake Buffalo
Mount Buffalo Alpine Resort
Powers Lookout
Paradise Falls
Blades
Tea Tree
Manna Gum
Abbeyards
McIver
Catherine Station
Lake William Hovell
Sandy Flat
Top Crossing Hut
Cherry Tree Junction
Bennies
Evans Creek Hut
The Razorback
A narrow, steep section of track. Spectacular views
Dandongadale Falls
Tomahawk Hut
See Craig's Hut & Mt Stirling for route notes to this area
Pineapple Flat
Lake Cobbler
The Staircase
A rough, rocky section of track. Careful wheel placement needed
Carters Road
Telephone Box Junction
King Hut
Razor/Viking
Wilderness Zone
Mirimbah
Mt Buller Alpine Resort
Craig's Hut
Great Alpine Road
Ovens River
Buffalo River
Wangaratta Road
King River
Whitfield Lake Buffalo Road
Boggy Creek Road
Whitfield Road
Mansfield Whitfield Road
Paradise Falls Road
Stony Creek
Wabonga Track
Long Spur Track
Upper King River
Basin Track
Burnt Track
Stockyard Track
Sandy Flat Track
Top Track
Myrtleford Whitfield Road
Upper Rose River Road
Rose River
Durling Track
Abbeyards Track
Mt Buggery Track
Buffalo River
Divide Track
Buffalo Dan Track
Yarrabula Track
Camp Creek Track
East Branch
Catherine River
West Branch
Lake Cobbler Road
Gap Track
Horse Wild
Dandongadale River
Williams Logging Road
Little Cobbler Track
Cobbler Lake Track
Speculation Road
King Basin Road
Circuit Road
Burnt
No 3 Road
Buckland Spur Track
Evans Creek
Mt Buller Road
Australian Alps Walking Track

TREK FOUR

THE COBBLER PLATEAU

TREK 4

On this trek you will take in some delightful and varied scenery and tackle a number of demanding four-wheel drive trails as you wind your way from Whitfield to Myrtleford.

Things to Do and See

Visit Lake William Hovell on the King River and enjoy its facilities.

There is some enjoyable four-wheel driving on the Wabonga Plateau and the traverse of The Razorback with its stunning views is a highlight. Some good camping is to be had at Pineapple Flat and along the King River to King Hut.

The 'Staircase' is a challenging four-wheel drive section on Speculation Road as it winds its way from the King River to the Cobbler Plateau and onto Lake Cobbler with its pleasant camping areas.

Down on the Buffalo River there are plenty of good picnic and camping spots and towards the end of the trek there are some great views across to the imposing Mt Buffalo.

Access

Whitfield, a small town in the King Valley is the start point for this trek. You can reach Whitfield via the all weather bitumen Whitfield-Wangaratta Road from Wangaratta (49km) or from Mansfield via the Whitfield-Mansfield Road (61km).

The Trek

From Whitfield take the King Valley Road to the village of Cheshunt where the route turns into the signposted Upper King River Road towards Lake William Hovell.

fast facts

Whitfield to Myrtleford via 'The Staircase' and Lake Cobbler

Trek distance: 150km

Standard: Medium/Hard (Dry weather only)

Fuel and supplies: Whitfield & Myrtleford

Trek highlights: Lake William Hovell, The Razorback, King River and Hut, The Staircase, Lake Cobbler, Dandongadale Falls and the Buffalo River

Track conditions:
Parks Vic/DNRE Bright
Ph 03/5755 1577

Parks Vic/DNRE Whitfield
Ph 03/5729 8266

Need help?: RACV Myrtleford (4WD Recovery) Ph 03/5752 1257 or 0418 107096

You can visit Lake William Hovell—a water supply dam on the King River by following this road, however our route turns down Long Spur Track and crosses the King River below the dam. After fording the river, which would be impassable during high water levels, follow Long Spur Track as it climbs from the river to the Wabonga Plateau. There are glimpses of Lake William Hovell from the track.

Continuing on, pass Sandy Flat Track on the left to the junction with Stockyard Track, which we follow until its juction with Burnt Top Track at Cherry Tree Junction. After following Burnt Top Track for about 3km you traverse a narrow steep ridge known as The Razorback, from which you obtain good views across to Mt Typo and Mt Cobbler.

After negotiating The Razorback, the trek passes Wild Horse Gap Track while continuing along Burnt Top Track to Pineapple Flat Camping Area beside the King River. From Pineapple Flat cross the river and follow Burnt Top Track until it meets with King Basin Road, which is then followed upriver, crossing the King River a number of times until reaching King Hut and its large grassed camping area. This section of the trek from Pineapple Flat to King Hut overlaps with Trek 3 - *Craig's Hut and Mt Stirling*.

Leaving King Hut continue on King Basin Road for a short distance to the junction with Speculation Road. Our route travels in an easterly direction along Speculation Road towards Lake Cobbler, whereas Trek 3 - *Craig's Hut and Mt Stirling* route turns south to travel to Circuit Road.

Continue on Speculation Road, passing Little Cobbler Track. A little over a kilometre from this point the track begins to deteriorate and then a further two kilometres on you come to a series of rocky steps known as The Staircase. Although these look a little daunting at first, the easiest route is to keep to the left close to the mossy rock wall (this will be on your right if following the route notes in reverse). After negotiating The Staircase you continue climbing until you reach the junction with Cobbler Lake Track. You are now on the Cobbler Plateau.

Turn left into Cobbler Lake Track (Speculation Road continues onto Mt Speculation) and follow this track across the often wet and boggy plateau to Lake Cobbler, a small man-made dam on the Dandongadale River. A camping and picnic area is located on the west side of the lake.

After enjoying Lake Cobbler pick up Lake Cobbler Road which is then followed to Abbeyards Track. From Lake Cobbler Road there are good views across to the impressive 255m drop of Dandongadale Falls, the highest waterfall in Victoria.

Follow Abbeyards Track as it descends to Buffalo River Road and its many pleasant camping areas beside the Buffalo River. Head north along the Buffalo River Road with the imposing massif of Mt Buffalo looming in the distance, passing the backed up waters of Lake Buffalo and the neatly rowed tobacco fields of the Buffalo River Valley to the conclusion of the route notes at Myrtleford.

Standard

This trek is given a medium/hard rating. The crossing of the King River below Lake William Hovell would be impassable at high water and care should be exercised here.

There are a couple of steep sections on Burnt Top Track and the numerous crossings of the King River at Pineapple Flat and along King Basin Road may require care. Care should also be exercised at The Staircase, which requires careful wheel placement to negotiate safely.

This is a dry weather only trek and should not be attempted during times of wet weather.

BELOW: *Long Spur Track enters Alpine National Park after crossing the King River.*

Camping

There are a number of very good camping opportunities to be had on this trek. For those visiting Lake William Hovell you will find good camp sites at the top end of the lake beside the King River at Sandy Flat and Top Hut (See *Camping Guide to Victoria* by Boiling Billy Publications for details).

Camping areas along the trek route are at Pineapple Flat and King Hut, both beside the King River, Lake Cobbler which has a shelter hut, and a number of camp sites with facilities along the Buffalo River Road on the banks of the Buffalo River. Camping is also available at Nug Nug Reserve which is located near Myrtleford. All camp sites, along with possible bush camping areas are listed in the route notes.

Please note that camping is not permitted at Lake William Hovell or Lake Buffalo.

Permits/Restrictions

This trek is restricted by seasonal road closures which are usually in force from after the Queen's Birthday Long Weekend to just after the Melbourne Cup in November.

Recommended Maps/Guides

Hema Maps *High Country - Victoria* map shows the trek route in its entirety as does the CFA *North East Rural Directory - Regions 23 and 24* (maps 331, 332, 369, 370, 333, 298).

The Brookes Bush Maps, Victoria *Wabonga Plateau* and *Watersheds of the King, Howqua and Jamieson Rivers* show part of the trek as does the *Mansfield - Mt Howitt Adventure Map* by Rooftop Mapping Services.

Topographic maps for this trek are the *Mansfield*, *Howitt*, *Whitfield* and *Buffalo* in the 1:100 000 series.

Further Information

Parks Victoria and Dept of Natural Resources and Environment
46 Bakers Gully Road, Bright VIC 3741 Ph 03/5755 1577 Fax 03/5755 1176

Dept of Natural Resources and Environment
Great Alpine Road, Ovens VIC 3738 Ph 03/5731 1222 Fax 03/5731 1223

Parks Victoria and Dept of Natural Resources and Environment
Main Street, Whitfield VIC 3733 Ph 03/5729 8266 Fax 03/5729 8479

Brochures - Parks Victoria: *Alpine National Park - valleys and bluffs around Mansfield and Whitfield*

HISTORY

Lake Cobbler

The delightful Lake Cobbler was originally a subalpine wetland area located on the Cobbler Plateau. The present day lake, which was formed by damming the Dandongadale River is believed to have been built in the 1950s by timber-getters for fishing and protection from bush fires.

Today, the shores of the snow gum lined lake provide for pleasant picnicking and camping. Basic facilities are provided for visitors.

Keen observers may catch glimpses of majestic peregrine falcons as they soar over the Cobbler Plateau. The falcons use the Mt Cobbler area and the cliffs of the Cobbler Plateau for nesting.

TREK 4

ROUTE NOTES

Trek commences in the town of Whitfield, 61km north of Mansfield and 49km south of Wangaratta.

▼ 0.0 (0.0)
Zero trip meter in Whitfield. Mountain View Hotel on right. PSA towards SP 5 Cheshunt.
▲ *150.0 (4.6)*
Whitfield. Mountain View Hotel on left. CSA to Wangaratta 49km or TL for Mansfield 61km.
GPS S:36 45.969 E:146 24.850
UTM Zone 55 0447714E 5930910N

▼ 4.6 (4.6)
Road junction. TR. SP Upper King River Rd. SP Lake William Hovell.
▲ *145.4 (14.0)*
Cross roads. TL. SP 5 Whitfield. SP 55 Wangaratta.

▼ 18.6 (14.0)
Road junction. TL. SP Long Spur Tk. Road SO leads 3km to Lake William Hovell, Sandy Flat and Top Crossing Hut Camping Areas.
▲ *131.4 (0.5)*
T junction with bitumen road. TR. This is Upper King River Rd.
GPS S:36 53.625 E:146 23.099
UTM Zone 55 0445206E 5916742N

▼ 19.1 (0.5)
Cross King River and enter Alpine National Park through seasonal closure gate.
▲ *130.9 (4.1)*
Cross King River.

▼ 22.0 (2.9)
Track begins to climb steeply. Glimpses of Lake William Hovell on right.

▼ 23.2 (1.2)
Track now levels out across Wabonga Plateau.
▲ *126.8 (3.3)*
Track begins steep decline from this point.

▼ 26.5 (3.3)
Track junction. CSA. SP Long Spur Tk. Track on right SP Sandy Flat Tk leads a short distance to Sandy Flat Camping Area on King River. *NB:* this track is steep in sections and is definitely a dry weather only track.
▲ *123.5 (1.9)*
Track junction. CSA. SP Long Spur Tk. Track on left SP Sandy Flat Tk.
GPS S:36 55.643 E:146 26.187
UTM Zone 55 0449803E 5913037N

▼ 28.4 (1.9)
Track junction. TR. SP Stockyard Tk.
▲ *121.6 (4.5)*
T junction. TL. SP Long Spur Tk.
GPS S:36 55.685 E:146 27.414
UTM Zone 55 0451631E 5912967N

▼ 32.9 (4.5)
Cross Stockyard Creek.
▲ *117.1 (3.0)*
Cross Stockyard Creek.

▼ 35.9 (3.0)
Track junction. This is Cherry Tree Junction. TR. SP Burnt Top Tk.
▲ *114.1 (3.0)*
Track junction. TL. SP Stockyard Tk.
GPS S:36 58.402 E:146 29.798
UTM Zone 55 0455195E 5907962N

▼ 38.9 (3.0)
The Razorback. This is a steep, rocky and narrow section of track. Excellent views to Mt Cobbler and Mt Buller. From The Razorback there is a short, steep descent.
▲ *111.1 (2.0)*
The Razorback.
GPS S:37 01.156 E:146 30.380
UTM Zone 55 0456087E 5902876N

▼ 40.9 (2.0)
SP Burnt Top. CSA.
▲ *109.1 (1.6)*
SP Burnt Top. CSA.

▼ 42.5 (1.6)
Track junction. TR. This is a continuation of Burnt Top Tk. Track on left SP Wild Horse Gap Tk.
▲ *107.5 (7.4)*
Track junction. TL. SP Burnt Top Tk. Track SO SP Wild Horse Gap Tk.
GPS S:37 02.273 E:146 31.549
UTM Zone 55 0457828E 5900815N

▼ 49.9 (7.4)
Pineapple Flat Camping Area. CSA through camping area on main track to river crossing.

▲ *100.1 (0.1)*
Pineapple Flat Camping Area. CSA through on main track.
GPS S:37 03.948 E:146 29.952
UTM Zone 55 0455479E 5897711N

▼ 50.0 (0.1)
Cross King River.

▲ *100.0 (0.6)*
Cross King River.

▼ 50.6 (0.6)
Track junction. Sharp TL. SP King Basin Rd.
NB: Craig's Hut & Mt Stirling trek joins here.

▲ *99.4(2.9)*
Track junction. Sharp TR. SP Pineapple Flat.
GPS S:37 04.162 E:146 29.814
UTM Zone 55 0455276E 5897312N

▼ 53.5 (2.9)
Minor track on right. KL.

▲ *96.5 (1.3)*
Minor track on left. CSA.

▼ 54.8 (1.3)
Tracks on left lead to camp site by river. Notes CSA.

▲ *95.2 (2.0)*
Tracks on right. CSA.

▼ 56.8 (2.0)
Track on left leads to camp site by river. Notes CSA.

▲ *93.2 (1.3)*
Track on right. CSA.

▼ 58.1 (1.3)
Cross King River and enter SP Alpine National Park.

▲ *91.9 (0.4)*
Cross King River.
GPS S:37 04.809 E:146 33.564
UTM Zone 55 0460833E 5896140N

▼ 58.5 (0.4)
Cross King River. Bush camp site on left over river.

▲ *91.5 (0.5)*
Bush camp site on right. CSA and cross King River.

ABOVE: A *section of 'The Staircase' on Speculation Road.*

▼ 59.0 (0.5)
Cross river.

▲ *91.0 (0.3)*
Cross river.

▼ 59.3 (0.3)
Cross river.

▲ *90.7 (0.4)*
Cross river.

▼ 59.7 (0.4)
Cross river.

▲ *90.3 (0.1)*
Cross river.

▼ 59.8 (0.1)
King Hut on right. Camping in this vicinity. Notes CSA.

▲ *90.2 (0.1)*
King Hut on left. CSA.
GPS S:37 05.298 E:146 34.336
UTM Zone 55 0461986E 5895245N

▼ 59.9 (0.1)
Track junction. KL.

▲ *90.1 (0.8)*
Track on left. CSA.

▼ 60.7 (0.8)
Track junction. CSA through gate. LAF. Track on right SP Speculation Rd.

▲ *89.3 (3.3)*
Track junction. CSA. SP King Hut. Track on left SP Speculation Rd. (Craig's Hut & Mt Stirling Trek joins here)
GPS S:37 05.343 E:146 34.894
UTM Zone 55 0462814E 5895172N

▼ 64.0 (3.3)
Seasonal closure gate at junction. CSA uphill. Track on left SP Little Cobbler Tk.

▲ *86.0 (1.3)*
Track junction. CSA through seasonal closure gate. Track on right SP Little Cobbler Tk.

▼ 65.3 (1.3)
Bridge. Track deteriorates from here.

▲ *84.7 (2.3)*
Bridge.

▼ 67.4 (2.1)
This rough rocky section is known as 'The Staircase'.

▲ *82.4 (1.3)*
Rough rocky downhill section of 'The Staircase'. Careful wheel placement required.

Alternative Route

If you do not wish to travel 'The Staircase' then this section can be detoured by VL at route note reading 64.0km into SP Little Cobbler Tk and following this for 12.5km to Cobbler Lake Road. At Cobbler Lake Road TR and travel for 3km to meet Abbeyards Track or continue on to Lake Cobbler.

▼ 68.9 (1.5)
Track junction. This is Cobbler Plateau. TL. This is Cobbler Lake Track. Track on right SP Mt Speculation.

▲ *81.1 (4.7)*
Track junction. TR. SP King River. Start descent down area known as SP "The Staircase". Track on left SP Mt Speculation.
GPS S:37 04.290 E:146 36.579
UTM Zone 55 0465300E 5897120N

▼ 73.6 (4.7)
Track junction. KR. Track on left SP Lake Cobbler leads 500m to camping area.

▲ *76.4 (1.5)*
Track junction. KL and CSA through seasonal closure gate. SP Mt Speculation. Track on right SP Lake Cobbler.
GPS S:37 02.970 E:146 37.836
UTM Zone 55 0467155E 5899572N

▼ 75.1 (1.5)
Views across valley to Dandongadale Falls.

▲ *74.9 (1.2)*
Views across valley to falls.

▼ 76.3 (1.2)
Track junction. VR. SP Abbeyard Tk. Track now climbs and declines steeply over the ridges before reaching the Buffalo Valley.

▲ *73.7 (2.5)*
Track junction. TL. SP Cobbler Lake Rd.
GPS S:37 02.195 E:146 38.103
UTM Zone 55 0467544E 5901007N

▼ 78.8 (2.5)
Track junction. CSA. SP Abbeyard-Cobbler Lake Tk. Track on left SP Williams Logging Rd.

▲ *71.2 (5.2)*
Track on right. CSA. SP Abbeyard-Cobbler Lake Tk. Track climbs steeply from here.

▼ 84.0 (5.2)
Lookout point. Good views from knoll.

▲ *66.0 (2.0)*
Lookout point. Good views.

▼ 86.0 (2.0)
Track junction. KR. Track on left SP Dan Buffalo Divide.

▲ *64.0 (8.8)*
Track junction. KL. SP Cobbler-Lake Tk. Track on right SP Dan Buffalo Divide.
GPS S:36 58.967 E:146 40.343
UTM Zone 55 0470839E 5906992N

▼ 94.8 (8.8)
Gate. LAF.

▲ *55.2 (1.1)*
Gate. LAF.

▼ 95.9 (1.1)
Minor track on left. CSA through gate. LAF.

▲ *54.1 (0.1)*
Gate. LAF. Through gate minor track on right. CSA.

▼ 96.0 (0.1)
Track junction. This is Abbeyards Road. TL. Track on right leads approximately 50km to junction of Zeka Spur Track and Rileys Creek Track for Wonnangatta Station.

▲ *54.0 (2.1)*
Track junction. TR. SP Cobbler-Lake Tk. This is directly opposite SP McIver Picnic Area.
GPS S:36 55.699 E:146 43.107
UTM Zone 55 0474924E 5913042N

▼ 98.1 (2.1)
SP Abbeyards Picnic Area on right. CSA.

▲ *51.9 (11.1)*
SP Abbeyards Picnic Area on left. CSA.

▼ 109.2 (11.1)
Track junction. CSA. Track on right SP Durling Tk.

▲ *40.8 (1.7)*
SP Durling Tk on left. CSA.

▼ 110.9 (1.7)
Manna Gum Picnic and Camping Area on right. CSA.

▲ *39.1 (1.2)*
Camping and picnic area on left. CSA.

▼ 112.1 (1.2)
Tea-Tree Picnic and Camping Area on right. CSA.

▲ *37.9 (0.3)*
Camping and picnic area on left. CSA.

▼ 112.4 (0.3)
SP Dan Buffalo Divide on left. CSA.

▲ *37.6 (1.8)*
SP Dan Buffalo Divide on right. CSA.

▼ 114.2 (1.8)
Road on left. CSA.

▲ *35.8 (0.4)*
Road on right. KL on main road.

▼ 114.6 (0.4)
Blades Picnic Area on right. CSA.

▲ *35.4 (2.8)*
Blades Picnic Area on left. CSA.

▼ 117.4 (2.8)
Road junction. CSA on bitumen towards Myrtleford. Road on left SP 35 Whitfield.

▲ *32.6 (19.5)*
Road junction. CSA onto gravel road. SP Abbeyards 19.

▼ 136.9 (19.5)
Road junction. CSA. Road on right SP Nug Nug Rd leads 1.2km to Nug Nug Reserve Camping Area.

▲ *13.1 (13.1)*
Road on left SP Nug Nug Rd leads to camping area. Notes CSA.

▼ 150.0 (13.1)
Myrtleford. Junction with Great Alpine Road.

▲ *0.0 (0.0)*
Zero trip meter on Great Alpine Road in Myrtleford. PSA south towards SP 21 Lake Buffalo.
GPS S:36 33.648 E:146 43.428
UTM Zone 55 0475286E 5953780N

HANDY TIP

First Aid Kits

It is essential that you carry a well stocked first aid kit with you on your travels throughout the High Country. Good first aid kits are available from the Red Cross, St Johns Ambulance, pharmacies and most camping and outdoor stores or you can make up your own to suit your individual needs.

As well as taking along a first aid kit it is vital that someone in your family or party has a good knowledge of applying first aid. Both the St Johns Ambulance Society and the Red Cross run First Aid Courses. These courses are conducted on a regular basis and are highly recommended. Check your local phone book for contact details.

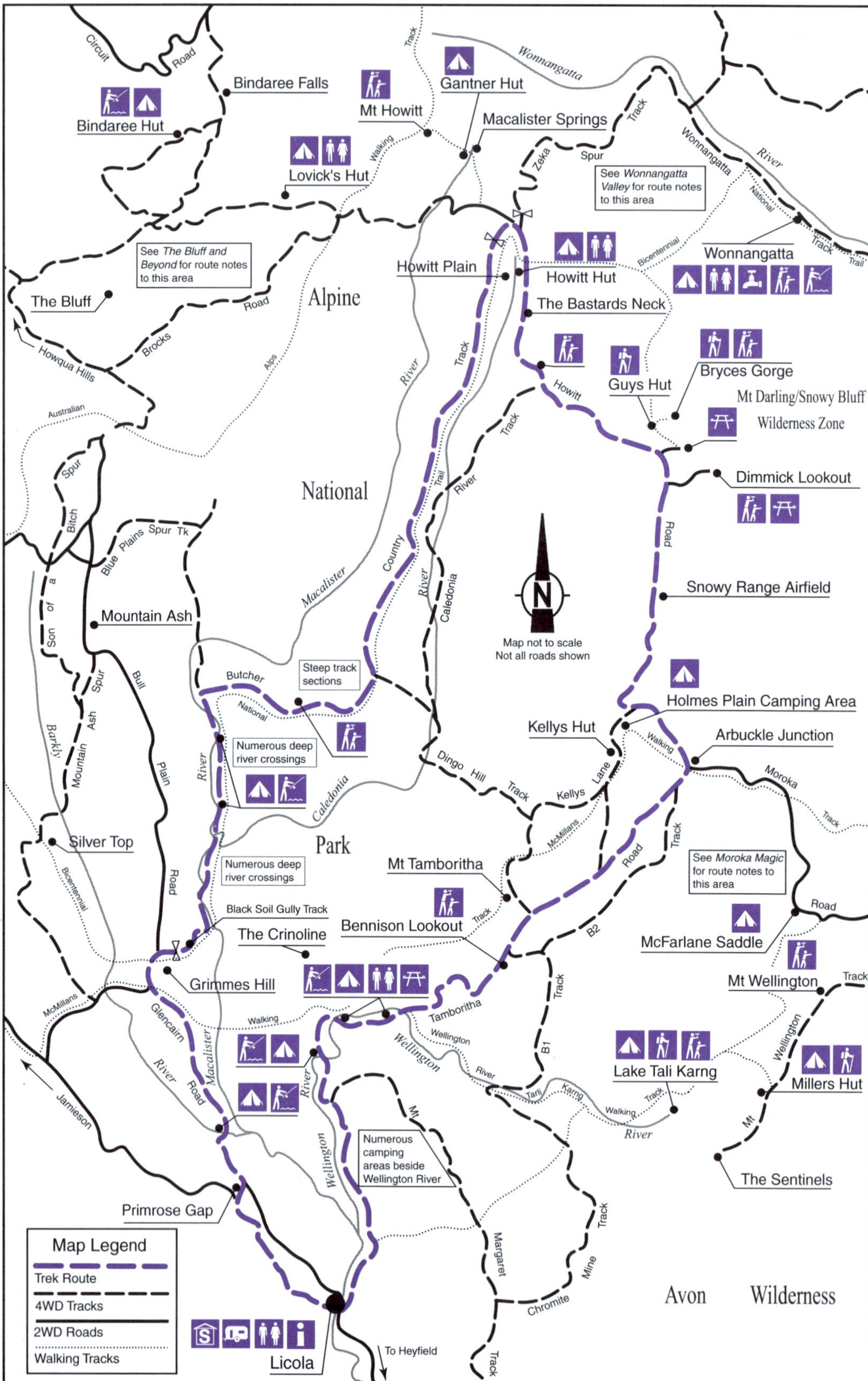
Bindaree Falls
Bindaree Hut
Mt Howitt
Gantner Hut
Macalister Springs
Lovick's Hut
Wonnangatta
Wonnangatta River
See Wonnangatta Valley for route notes to this area
See The Bluff and Beyond for route notes to this area
The Bluff
Howitt Plain
Howitt Hut
The Bastards Neck
Alpine
National
Park
Guys Hut
Bryces Gorge
Mt Darling/Snowy Bluff Wilderness Zone
Dimmick Lookout
Snowy Range Airfield
Map not to scale
Not all roads shown
Mountain Ash
Steep track sections
Numerous deep river crossings
Holmes Plain Camping Area
Kellys Hut
Arbuckle Junction
Silver Top
Mt Tamboritha
See Moroka Magic for route notes to this area
Black Soil Gully Track
The Crinoline
Bennison Lookout
McFarlane Saddle
Grimmes Hill
Mt Wellington
Lake Tali Karng
Millers Hut
Numerous camping areas beside Wellington River
The Sentinels
Primrose Gap
Map Legend
Trek Route
4WD Tracks
2WD Roads
Walking Tracks
Licola
To Heyfield
Avon Wilderness

TREK FIVE

BUTCHER COUNTRY

THE WILD AND REMOTE Macalister River and oddly named Butcher Country are explored in this interesting and challenging trek.

Things to Do and See

The camping and fishing along the Macalister River, along with the challenging four-wheel driving of Butcher Country Track are highlights of this trek.

Up on Howitt Plain you can walk to Mt Howitt (named in honour of explorer Alfred Howitt), Macalister Springs and Gantner Hut. On the edge of the plain is Howitt Hut and its camping area.

Off the Howitt Road is Guy's Hut and Bryce's Gorge, both of which can be accessed by a short walking track. In addition Dimmock Lookout offers superb views across the Mt Darling/Snowy Bluff Wilderness Area. You also pass by The Snowy Range Airstrip—the highest in Australia.

On the Tamboritha Road below Tamboritha Saddle is Bennison Lookout with its panoramic vistas over the Wellington River Valley.

Access

The village of Licola, situated on the banks of the Macalister River, is the start and finish point for this trek. Licola can be reached from Heyfield (54km) via the all weather Heyfield-Licola Road or from Mansfield via Jamieson (130km) on the Jamieson-Licola Road (95km gravel between Jamieson and Licola).

The Trek

From Licola, the route notes follow the Jamieson Road for around 8km to the Barkly River Road. Follow this road to Primrose Gap then to the Barkly River where there is a bush camping area near the bridge. The route now travels along Glencairn Road before joining with Bull Plain Road. A short distance along Bull Plain Road the trek turns into Black Soil Gully Road, which descends to the Macalister River.

fast facts

Licola to Licola via the Macalister River and Howitt Plain

Trek distance: 158km

Standard: Medium/Hard (Dry weather only)

Fuel and supplies: Licola

Trek highlights: Macalister River, Butcher Country Track, Howitt Hut, Guy's Hut and Bryce's Gorge

Track conditions:
Parks Vic/DNRE Heyfield
Ph 03/5139 7777

Arriving down on the Macalister River, we follow the Macalister River Track upstream, crossing the river on seven occasions until joining with Butcher Country Track.

Butcher Country Track climbs steeply from the river and continues to do so for much of its journey until you reach Howitt Plain. There are some excellent views to be had from Butcher Country Track.

Once on Howitt Plain, the last few kilometres of Butcher Country Track tends to be slippery and boggy as it crosses this low lying plain before reaching Howitt Road.

At Howitt Plain you have the option of continuing on with the route notes which follow Howitt Road to Arbuckle

Junction then Tamboritha Road to the Wellington River then onto Licola. At Arbuckle Junction you can pick up Trek 7 - *Moroka Magic* which will take you to Dargo or on Howitt Plain you can follow Zeka Spur Track which leads to Wonnangatta Valley (Trek 6 - *Wonnangatta Valley*). Another option is to join Brocks Road (known as King Billy Track at this point) at the end of Howitt Road which leads to Howqua Hills and Trek 2 - *The Bluff and Beyond*.

Standard

We have rated this trek medium/hard due to the number of deep river crossings (seven) of the Macalister River and the steep and rough nature of Butcher Country Track. This trek is best undertaken by experienced drivers with appropriate recovery gear, including a winch.

During late summer when the river flow is at its lowest these crossings should pose little problem, however in spring and after rain the Macalister River can carry quite a volume of water. It would be wise to check these crossings on foot before plunging in. Having a snorkle fitted to a diesel vehicle is always good insurance for water crossings.

There are some moderately steep sections to be negotiated on Butcher Country Track which will require careful wheel placement and judicious use of the throttle. In recent times the track has been re-routed around most of the steepest sections, although it is still a rough journey and many drivers will find Butcher Country Track challenging. The top end of Butcher Country Track where it crosses Howitt Plain can become very boggy in the wet and is best avoided in these conditions.

Camping

Bush camping is available at the Barkly River and a number of secluded sites beside the Macalister River. None of these sites have facilities.

Once on Butcher Country Track camping is limited to a few small clearings that would be suitable for an overnight stay. Up on Howitt Plain there is a camping area with facilities near Howitt Hut and camping is possible at Holmes Plain near Arbuckle Junction.

You can camp at Thomastown Camping Area on Tamboritha Road and there are a number of good camp sites with facilities beside the Wellington River before reaching Licola.

Permits/Restrictions

This trek is restricted by seasonal road closures which are usually in force from after the Queen's Birthday Long Weekend to just after the Melbourne Cup in November.

Recommended Maps/Guides

The best maps for this trek are the Brookes Bush Maps, Victoria *Macalister River Watershed*, *Jamieson - Licola Adventure Map* by Rooftop Mapping Services, the Hema Maps *High Country - Victoria* map and the CFA *North East Rural Directory - Regions 23 and 24* (maps 452, 409, 410).

Topographic maps for this trek are the *Licola - Wellington*, *Tamboritha - Moroka* and *Howitt - Selwyn* 1:50 000 series. These maps show good detail and are worthwhile having for this trek.

Further Information

Parks Victoria and Dept of Natural Resources and Environment
Licola Road, Heyfield VIC 3858 Ph 03/5139 7777 Fax 03/5139 7733

Licola General Store and Caravan Park
Jamieson Road, Licola Ph 03/5148 8786

Brochures - Parks Victoria: *Alpine National Park - walks around Howitt, Snowy Range and Tali Karng.*
Parks Victoria: *Alpine National Park - around Heyfield, Licola and Dargo in the Wonnangatta/ Moroka area*

ABOVE: *Travelling the Wombat Range Track between Eaglevale and Wonnangatta Valley (Trek 6)*

TOP: *There are great views across to the western face of the* Kosciuszko Main Range *from* Geehi (*Trek* 17)

ABOVE: Harrison's Cut *water diversion channel on the* Dargo River (*Trek* 10)

RIGHT: *Looking towards* The Cobberas *from near* The Playgrounds (*Trek* 16)

ABOVE: *One of a large number of camp sites scattered throughout the Wonnangatta Valley (Trek 6)*

BELOW: *Coolamine Homestead in Kosciuszko National Park was one of only a few permanently occupied (both summer and winter) grazing properties in the New South Wales Alps (Trek 20)*

TOP: *The remote Wonnangatta Valley is a four-wheel drive mecca and as such can be very popular over holiday periods, however this large valley can accommodate up to several hundred camp sites!* (Trek 6)

ABOVE: *The walking track to Guy's Hut and Conglomerate Gorge are well signposted. The walk leaves from Howitt Road* (Trek 5)

RIGHT: *Guy's Hut is a good example of a log cabin style cattlemen's hut. There are numerous huts like this scattered throughout the High Country* (Trek 5)

RIGHT: *Enjoying a breakfast 'cuppa' at Horse Yard Flat Camping Area on the banks of the Moroka River (Trek 7)*

BELOW: *Charlie's Plain and nearby Charlie's Plain Hut is a pleasant spot for an overnight camp (Trek 15)*

BOTTOM: *The historic Washington Steam Winch was used to haul saw logs out of a deep gully near Swifts Creek. The winch fell into disuse during the early 1960s and is now being restored (Trek 12)*

TOP: Admiring the vistas across the border into New South Wales from Ingeegoodbee Track (Trek 16)

ABOVE: Bluff Hut was built by Eadley Stoney in 1956 on his Bluff lease and is still used by the Stoney family as a base for their High Country horse treks. Visitors are welcome to use the hut when the Stoney's aren't in residence (Trek 2)

RIGHT: Passing through a stand of alpine ash on the way to Mt Pinnibar. Alpine ash is a highly valued timber and is found growing at altitudes up to 1400m above sea level (Trek 14)

TOP: *Remains of a boiler at Dogtown* (Trek 11)

ABOVE LEFT: *Paddy's River Dam* (Trek 19)

ABOVE: *Memorial at The Dog's Grave is a lasting reminder to the special friendship between a working dog and his master* (Trek 10)

LEFT: *The tranquil waters of Lake Cobbler. The lake was built by timber cutters in the 1950s by damming the Dandongadale River* (Trek 4)

ABOVE: *Jewellers Shop Mine - Grant Historic Area (Trek 8)*

ABOVE: *Tunnel through Tunnel Spur (Treks 1 & 2)*

ABOVE: *Historic Grant Cemetery (Trek 8)*

Travelling Howitt Road and The Snowy Plain

The trip along Howitt Road and the Snowy Plain is considered to be one of the most scenic and interesting jaunts in the Victorian High Country. Cutting across the Snowy Plain from Arbuckle Junction to Howitt Plain, Howitt Road takes in stunning views from a number of lookouts, provides access to interesting walks to places of natural beauty as well as highlighting reminders of our High Country heritage. Below is a list of highlights that you'll see while travelling this road.

Howitt Hut

Mt Howitt Walking Track – This 14km return walk (allow between 5-6 hrs) will take you past the source of the Macalister River, through snow gums and across snow plains to the 1742 metre high summit of Mt Howitt.

Butcher Country Track and Zeka Spur Track – Both these tracks join with Howitt Road on Howitt Plain. Butcher Country Track winds up from the Macalister River while Zeka Spur Track is an alternate route from the Wonnangatta Valley.

Howitt Hut – Built on Howitt Plain in the early 1900s and originally constructed of split timber slabs and a shingle roof, the present day hut is of corrugated iron sheets. It was not far from here that the body of John Bamford (see *The Wonnangatta Mystery* pages 74-77) was found.

Dry River Walking Track Head – This walking track follows the original route used to drive cattle from the Wonnangatta Valley to Howitt Plain for summer grazing. From the track head it is 11km to the Wonnangatta Valley and this track forms part of the Bicentennial National Trail.

Bastards Neck – A narrow ridge which connects Snowy and Howitt Plains which is traversed by Howitt Road. It was named by stockmen who often had difficulty driving their cattle over this route.

Bryce's Gorge Walk – This picturesque walking track (eight kilometre circuit suitable for families) leaves from a small car park and picnic area beside Howitt Road and leads one kilometre to Guy's Hut, a cattlemen's hut built in the 1940s, then continues onto Conglomerate Falls and Bryce's Gorge, returning via Piemans Falls. An alternative is to continue on past Guy's Hut for 19km to Wonnangatta Station.

Dimmock Lookout

Dimmick Lookout – A signposted track off Howitt Road leads two kilometres to this lookout with great views over the Conglomerate Creek Valley and the Mt Darling/Snowy Bluff Wilderness Zone.

Snowy Range Airstrip – The highest airfield in Australia (1620 metres above sea level) which was constructed by the DNRE to provide aerial firefighting facilities for the High Country.

Kellys Lane – Leads a short distance to Holmes Plain Camping Area (no facilities) and then to Kellys Hut and McMichaels Hut. Kellys Lane joins with the Tamboritha Road at Tamboritha Saddle.

Arbuckle Junction – Is the road junction of Moroka Road and Tamboritha Road with Howitt Road. It was named by explorer Angus McMillan after his friend, fellow Scot Dr Alexander Arbuckle, who often accompanied McMillan on his early expeditions.

Trek commences in the village of Licola.

▼ 0.0 (0.0)
Zero trip meter at Licola. General Store on right. Head in north-west direction towards Jamieson.
▲ *157.1 (8.8)*
Licola General Store on left.
GPS S:37 37.660 E:146 37.399
UTM Zone 55 0466760E 5835425N

▼ 8.8 (8.8)
Y junction. VR. SP Glen Cairn 10. SP Barkly River Road. Road on left SP Jamieson 84. SP 121 Mansfield.
▲ *148.3 (1.8)*
Road junction. CSA. SP Heyfield. Road on right SP Jamieson 84.
GPS S:37 35.299 E:146 34.255
UTM Zone 55 0462118E 5839775N

▼ 10.6 (1.8)
Track on right. KL and cross grid in fence. This is SP Primrose Gap.
▲ *146.5 (2.6)*
Cross grid and KR heading uphill.

▼ 13.2 (2.6)
KL.
▲ *143.9 (1.3)*
KR.

▼ 14.5 (1.3)
Barkly River bush camping. Notes CSA.
▲ *142.6 (0.1)*
Barkly River camping area. CSA.
GPS S:37 33.537 E:146 34.092
UTM Zone 55 0461864E 5843027N

▼ 14.6 (0.1)
Bridge over Barkly River.
▲ *142.5 (5.9)*
Bridge over Barkly River.

▼ 20.5 (5.9)
Y junction. KL uphill.
▲ *136.6 (3.8)*
Track on left. CSA.

▼ 24.3 (3.8)
Cross roads. TR.
▲ *132.8 (3.4)*
Cross roads. TL.
GPS S:37 30.355 E:146 31.379
UTM Zone 55 0457841E 5848895N

▼ 27.7 (3.4)
Track junction. TR. SP Black Soil Gully.
▲ *129.4 (2.6)*
Track junction. TL. This is Bull Plain Road.
GPS S:37 29.390 E:146 31.661
UTM Zone 55 0458246E 5850682N

▼ 30.3 (2.6)
Seasonal closure gate.
▲ *126.8 (0.9)*
Seasonal closure gate.

▼ 31.2 (0.9)
Track junction. TL.
▲ *125.9 (3.5)*
Track junction. TR.

▼ 34.7 (3.5)
Track junction. TL. Track on right leads to junction of Macalister and Caledonia Rivers and bush camp sites.
▲ *122.4 (0.1)*
Track junction. TR and head uphill.
GPS S:37 27.620 E:146 33.179
UTM Zone 55 0460466E 5853966N

▼ 34.8 (0.1)
Cross Macalister River for the first time.
▲ *122.3 (0.9)*
Cross Macalister River.

▼ 35.7 (0.9)
Wide river crossing.
▲ *121.4 (0.2)*
Wide river crossing.

▼ 35.9 (0.2)
River crossing. Small camp site on left prior to river.
▲ *121.2 (1.6)*
River crossing.

▼ 37.5 (1.6)
KR. Small camping area on left beside river.
▲ *119.6 (2.0)*
KL.

▼ 39.5 (2.0)
River crossing. Good camping area just over river.
▲ *117.6 (0.5)*
River crossing.

▼ 40.0 (0.5)
River crossing.
▲ *117.1 (0.8)*
River crossing.

▼ 40.8 (0.8)
Track on left. KR.
▲ *116.3 (1.3)*
Track on right. CSA.

▼ 42.1 (1.3)
Small camping area on left. CSA.
▲ *115.0 (0.4)*
Small camping area on right. CSA.

▼ 42.5 (0.4)
River crossing. Camp site on left just over river.
▲ *114.6 (1.3)*
River crossing.

▼ 43.8 (1.3)
Last crossing of Macalister River.
▲ *113.3 (0.4)*
First crossing of Macalister River.
GPS S:37 23.717 E:146 32.514
UTM Zone 55 0459453E 5861176N

▼ 44.2 (0.4)
Cross roads. TR. This is Butcher Country Track. Track now climbs steeply.
▲ *112.9 (7.0)*
Cross roads. TL.

▼ 51.2 (7.0)
Track junction. TL and head uphill. Track SO is Caledonia River Track.
▲ *105.9 (3.5)*
Track junction. TR and head uphill.
GPS S:37 23.722 E:146 36.288
UTM Zone 55 0465024E 5861193N

▼ 54.7 (3.5)
Track junction. TL. Track on right leads to Caledonia River Track.
▲ *102.4 (2.5)*
Track junction. TR. After turning KL on main track.

▼ 56.7 (2.0)
Short steep downhill section from here.
▲ *99.9 (11.4)*
Short steep climb ahead.

ABOVE: *The Macalister River at the junction with the Caledonia River.*

▼ 68.6 (11.9)
Minor track on left. CSA.
▲ *88.5 (4.3)*
Minor track on right. CSA.

▼ 72.9 (4.3)
Complete climb onto Howitt Plain. From here to next reading track is black soil and can be wet and very boggy.
▲ *84.2 (4.3)*
Howitt Plain. Begin descent from here.

▼ 77.2 (4.3)
Track junction. This is Howitt Road. TR.
▲ *79.9 (0.3)*
Track junction. TL. SP Butcher Country Trk.
GPS S:37 12.645 E:146 41.419
UTM Zone 55 0472522E 5881704N

▼ 77.5 (0.3)
Track junction. Notes CSA. Track on left SP Zeka Spur Tk. Refer to Trek 6 - Wonnangatta Valley.
▲ *79.6 (1.4)*
SP Zeka Spur Tk on right. CSA.

▼ 78.9 (1.4)
Dry River Walking Track car park on left. CSA.
▲ *78.2 (0.4)*
Dry River Walking Track car park on right. CSA.

▼ 79.3 (0.4)
Dry River Walking Track Head on left leads 11km to Wonnangatta. This walking track is part of the Bicentennial National Trail. Notes CSA.
▲ *77.8 (0.4)*
Dry River Walking Track Head on right. CSA.

▼ 79.7 (0.4)
SP Howitt Hut on right. CSA.
▲ *77.4 (0.6)*
Howitt Hut on left. CSA.

▼ 80.3 (0.6)
Good views on left over Wonnangatta Valley. CSA.
▲ *76.8 (11.9)*
Good views on right. CSA.

▼ 92.2 (11.9)
SP Bryce Gorge Car Park on left. Bryce's Gorge Walk leads 1km to Guy's Hut and 19km to Wonnanagatta Station. Notes CSA.
▲ *64.9 (2.0)*
Walking track car park on right. CSA.
GPS S:37 17.720 E:146 45.596
UTM Zone 55 0478723E 5872338N

▼ 94.2 (2.0)
Track junction. Notes CSA. Track on left SP Dimmick Lookout leads 2km to lookout over Mt Darling/Snowy Bluff Wilderness Zone.
▲ *62.9 (4.5)*
SP Dimmick Lookout on right. CSA.

▼ 98.7 (4.5)
Snowy Range Airstrip. Highest airfield in Australia – 1600m. CSA.
▲ *58.4 (2.5)*
Snowy Range Airstrip.

▼ 101.2 (2.5)
Seasonal closure gate.
▲ *55.9 (4.1)*
Seasonal closure gate.

▼ 105.3 (4.1)
Seasonal closure gate.
▲ *51.8 (0.3)*
Seasonal closure gate.

▼ 105.6 (0.3)
Track junction. Notes CSA. Track on right SP Kellys Lane leads to Holmes Plain Camping Area, 2.6km to Kellys Hut and 4km to McMichaels Hut.
▲ *51.5 (4.6)*
SP Kellys Lane on left. KR on main track.

▼ 110.2 (4.6)
SP Arbuckle Junction. CSA. SP Tamboritha Rd. Road on left SP Moroka Road.
▲ *46.9 (6.5)*
SP Arbuckle Junction. CSA. SP Howitt Rd. Road on right SP Moroka Road.
GPS S:37 25.177 E:146 47.034
UTM Zone 55 0480878E 5858551N

▼ 116.7 (6.5)
Track junction. Notes CSA. Track on right SP Thomastown and SP To Kellys Lane leads short distance to bush camp sites beside Shaws Creek.
▲ *40.4 (3.8)*
SP Thomastown on left. CSA.

▼ 120.5 (3.8)
Track junction. KL on main track. Track on right SP Tamboritha Saddle and SP Dingo Hill Tk.

▲ *36.6 (2.5)*
Track junction. KR on main track.

▼ 123.0 (2.5)
Track on left SP B1 Tk. CSA.
▲ *34.1 (1.7)*
Track on right SP B1 Tk. CSA.

▼ 124.7 (1.7)
SP Bennison Lookout on left. CSA.
▲ *32.4 (9.9)*
SP Bennison Lookout on right. CSA.
GPS S:37 30.366 E:146 41.280
UTM Zone 55 0472421E 5848937N

▼ 134.6 (9.9)
Bridge over Wellington River. Wellington River Walking Track on left before bridge. Bitumen road begins.
▲ *22.5 (0.3)*
Bridge over Wellington River. Gravel road begins.

▼ 134.9 (0.3)
Lake Tali Karng car park and bush camp sites on right. Notes CSA on bitumen road. *NB:* From here to park boundary are numerous bush camp sites beside the river, these are noted by numbered posts on the road at entrance to these areas – some have facilities.
▲ *22.2 (2.7)*
Lake Tali Karng car park on left. CSA.

▼ 137.6 (2.7)
SP Wellington Horse Yards and camping area on right. Notes CSA over bridge.
▲ *19.5 (0.7)*
Bridge. SP Wellington Horse Yards on left over bridge. Notes CSA.
GPS S:37 31.082 E:146 37.339
UTM Zone 55 0466626E 5847607N

▼ 138.3 (0.7)
SP M.G.S. Camp on right. Notes CSA.
▲ *18.8 (9.4)*
M.G.S. Camp on left. CSA.

▼ 147.7 (9.4)
Exit Alpine National Park.
▲ *9.4 (9.2)*
Enter Alpine National Park. NB: *There are numerous bush camp sites beside the river and these are noted by numbered posts on the road at entrance – some have facilities.*

ABOVE: *Butcher Country Track near Howitt Plain.*

▼ 156.9 (9.2)
Road junction. TL for 58 Heyfield. TR for Jamieson 95. Notes TR over bridge.
▲ *0.2 (0.2)*
Bridge. At junction over bridge TL. This is Tamboritha Road. Road SO leads to Heyfield.

▼ 157.1 (0.2)
Licola General Store on right.
▲ *0.0 (0.0)*
Licola General Store on left. PSA in southerly direction over bridge.
GPS S:37 37.660 E:146 37.399
UTM Zone 55 0466760E 5835425N

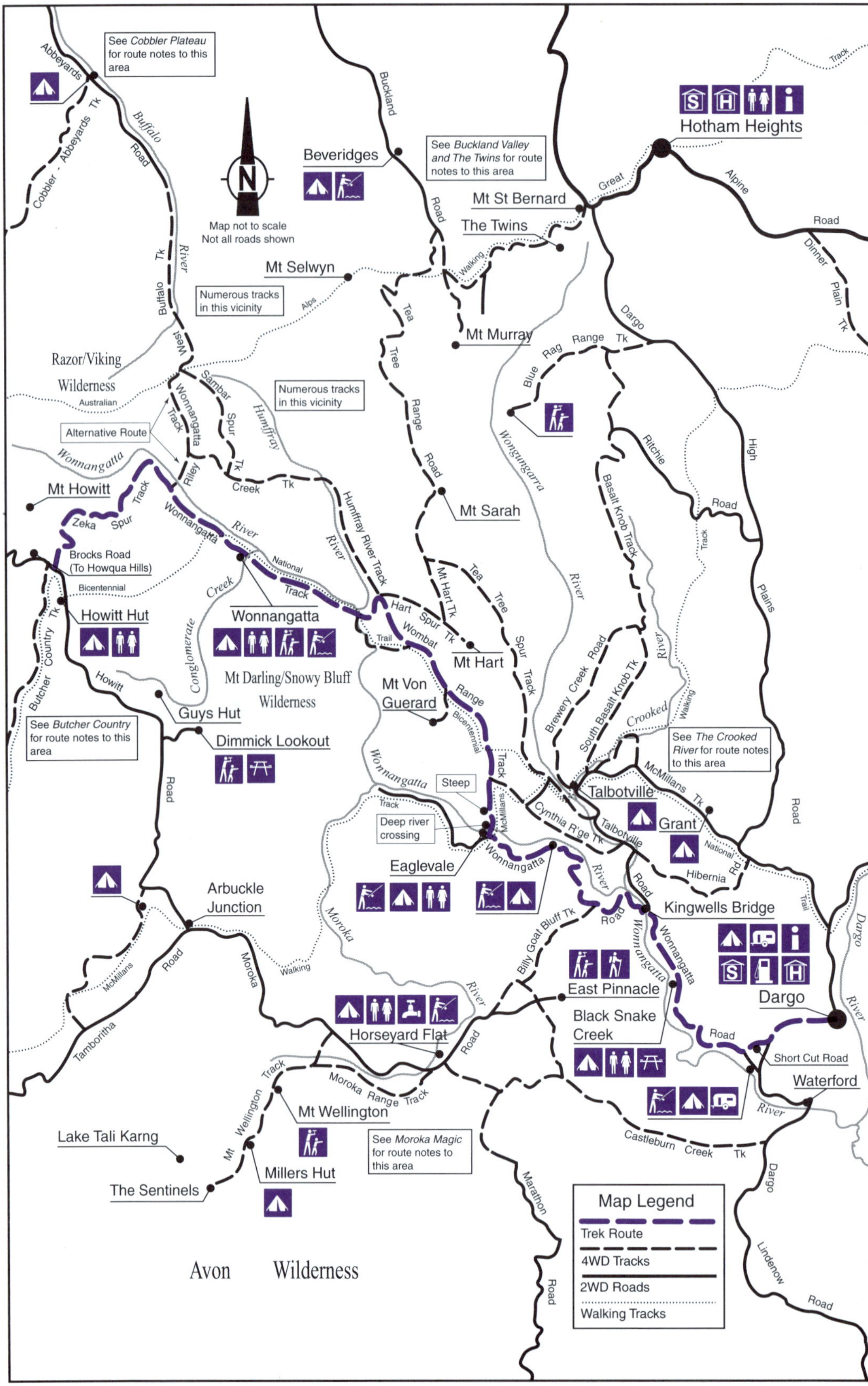

See Cobbler Plateau for route notes to this area
Abbeyards
Cobbler - Abbeyards Tk
Buffalo River
Buffalo Road
Map not to scale
Not all roads shown
Beveridges
Buckland Road
See Buckland Valley and The Twins for route notes to this area
Hotham Heights
Great Alpine Road
Mt St Bernard
The Twins
Walking
Mt Selwyn
Alps
Numerous tracks in this vicinity
West Buffalo Tk
Razor/Viking
Wilderness
Australian
Alternative Route
Wonnangatta Track
Sambar Spur Tk
Humffray
Creek Tk
Riley
Tea Tree Range Road
Mt Murray
Dinner Plain Tk
Dargo
Blue Rag Range Tk
Wongungarra
Ritchie
High Plains Road
Basalt Knob Track
Mt Howitt
Zeka Spur Track
Wonnangatta River
National Track
Brocks Road
(To Howqua Hills)
Bicentennial
Howitt Hut
Butcher Country Tk
Creek
Conglomerate
Wonnangatta
Mt Darling/Snowy Bluff
Wilderness
Humffray River Track
Mt Sarah
Mt Hart Tk
Tea Tree Spur Track
Hart Spur Tk
Trail
Wombat Range
Mt Hart
Mt Von Guerard
Bicentennial Track
Howitt
Guys Hut
Dimmick Lookout
See Butcher Country for route notes to this area
Road
Brewery Creek Road
South Basalt Knob Tk
Crooked
Walking
River
See The Crooked River for route notes to this area
Talbotville
McMillans Tk
Cynthia R'ge Tk
Talbotville Road
Grant
National
Hibernia Rd
Steep
Deep river crossing
Wonnangatta
Track
McMillan's
Eaglevale
Wonnangatta River
Kingwells Bridge
Trail
Dargo River
Arbuckle Junction
Moroka
Walking
Billy Goat Bluff Tk
Road
McMillans
Road
Tamboritha
Moroka
East Pinnacle
Black Snake Creek
Dargo
River
Horseyard Flat
Road
Road
Short Cut Road
Waterford
Mt Wellington Track
Moroka Range Track
Mt Wellington
See Moroka Magic for route notes to this area
Castleburn Creek Tk
River
Lake Tali Karng
Millers Hut
The Sentinels
Marathon Road
Dargo
Lindenow Road
Avon Wilderness
Map Legend
Trek Route
4WD Tracks
2WD Roads
Walking Tracks

TREK 6

TREK SIX

WONNANGATTA VALLEY

SURROUNDED BY MOUNTAINS in the heart of the Victorian Alps is the remote Wonnangatta Valley. Not only is the valley known as a mecca for four-wheel drive touring due to its spectacular scenery and isolation, but for the mysterious and still unsolved murders of Wonnangatta Station manager Jim Barclay and his farmhand John Bamford in 1917.

The Wonnangatta Valley was first settled by an American, Oliver Smith in the late 1860s. Shortly after, William Bryce and his family moved to the property forming a partnership with Smith. In 1872 Oliver Smith moved from Wonnangatta to Sale after the death of his wife and two infant children. William Bryce then took over the property, and for the next forty years built Wonnangatta Station into a major cattle and horse property.

The Bryce family continued on with the property after William Bryce's death in 1902 until 1915 when Wonnangatta Station was sold to a syndicate from Mansfield headed by Arthur Phillips. It was not long after this that the still unsolved Wonnangatta murder mystery (see *Who Done It? - The Wonnangatta Mystery* pages 74-77) occured.

Wonnangatta Station changed hands a number of times over the next 15 or so years, with the Guy family purchasing Wonnangatta in 1934. However, by the mid 1950s there was no longer a resident station manager at Wonnangatta and with the increasing popularity of the valley as a bushwalking destination, saw the Wonnangatta Station Homestead burnt to the ground in 1957 by careless bushwalkers who left a fire unattended.

The property changed hands again in 1970 and in 1988 it was acquired by the Victorian government and is now part of the Alpine National Park.

fast facts

Dargo to Howitt Plain via Eaglevale and the Wonnangatta Valley

Trek distance: 112km

Standard: Medium/Hard (Dry weather only)

Fuel and supplies: Dargo and Licola

Trek highlights: Wonnangatta River, excellent camping and fishing, Wonnangatta Station ruins, Zeka Spur Track and Howitt Plain

Track conditions:
Parks Vic/DNRE Dargo
Ph 03/5140 1243

Need help?: D.Guy Autos, Waterford (4WD Recovery) Ph 03/5140 1265

Things to Do and See

The Wonnangatta Valley is Victoria's premier four-wheel destination—and for good reason. This remote and scenic valley is hidden between imposing mountain ranges on all sides. And apart from its chequered history it's a journey in itself just getting in and out of the place!

Once down in the valley you can explore the old homestead site and wander around the small cemetery that is the final resting place for some of the valley's pioneer families.

Camping and fishing is also well catered for with an abundance of bush camping areas to choose from beside the Wonnangatta River. There are also a couple of walking tracks, including a walk upstream on Conglomerate Creek and the Dry River Walking Track to Howitt Plain.

Access

The village of Dargo is the starting point for this trek. To reach Dargo travel north via the bitumen Dargo Road from Bairnsdale on the Princes Highway or via Briagalong or Stratford. Alternatively, from the north take the gravel Dargo High Plains Road from The Great Alpine Road at Mount St Bernard.

The Trek

From Dargo head south along Dargo Road to Short Cut Road which joins with Wonnangatta Road. Follow Wonnangatta Road, which at times parallels the Wonnangatta River, passing Black Snake Creek Camping Area before arriving at Kingwell's Bridge (the road on the right before the bridge goes to Talbotville) where you cross to the left bank of the Wonnangatta River.

The trek continues on Wonnangatta Road, passing Billy Goat Bluff Track then onto Eaglevale. At Eaglevale cross the river (which at times can be deep here) at the camping area and pass by the homestead before joining with Wombat Range Track which will take you to Mt Cynthia. From here keep on Wombat Range Track, passing Mt Von Guerard (named in honour of the artist Eugene von Guerard who visited the area with Alfred Howitt) and the very steep Herne's Spur Track before arriving at the Hummffray River, a tributary of the Wonnangatta.

After crossing the Hummffray River a couple of times you will be faced with a crossing of the Wonnangatta River. Once across keep on Wonnangatta Station Track until you cross Conglomerate Creek where you will come to the site of the old Wonnangatta Station Homestead. Little now remains of the weatherboard and iron building which looked out over the valley from a small rise behind the present day Guy's Hut—constructed from material salvaged from the original homestead. There is a small cemetery located a little to the north of the homestead site.

Continuing along the valley there are many tracks that lead off the main Wonnangatta Track to bush camping areas, mostly beside the river.

At the head of the valley you reach a track junction. Our route continues straight ahead which soon becomes Zeka Spur Track. The track to the right is Riley's Creek Track which leads to Myrtleford via the Buffalo River and the Abbeyards. This route is now the major and easiest route in and out of the Wonnangatta Valley.

Zeka Spur Track, like many of the High Country's more infamous routes has been realigned over the years, with most of the more difficult and dangerous sections having been eliminated, although many drivers will still find this track quite enjoyable, if not a little challenging.

The trek concludes at the junction of Zeka Spur Track and Howitt Road on Howitt Plain. From here there is the option to explore Trek 5 - *Butcher Country*, or follow Howitt Road to Arbuckle Junction to pick up Trek 7 - *Moroka Magic* or head down Brocks Road to Howqua Hills to join with Trek 1 - *Howqua-Mitchell's Trek* or Trek 2 - *The Bluff and Beyond*.

Standard

Trek rating is medium/hard. Although the area visited on this trek is popular among four-wheel drivers, nevertheless it is remote and your level of preparation and equipment carried should reflect this.

You will encounter some moderately steep track sections on Wombat Range Track and as you climb out of the valley on Zeka Spur Track. The crossings of the Wonnangatta River at Eaglevale and on Wonnangatta Station Track near the Hummffray River junction can at times be quite deep and deserve caution. If in doubt check the water depth by walking the crossing first.

The Wonnangatta Station Track running through the valley, has, over the last few years been realigned to follow higher ground and is no longer the bogholed route that it once was.

Camping

There are numerous camping opportunities on this trek ranging from established camping areas with facilities to secluded bush camp sites, with some excellent sites beside the Wonnangatta River.

There are established camping areas with varying facilities located at Black Snake Creek, Kingwell's Bridge, Bullock Flat and Eaglevale as well as scattered sites beside the river along Wonnangatta Road.

In the Wonnangatta Valley itself there is a plethora of secluded bush camp sites beside the river. Even though it is very busy here over the summer holidays, Easter and long weekends, you will generally be able find a spot to yourself.

At the conclusion of the trek you can camp at Howitt Hut Camping Area on Howitt Plain.

Permits/Restrictions

This trek is restricted by seasonal road closures which are usually in force from after the Queen's Birthday Long Weekend to just after the Melbourne Cup in November.

Recommended Maps/Guides

We recommend the Brookes Bush Maps, Victoria *Crooked River - Dargo Area* and *Macalister River Watershed*. The Hema Maps *High Country - Victoria* map also shows the trek route.

Topographic maps for this trek are the *Crooked River - Steve*, *Howitt - Selwyn* and *Tamboritha - Moroka* 1:50 000 series.

Further Information

Parks Victoria and Dept of Natural Resources and Environment
Lind Ave, Dargo VIC 3862 Ph 03/5140 1243 Fax 03/5140 1216

Dargo General Store
16A Lind Ave, Dargo Ph 03/5140 1219

Licola General Store and Caravan Park
Jamieson Road, Licola Ph 03/5148 8786

Brochures - Parks Victoria: *Alpine National Park - valleys and bluffs around Mansfield and Whitfield*
Parks Victoria: *Alpine National Park - walks around Howitt, Snowy Range and Tali Karng*
Parks Victoria: *Alpine National Park - around Heyfield, Licola and Dargo in the Wonnangatta/ Moroka area*

Further Reading - *The Wonnangatta Mystery - An inquiry into the unsolved murders* by Keith Leydon and Michael Ray
The History of Wonnangatta Station and *Wonnangatta Station - The Next Twenty Years* both by Wallace Malcolm Mortimer

BELOW: *Crossing of the Wonnangatta River near the Humffray River junction.*

Who Done It? - The Wonnangatta Mystery

The mysterious deaths of Jim Barclay, a well liked horse trainer and cattle trader, and John Bamford, a farmhand with a bad temper, that took place in this remote and tranquil valley nearly 85 years ago are still the subjects of much conjecture today as they were after that fateful day in late 1917.

Jim Barclay

Jim Barclay, born James Barclay on February 18, 1869 was the fourth child of James and Mary Barclay of Hastings, Victoria. Throughout his childhood the young Barclay had several minor encounters with the authorities for fighting and finally left his Hastings school after being 'sufficiently educated' in 1883. Jim then left his family home in 1886, apparently to seek his fortune on the new goldfields in north-eastern Victoria. With no luck on the goldfields, Barclay went to Queensland.

ABOVE: *Jim Barclay.*

After roving around Queensland working as a shearer and unsuccessfully prospecting for gold, Barclay arrived back in the Mansfield district and in 1909 took out a lease on the Howqua River. His nearest neighbours were the Fry family who became very good friends of Barclay's. At this time Jim Barclay was doing various labouring jobs and actively pursuing cattle for purchase as well as improving his cattle and horse handling skills for which his reputation grew.

On December 23, 1910 at the age of 41 Jim Barclay married Elizabeth (Lizzie) Beatrice Cantienie whom he had met whilst she was staying with the Fry family. Lizzie was seven months pregnant at the time of their marriage.

It was also at this time that Barclay was charged with taking a bull from its owner without consent. Originally Barclay denied any knowledge of the bull to Mansfield Detective Sullivan, however after being charged and on his way to the police station Barclay changed his story, saying that he did take the bull but when he found out it was not one from his mob he had tried to cut it out, but this proved unsuccessful.

When the case went to court in Mansfield in January 1911 there were some fiery courtroom scenes between Barclay's solicitor and police Detective Sullivan. Barclay was eventually found guilty by the magistrate and fined five pounds.

On February 22 of that same year Jim's wife Lizzie gave birth to their son James. However Lizzie, who had been diagnosed with a form of tuberculosis finally succumbed to the chronic illness and died in September that year. She was only 20 years old when she died.

With young Jim being cared for by various people, mostly the Hearn family, Jim snr was able to continue working at Glenroy Station near Mansfield, which was owned by Mr Arthur Phillips. Phillips obviously regarded Barclay as a valuable employee as he was paid double that of the other employees. Barclay still traded in cattle and horses and also took up a cattle lease, The Bluff Run with friend Jack Bullock. There is an area on The Bluff, which is now part of the Alpine National Park, known as Barclay's Flat.

Wonnangatta Station

In April 1915 Jim Barclay took on the position of manager of Wonnangatta Station which had been newly acquired by a syndicate from Mansfield, headed by Arthur Phillips. As well as his role of manager, Barclay was apparently still free to continue his own trading of cattle and horses.

Access in and out of the rugged and remote Wonnangatta Valley was only possible by foot or horse. From the station the Dry River Track was taken up over the tablelands, then a zigzag down Mt Howitt via Howitt Spur Track into Mansfield. The trip taking about three days.

Although access was difficult, Barclay's life at Wonnangatta was not entirely solitary. Barclay had frequent visits from his neighbour and good friend Harry Smith from Eaglevale and during the spring of 1916 Jim's brother John visited along with his son Jack and son-in-law Owen Bryant. Also in 1916 a cook, Mrs Rebecca Wilson, had moved in, however it is not known how long she stayed.

John Bamford

By December 1917 Barclay had started looking for a general hand, as harvest season was soon about to start. John Bamford, a 61 year old Yorkshireman, who had migrated to Australia at age 18 took up the position in mid December. Not much is known of Bamford before this time, except that by 1916 he was living in a hut at Black Snake Creek close to Talbotville.

On Thursday December 20, about a week after Bamford had taken up his position at Wonnangatta, both Barclay and Bamford rode to Talbotville to vote in the national referendum on conscription. When in town Barclay was heard to have said that his crop needed another fourteen days before they could cut it. Also in town at that time was Harry Smith, who apparently questioned Barclay, "What sort of a bugger have you hired?" referring to Bamford who Smith later described as a man with a bad temper. Barclay's reply to Smith, "He was all I could get".

As Christmas was fast approaching, Barclay was expecting some mail so visited his friend, Albert Stout, the local post office and store owner at Talbotville. Barclay had received a letter from his sister Molly and from Jim jnr, now aged six. Whilst there he attended to his mail, replying to both his son and Molly.

Both Barclay and Bamford stayed overnight in Talbotville with Albert Stout and his wife, leaving early on Friday morning. Both men were never seen alive again.

The Murder Mystery

About 6.00pm on the evening of Wednesday January 23, 1918 Harry Smith, who Barclay and Bamford had seen in Talbotville at the referendum vote just prior to Christmas, had just made the 16 mile (25km) journey from his home at Eaglevale to Wonnangatta Station. Smith used these opportunities to see his friend Jim Barclay and also to deliver some mail he had collected from Talbotville for Barclay.

On Smith's arrival he found no-one home and a message, that he believed to be written by John Bamford on the kitchen door in chalk, 'home tonight'. Harry made himself at home in the kitchen, cooked a meal and stayed overnight waiting for his friend's return. When no-one returned the following morning, Thursday January 24, Smith left the mail on the kitchen table and rode back home to Eaglevale.

It was another three weeks before Harry Smith returned—on Thursday February 14. He arrived in the late afternoon and on entering the kitchen was shocked, as well as surprised, to see that the mail and everything else for that matter at the station was exactly as it was when he left three weeks previous. The only difference on this trip was that Barclay's favourite dog, Baron, was running loose and obviously hungry. Smith knew that Barclay would never leave Baron hungry or without food and guessed, at this point, that something must be wrong.

Smith stayed overnight and the next morning, after a quick search around the homestead and yards, left for Eaglevale taking Baron with him.

On his way out Smith met up with William Riggall of Dargo who was travelling to his properties on the Bennison High Plains. Smith, concerned about the extended absence of Barclay and Bamford from the station homestead, arranged for Riggall to send a telegram to Arthur Phillips of Mansfield on his return to Dargo, advising him of the situation. Smith then continued on his way home to Eaglevale.

The Search for Barclay and Bamford Begins

Arthur Phillips, who was the station owner at the time, arrived at Wonnangatta on Friday, February 22 with Jack Jebb to find that the homestead had not been occupied for sometime. The next day they rode over to Eaglevale to see Harry Smith. Phillips and Jebb stayed the night with Smith before the three men returned to Wonnangatta on Sunday 24. They arrived around 3.00pm in the afternoon and spent until dark fruitlessly searching the areas close to the homestead and Conglomerate Creek, or Home Creek as it was also known.

The next morning the three men resumed their search for the missing Barclay and Bamford, with Harry Smith suggesting that another recce up Home Creek should be made. It wasn't long before they found something along the banks of Home Creek.

On their arrival at the site, which was marked by a red blanket, the men were met with a frightening sight—a human skull protruding from the sand which some wild animal had attacked. Further inspection showed that the skull was attached to a body buried in a shallow grave. As both Barclay and Bamford were missing it was necessary for the three to identify who was in the grave. After removing some sand from around the feet of the body they were able to ascertain from the boots and the pants that the body was in fact Jim Barclay's.

Later that day Arthur Phillips made a search of the homestead and found some items missing. He and Jack Jebb then left for Mansfield to advise the police, arriving there on February 26. It wasn't long before the newspapers picked up the story of the disappearance of both Barclay and Bamford and the subsequent discovery of Barclay's body. At the same time Harry Smith had gone back to Eaglevale.

The Police Investigation

The police investigator placed in charge of the case, Detective Alex McKerral and his party arrived at Wonnangatta Station on Saturday March 2, with Harry Smith and Constable Hayes already there awaiting their arrival. Whilst at Wonnangatta McKerral arranged for Barclay's body to be retrieved from the grave and transported back to Mansfield Hospital for an autopsy while he investigated the homestead and searched both Barclay's and Bamford's rooms.

From his investigations McKerral concluded that a shotgun in Barclay's room had recently been fired, some sort of struggle had taken place on Barclay's bed and that marks on the floor of Barclay's room were consistent of boots being dragged. In Bamford's room he found a pile of clothes on the floor looking like they had been taken off in a hurry and an old blue blanket was missing. The autopsy carried out on Barclay's body found there were fifteen pellets in the body and from the wounds the shot/shots came from behind.

The inquest in Jim Barclay's death opened on March 7, 1918 and was adjourned and again reopened on April 25, 1918. After hearing all witnesses and receiving all evidence, Deputy Coroner Harrie Amor read his official finding to the court as thus –

> *"Having duly inquired upon the part of the Lord the King when, where, how and by what means the said James Barclay came by his death, I say that the said James Barclay died at Wonnangatta Station between the twenty first day of December, 1917, and fourth day of January 1918, from a gunshot wound in the back; the verdict that the deceased, James Barclay, was murdered by some person or persons unknown."*

Jim Barclay's body was handed over to his family who buried him in his parent's plot in the Hastings Cemetery on Saturday 9 March, 1918. Jim Barclay was 48 years old.

The Suspect

The search for Barclay's murderer remained open throughout 1918. John Bamford, who had not been seen since both men were at Talbotville the previous December remained the main suspect. A reward was offered and a notice to police Australia wide to have any suspects held.

In the spring of 1918, Harry Smith went to Dargo police station to see what the police were doing about the search for Bamford, advising them he felt that Bamford would be found on Mount Howitt. In November of that year Smith was met by Mounted Constable Daniel Hayes of Dargo at Smith's home at Eaglevale. From there they rode to Wonnangatta Station to collect Bill Hearn, the new manager at the station, and Jim Fry, who was there helping Hearn.

ABOVE: *All that remains of* Wonnangatta Homestead *today*.

The group left Wonnangatta Station and rode to Howitt Hut, camping there the night of Wednesday 6 November. They started their search the next day at a place called Terrible Hollow (where in April, Fry and Hearn had seen a pair of hobbles on a tree and a bell), which is about six miles from the hut. After searching the area with no result, they decided to return back to Howitt Hut. However, on the way back Hearn had spotted the remains of a fire on the track; possibly a camp fire or a fire for cattle branding. When he rode back to where he had seen the fire Hearn noticed some boots sticking out from under a log. There they found John Bamford's body lying under a large log with other logs, sticks and stones covering parts of the body. The group removed Bamford's body from its makeshift grave, wrapped it up and took the corpse to Dargo where they arrived on November 9.

After an autopsy was conducted by Dr Backhouse on Bamford's remains, it was found there was a small bullet from a revolver in Bamford's skull and evidence of a bullet wound on the left side of the temple along with a bullet inside. It was Dr Backhouse's opinion that the shot would have caused instant death, it was not self-inflicted and that the shot would have been fired from a distance.

On November 12, the coroner Mr Grey presided over the inquest into John Bamford's death where evidence was presented on the identification of the body. The inquest was adjourned until December 23. Harry Smith and Mounted Constable Daniel Hayes gave further evidence at this time about the search and the finding of Bamford's body. Evidence was also given by Dr Backhouse.

Upon hearing all the evidence Coroner Grey found that –

> "The deceased John Bamford met his death between December 1917 and January 1918 and was willfully murdered by some person or persons unknown".

John Bamford was buried at the Dargo Cemetery.

The Conclusion

Was Barclay killed for cattle duffing? Or was he killed over a lady? And the unfortunate Bamford, was he a witness to the murder, therefore naming his own fate? Was this a murder suicide? Did Bamford kill Barclay then kill himself at a different location? Did Bamford kill Barclay, for whatever reason, then was he himself killed by someone else? Were they killed by others that had come to help with the harvest? Or was it others who had come to steal their cattle? Rumours and theories abound as to who killed Barclay and Bamford, and why!

A full account into the Wonnangatta murders is detailed in the excellent book, *The Wonnangatta Mystery - An inquiry into the unsolved murders* by Keith Leydon and Michael Ray. It is published by Warrior Press, Mansfield.

ROUTE NOTES

Trek commences in the village of Dargo.

▼ 0.0 (0.0)
Zero trip meter in village of Dargo. Dargo Hotel on left and General Store on right. PSA in a southerly direction towards Bairnsdale.
▲ *82.8 (5.9)*
Dargo village. Dargo Hotel on right and Dargo General Store on left.
GPS S:37 27.710 E:147 15.054
UTM Zone 55 0522192E 5853872N

▼ 5.9 (5.9)
Y junction. VR onto gravel. This is Short Cut Road.
▲ *76.9 (2.2)*
Road junction. CSA onto bitumen.
GPS S:37 28.975 E:147 12.329
UTM Zone 55 0518163E 5851533N

▼ 8.1 (2.2)
T junction. TR. Road to left. SP Stratford.
▲ *74.7 (12.9)*
Track junction. TL. Road SO SP Stratford.
GPS S:37 29.570 E:147 11.234
UTM Zone 55 0516550E 5850437N

▼ 21.0 (12.9)
Track junction. Notes CSA over bridge. Track on left leads to Black Snake Creek Camping Area.
▲ *61.8 (7.9)*
Bridge. CSA uphill. Track on right leads to Black Snake Creek Camping Area.
GPS S:37 26.796 E:147 08.404
UTM Zone 55 0512386E 5855574N

▼ 28.9 (7.9)
Road junction. CSA over Kingwell Bridge. SP Eaglevale 22. Road on right SP Talbotville 14.
▲ *53.9 (1.6)*
Kingwell Bridge. CSA. SP Dargo 30.
GPS S:37 24.635 E:147 06.936
UTM Zone 55 0510230E 5859574N

▼ 30.5 (1.6)
Bridge.
▲ *52.3 (3.7)*
Bridge.

▼ 34.2 (3.7)
Track junction. KL on upper road. Track on right SP Private Property. No Through Rd.
▲ *48.6 (0.4)*
CSA. Track on left SP Private Property.

▼ 34.6 (0.4)
Track junction. CSA. Track on left SP Billy Goat Bluff Tk. SP Pinnacles.
▲ *48.2 (0.7)*
CSA. Track on right SP Billy Goat Bluff Tk.

▼ 35.3 (0.7)
Track junction. CSA. Track on right leads to possible bush camp sites beside river.
▲ *47.5 (7.1)*
CSA. Track on left leads to possible bush camp sites.

▼ 42.4 (7.1)
SP Bullock Flat Camping Area on right. Notes CSA.
▲ *40.4 (7.5)*
SP Bullock Flat Camping Area on left. Notes CSA.
GPS S:37 22.480 E:147 03.404
UTM Zone 55 0505022E 5863562N

▼ 49.9 (7.5)
Track junction. VR. SP Eaglevale Tk. SP Eaglevale Camping Area on right.
▲ *32.9 (0.2)*
SP Eaglevale Camping Area on left. Notes CSA on main track uphill. This is Wonnangatta Road.
GPS S:37 22.126 E:147 00.454
UTM Zone 55 0500669E 5864215N

▼ 50.1 (0.2)
Track junction. TR and cross Wonnangatta River. Continue on track past homestead on right and footbridge on left.
▲ *32.7 (0.6)*
CSA pass footbridge on right and homestead on left and cross Wonnangatta River. Track junction immediately over river. TL and follow fenceline.

▼ 50.7 (0.6)
CSA. SP McMillans Track on right. Track climbs steeply from here.

▲ *32.1 (3.6)*
CSA. SP McMillans Track on left.

▼ 54.3 (3.6)
Track junction. This is Mt Cynthia. TL. SP Wombat Range. Track SO SP Cynthia Range Tk.
▲ *28.5 (1.9)*
Track junction. TR. SP Eaglevale Tk. Track on left SP Cynthia Range Tk.
GPS S:37 20.169 E:147 00.360
UTM Zone 55 0500533E 5867834N

▼ 56.2 (1.9)
Track junction. VL.
▲ *26.6 (0.3)*
Track on left. CSA.

▼ 56.5 (0.3)
Track rejoins on right. CSA.
▲ *26.3 (1.3)*
Track junction. VR.

▼ 57.8 (1.3)
SP Bicentennial National Trail on right. CSA.
▲ *25.0 (4.0)*
SP Bicentennial National Trail on left. CSA.

▼ 61.8 (4.0)
Track junction. CSA. Track on left leads 1.1km to Mt Von Guerard – excellent views.
▲ *21.0 (5.0)*
Track on right. CSA.

▼ 66.8 (5.0)
Track junction. CSA. SP Wombat Range. Track drops steeply to river from here. Track on left SP Herne Spur.
▲ *16.0 (4.2)*
CSA. SP Wombat Range. Track on right SP Herne Spur.
GPS S:37 15.345 E:146 56.767
UTM Zone 55 0495221E 5876752N

▼ 71.0 (4.2)
Track junction. Hard TL through seasonal closure gate. Track SO SP Mt Hart Spur.
▲ *11.8 (0.2)*
Track junction. Hard TR. SP Wombat Range. Track climbs steeply from here. Track on left SP Mt Hart Spur.
GPS S:37 13.780 E:146 55.420
UTM Zone 55 0493234E 5879644N

▼ 71.2 (0.2)
Track on right. CSA. SP Humffray Riv Tk.
▲ *11.6 (0.2)*
Track junction. VR. SP To Wombat Range.

▼ 71.4 (0.2)
Cross Humffray River. Small bush camp site on right over river.
▲ *11.4 (0.6)*
Cross Humffray River.

▼ 72.0 (0.6)
River crossing.
▲ *10.8 (1.2)*
River crossing.

▼ 73.2 (1.2)
River crossing.
▲ *9.6 (0.4)*
River crossing.

▼ 73.6 (0.4)
Track on left is Herne Spur. CSA and cross Wonnangatta River. This is Wonnangatta Track.
▲ *9.2 (0.4)*
Cross Wonnangatta River. CSA over river past Herne Spur on right.
GPS S:37 14.379 E:146 54.393
UTM Zone 55 0491709E 5878537N

▼ 74.0 (0.4)
Bush camp site on right. CSA.
▲ *8.8 (1.4)*
Bush camp site on left. CSA.

▼ 75.4 (1.4)
Track junction. KL.
▲ *7.4 (3.2)*
Track on left. CSA.

▼ 78.6 (3.2)
Track on right. CSA.
▲ *4.2 (1.2)*
Track on left. CSA.

▼ 79.8 (1.2)
Track on right. CSA.
▲ *3.0 (1.4)*
Track on left. CSA.

▼ 81.2 (1.4)
Track on right leads to possible bush camp sites beside river. Notes CSA.
▲ *1.6 (0.9)*
Track on left. CSA.

ABOVE: *Wombat Range Track near Eaglevale.*

▼ 82.1 (0.9)
Track on right. CSA and cross creek. Over creek KL. Track on right leads to bush camp sites.

▲ *0.7 (0.6)*
Creek crossing. SP Humffray Rv. KR over creek.

▼ 82.7 (0.6)
SP Duffys Camp Camping Area on left. CSA and cross Conglomerate Creek.

▲ *0.1 (0.1)*
SP Duffys Camp on right. CSA.

▼ 82.8 (0.1)
Track junction over Conglomerate Creek. Enter Wonnangatta Valley. Track on left leads to hut and site of old Bryce Homestead and camp sites on creek. Track on right leads to camp sites on river. Zero trip meter here.

▲ *0.0 (0.0)*
Track junction before Conglomerate Creek. CSA over Conglomerate Creek.
GPS S:37 12.445 E:146 49.939
UTM Zone 55 0485122E 5882103N

▼ 0.0 (0.0)
Track junction after crossing Conglomerate Creek. Notes CSA. Numerous tracks lead off from the main track to camp sites by the river.

▲ *30.0 (0.4)*
Track junction before Conglomerate Creek. Zero trip meter here.

▼ 0.4 (0.4)
Cemetery on left. Notes CSA.

▲ *29.6 (3.0)*
Cemetery on right. CSA.

▼ 3.4 (3.0)
SP Dry River Track on left. CSA.

▲ *26.6 (0.4)*
SP Dry River Track on right. CSA.

▼ 3.8 (0.4)
Cross Dry River.

▲ *26.2 (3.5)*
Cross Dry River.

▼ 7.3 (3.5)
Track junction. CSA. SP Howitt Plain. This is Zeka Spur Track. Track on right SP Rileys Creek Track. SP Myrtleford.

▲ *22.7 (22.7)*
Track junction. CSA. SP Wonnangatta Stn. Track on left SP Rileys Creek Tk. SP Myrtleford.
GPS S:37 10.171 E:146 46.545
UTM Zone 55 0480094E 5886296N

▼ 30.0 (22.7)
Track junction. This is Howitt Road. TL for Arbuckle Junction and Licola 80km. TR for 300m to join Trek 5 - Butcher Country.

▲ *0.0 (0.0)*
Zero trip meter on Howitt Plain at junction of Howitt Road and SP Zeka Spur Tk. This junction is 80km from Licola. Proceed along SP Zeka Spur Tk.
GPS S:37 12.740 E:146 41.624
UTM Zone 55 0472826E 5881530N

OPPOSITE: *A number of the Bryce family are buried in the Wonnangatta Station cemetery.*

Sacred
to
THE MEMORY OF
JESSIE BRYCE
DIED DEC 8TH 1891.
AGED 22 YEARS.
"AT REST"
IN
Memory
of
our
Mother,
DIED APRIL
23RD 1919,

TREK 6

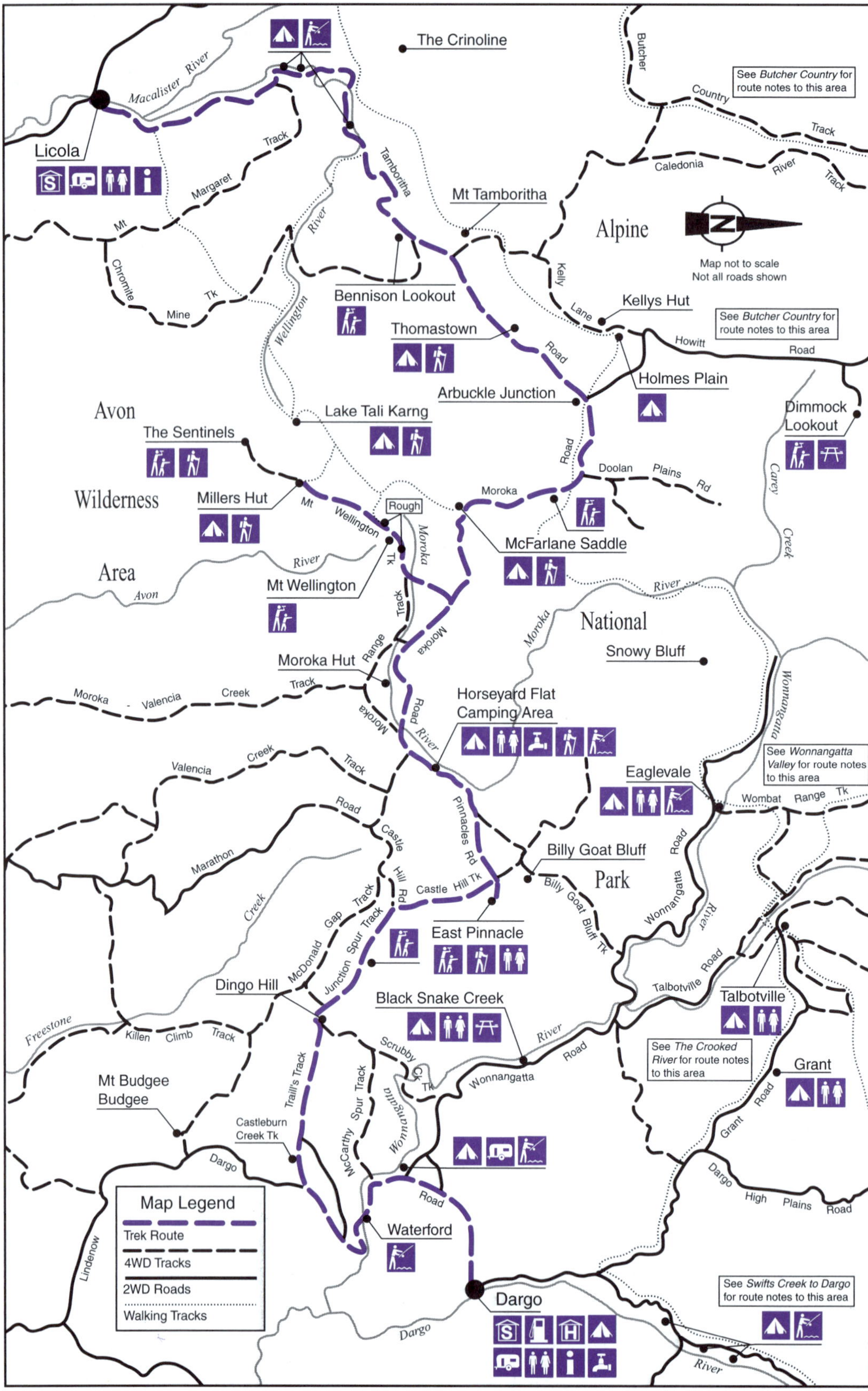
The Crinoline
Macalister River
Licola
Margaret Track
Mt
Chromite Mine Tk
Tamboritha
Mt Tamboritha
Bennison Lookout
Thomastown
Wellington River
Butcher Country Track
See Butcher Country for route notes to this area
Caledonia River Track
Alpine
Map not to scale
Not all roads shown
Kelly Lane
Kellys Hut
See Butcher Country for route notes to this area
Howitt Road
Road
Holmes Plain
Arbuckle Junction
Lake Tali Karng
Avon
The Sentinels
Wilderness
Millers Hut
Mt Wellington Tk
Rough
Moroka River
Moroka Road
Doolan Plains Rd
McFarlane Saddle
Dimmock Lookout
Carey Creek
Area
Avon River
Mt Wellington
National
Snowy Bluff
Moroka Hut
Range Track
Moroka - Valencia Creek Track
Moroka Road
Horseyard Flat Camping Area
Wonnangatta
See Wonnangatta Valley for route notes to this area
Eaglevale
Wombat Range Tk
Valencia Creek Track
Road
Castle Hill Rd
Marathon
Pinnacles Rd
Castle Hill Tk
Billy Goat Bluff
Billy Goat Bluff Tk
Park
Wonnangatta Road
River
Creek
McDonald Gap Track
Junction Spur Track
East Pinnacle
Dingo Hill
Black Snake Creek
Talbotville Road
Talbotville
Freestone
Killen Climb Track
Scrubby Ck Tk
River
Wonnangatta Road
See The Crooked River for route notes to this area
Grant
Grant Road
Mt Budgee Budgee
Traill's Track
McCarthy Spur Track
Wonnangatta
Castleburn Creek Tk
Dargo
Dargo High Plains Road
Road
Map Legend
Trek Route
4WD Tracks
2WD Roads
Walking Tracks
Lindenow
Waterford
Dargo
See Swifts Creek to Dargo for route notes to this area
Dargo
River

TREK SEVEN

MOROKA MAGIC

THE OVERPOWERING 360° views of the valleys and mountains of the Alpine National Park and the Avon Wilderness Area are features of this trek. From The Pinnacles the vistas are stunning and from here you can see Mt Hotham to the north and as far south as the Gippsland Lakes. Directly below you is the Wonnangatta Valley.

Along the Moroka Road you pass some excellent camping areas at Horseyard Flat and also at the Moroka River. There is a short signposted walking track to Moroka Hut, a log cattlemen's hut that was built in 1946, just after the river crossing.

A little further on the track to Mount Wellington is reached and from here it's a slow bumpy climb to the summit where once again you will be astounded by the views. To the south you look over the Avon Wilderness and The Razorback Range whilst to the north you'll see Doolans Plains. Continuing on past the summit you will arrive at Millers Hut, a good place to base yourself if you plan to walk to the hidden Lake Tali Karng or the Sentinels.

Things to Do and See

As mentioned the views from the peaks visited on this trek are nothing short of astounding and are the main highlights of this trek. There are great views from The Pinnacles as well as Mount Wellington.

Visit a number of cattlemen's huts; Horseyard Flat Hut, Moroka Hut and Millers Hut. All these huts display the unique style and craftsmanship of those who built them.

In addition to visiting the huts, you can set up camp at a number of spots beside the Moroka River. You could even throw a line in the river and try your luck tickling a trout or two for dinner.

fast facts

Dargo to Licola via The Pinnacles and Mt Wellington

Trek distance: 110km

Standard: Hard (Dry weather only)

Fuel and supplies: Dargo, Waterford and Licola

Trek highlights: Good four-wheel driving, views from The Pinnacles and Mt Wellington, Moroka River, walk to Lake Tali Karng

Track conditions:
Parks Vic/DNRE Dargo
Ph 03/5140 1243

Need help?: D. Guy Autos, Waterford (4WD Recovery) Ph 03/5140 1265

From Millers Hut you can walk to Lake Tali Karng, or drive further past Millers Hut to the start of the walk to The Sentinels. If undertaking either walk it is recommended that you be well equipped and self-sufficient.

Alternatively, you can set up camp at McFarlane Saddle along the Moroka Road and walk to Lake Tali Karng and The Sentinels from there.

Bennison Lookout on the Tamboritha Road provides impressive views towards Mt Wellington and The Sentinels.

Further along the Tamboritha Road you will come to the Wellington River with numerous camp sites beside the river. A walking track to Lake Tali Karng also starts here.

For those who like their walks a little longer, you can join the McMillan's Walking Track from Arbuckle Junction and along the Tamboritha Road at the MGS camp site.

Access

The village of Dargo at the base of the Dargo High Plains is the starting point for this trek. To reach Dargo travel north via the bitumen Dargo Road from Bairnsdale on the Princes Highway or via Briagalong or Stratford. Alternatively, from the north take the gravel Dargo High Plains Road from The Great Alpine Road at Mount St Bernard.

The Trek

From Dargo the route heads towards Bairnsdale where it turns west 8km after crossing the Waterford Bridge. From here the track begins its steep climb to the ridgeline and Dingo Hill.

From Dingo Hill the track drops steeply to cross Castleburn Creek South before it once again climbs the ranges to meet The Pinnacles Road.

At the junction with The Pinnacles Road it's an easy drive along a well maintained gravel road to the lookout car park. From the car park it's a short walk to the fire tower perched on The Pinnacles and its stunning panoramas.

From the car park we return via The Pinnacles Road, then west towards Arbuckle Junction along Moroka Road. En route we pass Horseyard Flat and cross the Moroka River. At the junction of Mt Wellington Track we turn south and cross the Moroka River once again before reaching the seasonal closure gates to Mt Wellington.

Although it's only a short distance to the summit, the Mt Wellington Track is quite rough and rocky, with some steep sections to be negotiated. This track is slow going, requiring careful wheel placement in some sections. Once at the summit you can continue onto Millers Hut—the track surface remaining rough and rocky. There is a short and steep descent just prior to reaching the hut.

From Millers Hut the route backtracks over Mt Wellington to the all weather Moroka Road to Arbuckle Junction. At Arbuckle Junction you can turn south towards Licola via the well maintained Tamboritha Road or head north along Howitt Road to meet with Trek 5 - *Butcher Country* or Trek Six - *Wonnangatta Valley*.

ABOVE: *Looking over the Wonnangatta River Valley from the Pinnacles Lookout.*

Standard

This trek has been rated hard. Part of the trek is via maintained gravel roads, although the climb at the beginning of the trek off the Bairnsdale Road is short and steep. From Dingo Hill the track drops steeply before climbing to The Pinnacle.

The rocky climb to Mount Wellington and onto Millers Hut will require careful wheel placement.

Camping

There is an abundance of camping along this trek. Horseyard Flat has some excellent flat grassy sites, with facilities including fire pits and a pit toilet. There is some good bush camping in the vicinity of Moroka and Millers Huts however neither have facilities. Moroka Hut is a walk-in only site. Along the Moroka Road you can camp beside the Moroka River at the bridge crossing and at MacFarlane Saddle. Neither of these sites have facilities.

Along Tamboritha Road there are numerous camp sites beside the Wellington River and these are indicated by numbered posts along the road. Some sites have facilities.

Permits/Restrictions

The main part of this trek has no restrictions, however Mt Wellington Track has a seasonal road closure which is in force from after the Queen's Birthday Long Weekend to just after the Melbourne Cup in November.

Recommended Maps/Guides

The best maps for this trek are the Brookes Bush Maps, Victoria *Crooked River - Dargo* and *Snowy Plains, Mt Kent & Lake Tali Karng*. Hema Maps *High Country - Victoria* map also shows the route.

Topographic maps for the area are the *Crooked River - Steve, Cobbannah - Tabberabbera, Licola - Wellington* and *Tamboritha - Moroka* 1:50 000 series.

Further Information

Parks Victoria and Dept of Natural Resources and Environment
Lind Avenue Dargo VIC 3862 Ph 03/5140 1243 Fax 03/5140 1216

Dargo General Store
16A Lind Avenue, Dargo Ph 03/5140 1219

Licola General Store and Caravan Park
Jamieson Road, Licola Ph 03/5148 8786

Brochures - Parks Victoria: *Alpine National Park - walks around Howitt, Snowy Range and Tali Karng.*
Parks Victoria: *Alpine National Park - around Heyfield, Licola and Dargo in the Wonnangatta/ Moroka area*

ROUTE NOTES

Trek starts in the village of Dargo.

▼ 0.0 (0.0)
Zero trip meter in Dargo. Dargo Hotel on left and General Store on right. PSA south towards Bairnsdale.
▲ *45.8 (8.6)*
Dargo village. Hotel on right and store on left.
GPS S:37 27.710 E:147 15.054
UTM Zone 55 0522192E 5853872N

▼ 8.6 (8.6)
Road on right SP Wonnangatta Road. CSA.
▲ *37.2 (1.4)*
SP Wonnangatta Road on left. CSA. SP Dargo 9km.

▼ 10.0 (1.4)
Waterford Bridge over Wonnangatta River.
▲ *35.8 (7.8)*
Waterford Bridge over Wonnangatta River.

▼ 17.8 (7.8)
Road junction. Sharp TR. SP Castleburn Ck Tk. Once in Castleburn Ck Tk, TL and cross creek. Track climbs steeply from creek.
▲ *28.0 (2.1)*
Cross creek. At road junction with bitumen TL for Dargo. This is Dargo Road. TR for Bairnsdale/Stratford.
GPS S:37 32.367 E:147 12.469
UTM Zone 55 0518358E 5845259N

▼ 19.9 (2.1)
Track junction. TL. SP Traills Tk.
▲ *25.9 (2.0)*
Track junction. TR. Track declines steeply to creek from here.
GPS S:37 32.211 E:147 11.392
UTM Zone 55 0516775E 5845554N

▼ 21.9 (2.0)
Enter SP Alpine National Park.
▲ *23.9 (4.9)*
Exit Alpine National Park.

▼ 26.8 (4.9)
Track junction. This is Dingo Hill. TL. Track drops steeply off Dingo Hill. Track on right SP McCarthy Spur. SP To Scrubby Crk Tk.
▲ *19.0 (2.1)*
Track junction. TR. SP Trails Tk. Track SO SP McCarthy Spur.
GPS S:37 31.058 E:147 07.662
UTM Zone 55 0511283E 5847694N

▼ 28.9 (2.1)
Track junction. TR. SP Junction Spur Tk. Track on left SP Castleburn Ck Tk.
▲ *16.9 (0.6)*
Track junction. TL. SP Traill Tk. Track now climbs steeply to Dingo Hill. Track SO SP Castleburn Ck Tk.
GPS S:37 31.682 E:147 07.233
UTM Zone 55 0510653E 5846545N

▼ 29.5 (0.6)
Cross Castleburn Creek South.
▲ *16.3 (0.4)*
Creek crossing.

▼ 29.9 (0.4)
Creek crossing. Track climbs from creek.
▲ *15.9 (2.7)*
Cross Castleburn Creek South.

▼ 32.6 (2.7)
Helipad.
▲ *13.2 (4.4)*
Helipad. Track drops to creek.

▼ 37.0 (4.4)
Track junction. TR. SP Castle Hill Tk.
▲ *8.8 (0.9)*
Track junction. TL. SP Junction SP Tk.
GPS S:37 30.445 E:147 03.377
UTM Zone 55 0504974E 5848837N

▼ 37.9 (0.9)
Minor track on left. KR on main track.
▲ *7.9 (2.3)*
Minor track on right. CSA.

▼ 40.2 (2.3)
Good views over surrounding valleys on right.
▲ *5.6 (3.7)*
Good views on left. CSA on main track.

▼ 43.9 (3.7)
Minor track on right. CSA.
▲ *1.9 (0.2)*
Minor track on left. CSA on main track.

▼ 44.1 (0.2)
T junction. TR. This is The Pinnacles Road.
▲ *1.7 (0.1)*
Track junction. TL. SP Castle Hill Tk.
GPS S:37 27.818 E:147 02.404
UTM Zone 55 0503542E 5853689N

▼ 44.2 (0.1)
KR. SP The Pinnacles. Track on left SP To Billy Goat Bluff.
▲ *1.6 (1.4)*
Track on right SP To Billy Goat Bluff. CSA.

▼ 45.6 (1.4)
Track on right leads to possible bush camping and helipad. CSA.
▲ *0.2 (0.2)*
Track on left. CSA.

▼ 45.8 (0.2)
The Pinnacles car park. Zero trip meter here.
▲ *0.0 (0.0)*
Pinnacles car park. Return the way you came.
GPS S:37 27.668 E:147 03.221
UTM Zone 55 0504744E 5853973N

▼ 0.0 (0.0)
Pinnacles car park. Return the way you came.
▲ *39.9 (0.2)*
The Pinnacles car park. Zero trip meter here.

▼ 0.2 (0.2)
Track on left. CSA.
▲ *39.7 (1.4)*
Track on right leads to possible bush camping and helipad. CSA.

▼ 1.6 (1.4)
Track on right SP To Billy Goat Bluff. CSA.
▲ *38.3 (0.1)*
KR. SP The Pinnacles. Track on left SP To Billy Goat Bluff.

▼ 1.7 (0.1)
Track on left SP Castle Hill Tk. CSA.
▲ *38.2 (2.4)*
Track on right SP Castle Tk. CSA.

▼ 4.1 (2.4)
Track on left. CSA.
▲ *35.8 (1.2)*
Y junction. KL. SP Pinnacles.

▼ 5.3 (1.2)
Track junction. KL.
▲ *34.6 (3.9)*
Y junction. VR. SP Pinnacles. SP Billy Goat Bluff Tk.
GPS S:37 28.319 E:147 00.478
UTM Zone 55 0500698E 5852767N

▼ 9.2 (3.9)
Track junction. CSA. Track on right SP Horseyard Flat leads to camping area.
▲ *30.7 (2.0)*
SP Horseyard Flat on left to camping area. Notes CSA.

▼ 11.2 (2.0)
Track junction. CSA. Track on left SP Marathon Rd.
▲ *28.7 (1.7)*
Track junction. CSA. SP Pinnacles. SP Shanty Hollow. Track on right SP Marathon Rd.

▼ 12.9 (1.7)
Track on left. CSA.
▲ *27.0 (0.6)*
Track on right. CSA.

▼ 13.5 (0.6)
Track on left SP Moroka Range Tk. CSA over bridge over Moroka River. *NB:* possible bush camping on right over bridge.
▲ *26.4 (2.7)*
Bridge over Moroka River. CSA past SP Moroka Range Tk on right. NB: *possible bush camping on left prior to bridge.*

▼ 16.2 (2.7)
SP Moroka Hut on left. This is a 300m walking track to hut and camping area. Notes CSA.
▲ *23.7 (2.6)*
SP Moroka Hut on right. CSA.
GPS S:37 30.341 E:146 55.922
UTM Zone 55 0493994E 5849027N

▼ 18.8 (2.6)
Track on left. CSA.
▲ *21.1 (2.8)*
Track on right. KL on main track.

TOYOTA
BBP·001

▼ 21.6 (2.8)
Track on right. CSA.
▲ *18.3 (0.9)*
Track on left. CSA.

▼ 22.5 (0.9)
Track junction. CSA. Track on left SP Mt Wellington Tk.
▲ *17.4 (5.3)*
SP Mt Wellington Tk on right. CSA.
GPS S:37 28. 756 E:146 53.288
UTM Zone 55 0490110E 5851950N

Mt Wellington Route Notes

At junction turn into SP Mt Wellington Tk and zero trip meter.

▼ (2.3) Cross Moroka River.

▼ (1.0) Track junction. Sharp TR through seasonal closure gate. SP Mt Wellington Tk.
GPS S:37 30.047 E:146 52.451
UTM Zone 55 0488886E 5849573N

▼ (4.2) Mt Wellington summit. CSA.
GPS S:37 30.482 E:146 50.711
UTM Zone 55 0486318E 5848757N

▼ (4.1) Track on left leads to small bush camp site. CSA.

▼ (0.7) Millers Hut. Camping in hut vicinity. Walk to Tali Karng. Track continues past the hut to The Sentinels walking track.
GPS S:37 32.387 E:146 49.337
UTM Zone 55 0484294E 5845234N

Millers Hut

OPPOSITE: *The Mt Wellington Track near Mt Wellington summit.*

▼ 27.8 (5.3)
SP McFarlanes Saddle camping area on left. CSA.
▲ *12.1 (2.2)*
SP McFarlanes Saddle on right. CSA.

▼ 30.0 (2.2)
Track on left. CSA.
▲ *9.9 (1.8)*
Track on right. KL on main track.

▼ 31.8 (1.8)
Track on right. CSA.
▲ *8.1 (2.8)*
Track on left. CSA.

▼ 34.6 (2.8)
Track on right. CSA.
▲ *5.3 (0.6)*
Track on left. CSA.

▼ 35.2 (0.6)
SP Moroka Rd Lookout on right. CSA.
▲ *4.7 (0.7)*
Moroka Rd Lookout on left. CSA.

▼ 35.9 (0.7)
Track on right. CSA.
▲ *4.0 (4.0)*
Track on left. CSA.

▼ 39.9 (4.0)
SP Arbuckle Junction. Road on left SP Tamboritha Rd. Road on right SP Howitt Rd. TL for Licola. TR to meet Trek 5 - Butcher Country or Trek 6 - Wonnangatta Valley.
▲ *0.0 (0.0)*
Zero trip meter at Arbuckle Junction. Turn into SP Moroka Rd.
GPS S:37 25.187 E:146 47.043
UTM Zone 55 0480891E 5858537N

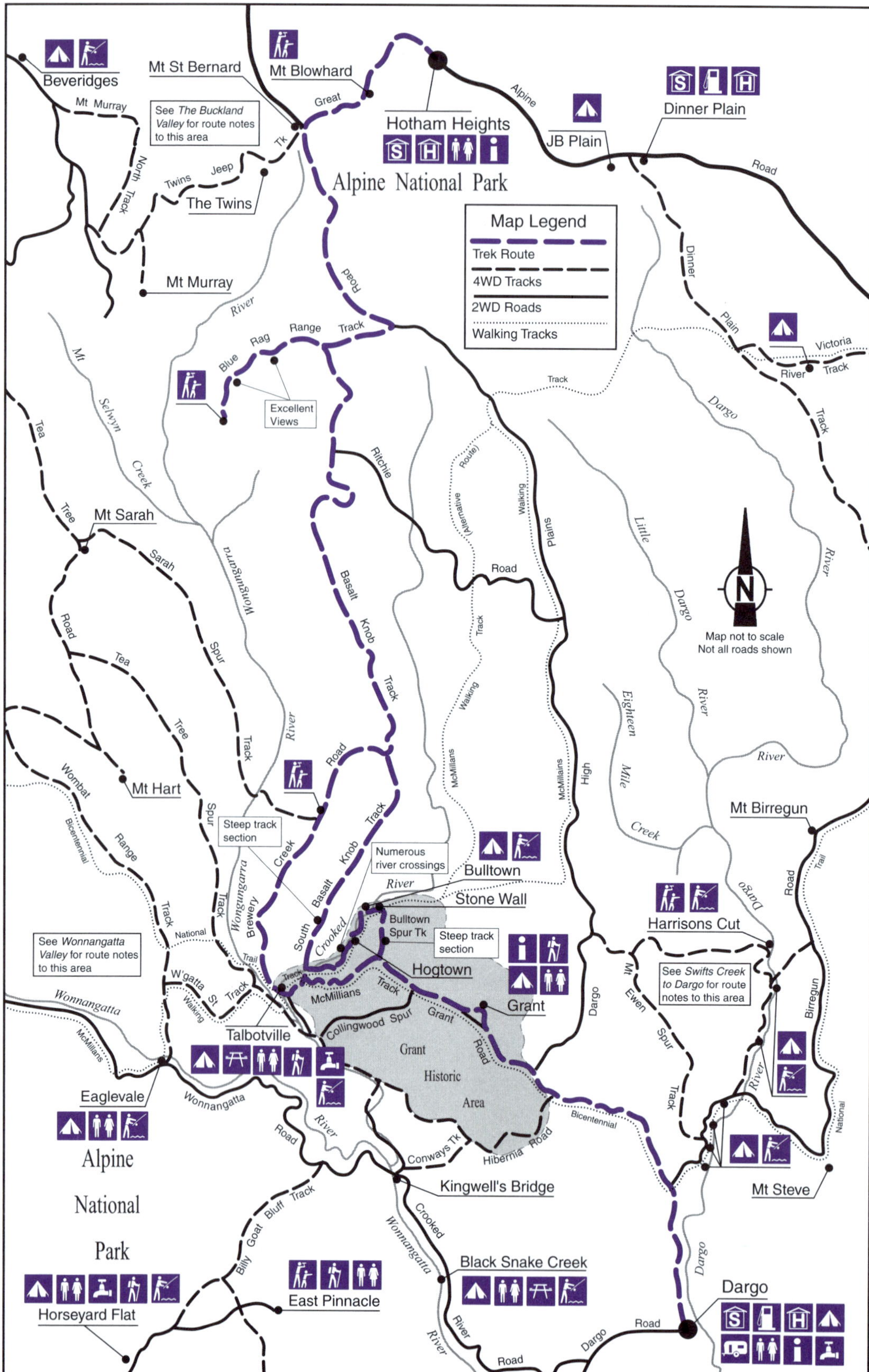
Map Legend
Trek Route
4WD Tracks
2WD Roads
Walking Tracks
Map not to scale
Not all roads shown
N
Beveridges
Mt St Bernard
Mt Blowhard
Hotham Heights
Alpine National Park
JB Plain
Dinner Plain
See The Buckland Valley for route notes to this area
Mt Murray
North Track
Twins Jeep
The Twins
Great Alpine Road
Tk
Mt Murray
River
Road
Blue Rag Range Track
Excellent Views
Mt Selwyn Creek
Tea Tree Road
Mt Sarah
Sarah Spur Track
Tea Tree Spur Track
Wonnangatta River
Ritchie Road
Basalt Knob Track
(Alternative Route)
Walking Track
Plains
High Plains Road
Track
Dinner Plain Track
Victoria River Track
Dargo River
Little Dargo River
Eighteen Mile Creek
Mt Hart
Wombat Range Track
Bicentennial
Road
Steep track section
Creek Track
Basalt Knob Track
Numerous river crossings
River
Bulltown
Stone Wall
McMillians
McMillians
Wongungarra
Brewery Trail
Track
National
South Basalt
Crooked
Bulltown Spur Tk
Steep track section
Hogtown
Grant
McMillians Track
Collingwood Spur
Grant Road
Grant Historic Area
See Wonnangatta Valley for route notes to this area
W'gatta St Track
Walking
Wonnangatta
McMillians
Talbotville
Eaglevale
Alpine National Park
Wonnangatta Road
River
Conways Tk
Hibernia Road
Bicentennial
Kingwell's Bridge
Crooked
Wonnangatta
Black Snake Creek
River
River
Road
Dargo Road
Road
Dargo
Billy Goat Bluff Track
East Pinnacle
Horseyard Flat
Mt Birregun
Road
Trail
Dargo
Harrisons Cut
See Swifts Creek to Dargo for route notes to this area
Mt Ewen Spur Track
Dargo
Birregun
River
National
Mt Steve
Dargo

TREK EIGHT

THE CROOKED RIVER

LOCATED IN A STEEP valley and enveloped from all sides by sheer sided mountains are the Crooked River Goldfields, which were first discovered by the then government geologist Alfred Howitt in 1860. At the time these were the most remote and isolated fields in Victoria. Howitt's initial find was at Good Luck Creek, a tributary of the Crooked River.

Although the fields were isolated, prospectors soon flooded the area with the towns of Grant, Talbotville, Hogtown, Bulltown and Howittville being established. Grant became the main centre of the goldfields and at its peak had a population of almost 3000.

Things to Do and See

Those with an interest in our pioneering past and its gold mining history will find numerous sites to explore on this trek, ranging from the once grand settlement of Grant, where you can visit the cemetery, walk to the Jolly Sailor Mine or view the water filled tunnel of the Jeweller Shop Mine, to the long gone mining villages of Bulltown, Hogtown and Talbotville on the Crooked River. *Please note*: There are many old mine shafts in these areas and care is required when exploring on foot.

Along the Crooked River Track take the walking track to the New Good Hope Mine where an abandoned ore crusher and boiler still remain.

At Talbotville you can explore the cemetery or wander down to the Crooked River via the Dry Foot Walking Track.

Towards the end of the trek there are great views to be had from Blue Rag Range and on a clear day you seem almost to be standing on the top of the world.

fast facts

Dargo to Mt St Bernard via Grant, Talbotville and Blue Rag Range

Trek distance: 100km

Standard: Route Option A - Easy/Medium
Route Option B - Hard
Both routes are dry weather only

Fuel and supplies: Dargo & Harrietville/Bright. Limited supplies at Hotham Heights

Trek highlights: Grant Historic Area, Talbotville, Blue Rag Range, Bulltown, Crooked River, old mines.

Track conditions:
Parks Vic/DNRE Dargo
Ph 03/5140 1243

Need help?: D. Guy Autos, Waterford (4WD Recovery) Ph 03/5140 1265

RACV Bright 0500 550 230

Access

The village of Dargo, located 50km north west of Bairnsdale, is the start point for this trek. To reach Dargo travel north via the bitumen Lindenow - Dargo Road from Bairnsdale on the Princes Highway or via Briagalong or Stratford. Alternatively, from the north take the gravel Dargo High Plains Road from The Great Alpine Road at Mount St Bernard.

The Trek

From Dargo take the Dargo High Plains Road (Lind Ave), heading north towards Mt Hotham. Before long you come to a junction with Upper Dargo Road which leads to a number of good camp sites beside the Dargo River. This junction is known as Farm Junction.

Continue on Dargo High Plains Road as it winds up through The Long Cutting until you reach Grant Junction. At this point turn left into Grant Road (also known as McMillan's

Track), passing Jolly Sailor Spur Track and Grant Cemetery before arriving at the now abandoned ghost town of Grant.

After exploring Grant continue on towards Talbotville—the road now has become McMillan's Track. Pass Collingwood Spur Track on the left before you reach Bulltown Spur Track branching off to the right. If you have chosen the easy/medium trek continue along McMillan's Track, dropping to the Crooked River and Talbotville which is located in the deep valley below.

The hard trek turns into Bulltown Spur Track, which is a steep downhill run to the Crooked River at the one time mining village of Stonewall. Like other mining villages along the Crooked River not much remains except for a few crumbling ruins of miners huts and chimneys. From Stonewall follow the Crooked River Track, passing the sites of Bulltown (or Naarun) and Hogtown. To stretch your legs there is a walking track to the New Good Hope Mine which is worthwhile exploring.

Both treks meet again at Talbotville with its good camping. From Talbotville the easy trek crosses the Crooked River and winds its way up the Louisa Range on Brewery Creek Track with views across the Wongungarra River Valley to the Mt Darling/Snowy Bluff area before meeting with South Basalt Knob Track.

From Talbotville, route option B recrosses the Crooked River and backtracks along Crooked River Track for a short distance to South Basalt Knob Track. From here it is a sustained low range climb for 1½km before the track begins to level out. The trek then continues onto join with route option A at the Ritchie Road - South Basalt Knob Track intersection.

From the Ritchie Road - South Basalt Knob Track junction the trek continues in a northerly direction, passing Basalt Knob before joining with the northern end of Basalt Knob Track which then joins with Blue Rag Range Track. It is a short and spectacular drive along the dead-end Blue Rag Range Track and on a fine day the vistas from the ridge are stunning. From Blue Rag Range the trek then goes out to the Dargo High Plains Road and onto Mt St Bernard (where you can join Trek 9 - *The Buckland Valley*) before concluding on the Great Alpine Road at Hotham Heights.

Standard

This trek has both an easy/medium option and a hard option. Which option you choose will depend on your level of experience and the current weather conditions. Although it is possible to travel route option A in damp conditions, route option B is best avoided during these times as Bulltown Spur Track and South Basalt Knob Track can become extremely slippery and dangerous.

Route option A, the easier of the two, is of an easy/medium standard and traverses mostly well made forest roads that are in good condition. This route is suitable for novice four-wheel drive tourers. The gradients are not overly steep, however care should be taken at the Crooked River crossing when the water level is high.

The more difficult route option B, which is given a hard rating, travels the steep Bulltown Spur Track to the Crooked River at Stonewall. From here the trek follows the river downstream to Talbotville, crossing the twisting Crooked River on 21 separate occasions. From Talbotville, this route climbs very steeply on the South Basalt Knob Track before rejoining with route option A at Ritchie Road.

Camping

You can camp at a number of sites on Upper Dargo Road at the start of this trek. All sites are beside the Dargo River and some have facilities (see Trek 10 - *Swifts Creek to Dargo* for details).

A small camping area with facilities is located at Grant near the old township site, however much better camping is available down on the Crooked River at Talbotville. This is a large grassed area beside the river and has fireplaces, picnic tables and toilets. It is also a good base from which to explore the surrounding area. This area is very popular over the summer and Easter holiday periods.

If you chose to follow route option B, then there is an array of secluded bush camp sites along the Crooked River between Bulltown and Talbotville. There are no facilities at these sites.

Permits/Restrictions

This trek is restricted by seasonal road closures which are usually in force from after the Queen's Birthday Long Weekend to just after the Melbourne Cup in November.

Recommended Maps/Guides

There is a large choice of maps for this trek, including the Brookes Bush Maps, Victoria *Crooked River - Dargo Area*, the *Grant Historic Adventurer* by Paoletti's Maps and Hema Maps *High Country - Victoria* map.

Topographic maps for this trek are the *Crooked River - Steve* and the *Dargo Plains - Cobungra* in the 1:50 000 series or the 1:100 000 *Dargo* map sheet.

Further Information

Parks Victoria and Dept of Natural Resources and Environment
Lind Ave, Dargo VIC 3722 Ph 03/5140 1243 Fax 03/5140 1216

Dargo General Store
16A Lind Ave, Dargo VIC Ph 03/5140 1219

Brochures - Parks Victoria: *Grant Historic Area - around Dargo and the Crooked River Goldfields*
Parks Victoria: *Alpine National Park - around Heyfield, Licola and Dargo in the Wonnangatta/ Moroka area*

Further Reading - *Secrets of Ghost Towns of the High Country* by Luke Steenhuis 1998

ABOVE: *Remains of a boiler engine and battery stamp at New Good Hope.*

The Golden Age of Grant

During the boom days of the late 1800s the town of Grant, which was situated on a ridge high above Crooked River was known as the 'capital' of the Crooked River Goldfields. Grant's population peaked at 2000 with the town having fifteen hotels, a courthouse, police station and lockup, four banks, a church, medical hall, a newspaper office that published the Crooked River Chronicle once a week and several other stores located along the town's two main streets.

ABOVE: *Grant in its heyday circa* 1870s

The first notable exploration of the area was undertaken by surveyor John Wilkinson who was sent to survey the upper reaches of the Mitchell River in 1850. Although Wilkinson reported the presence of gold in the Wonnangatta and Wongungarra Rivers, it wasn't until May of 1860 that Alfred Howitt was engaged by the government's Prospecting Board to open up the area as a new goldfield in the hope of holting the colonies downward sliding economy.

Howitt found evidence along the Dargo River in the way of mine workings, sluice boxes, water races and a number of huts to indicate that prospectors had already moved to the area. However, with winter not far off Howitt found the camps deserted.

Howitt, having only meagre success on the Dargo River, moved his attention to the Wonnangatta River which he followed to its junction with the Wongungarra River. Howitt and his party then came upon a branch of this river, which, due to its winding course he named Crooked River. At Good Luck Creek, a tributary of Crooked River, Howitt washed several pennyweight nuggets, totalling £7/6/- (about $30). With this success most of Howitt's party resigned to take up claims along the river. By 1861 there were seven hundred prospectors working the Crooked River fields.

With new fields being discovered at Jordan (near Woods Point) and at the head of the Dargo River at Maytown, veteran explorer Angus McMillan was called out of semiretirement in 1864 to lead the Alpine Exploring Expedition to clear a route of 220 miles (about 355km) from Omeo to Crooked River to Woods Point. In April, while the party were working on a spur dividing the Wongungarra and Crooked Rivers, two of McMillan's men found a lump of quartz impregnated with gold. Like Howitt, most of McMillan's party resigned to stake claims. The new find was named 'Pioneer' Reef in honour of McMillan's favourite horse.

ABOVE: *Grant today*

Over the next few months new reefs were being uncovered almost daily. At its peak there were eight crushing mills in the surrounding areas and 250 registered reefs. The most productive mine was the Good Hope Mine which was worked from 1865 to 1915.

To cater for this second influx of prospectors to the area a settlement began at a place known as Mt Pleasant. By 1865 the town's population was around 750 with another 1500 or so in the vicinity. In March of that year the town's name was changed from Mt Pleasant to Grant in honour of the impending visit of the then Lands Commissioner.

As with other areas relying on the fortunes of gold, the town's boom days were short lived. By 1867 the majority of the businesses in Grant had closed their doors and in 1916 the last residents departed.

ROUTE NOTES

Trek commences in village of Dargo.

▼ 0.0 (0.0)
Zero trip meter in Dargo. Hotel on right and General Store on left. PSA along Dargo High Plains Road in a northerly direction.

▲ *22.4 (5.6)*
Dargo village. Hotel on left and General Store on right.
GPS S:37 27.710 E:147 15.054
UTM Zone 55 0522192E 5853872N

▼ 5.6 (5.6)
SP Upper Dargo Rd on right. Leads to camping areas and Trek Ten - Swifts Creek to Dargo. CSA uphill.

▲ *16.8 (10.1)*
SP Upper Dargo Rd on left. CSA downhill.

▼ 15.7 (10.1)
SP Hibernia Rd on left. CSA.

▲ *6.7 (1.1)*
SP Hibernia Rd on right. CSA.

▼ 16.8 (1.1)
Track junction. TL. SP Grant. SP McMillan Rd. Enter SP Grant Historic Area.

▲ *5.6 (0.9)*
Road junction with bitumen. TR. SP Dargo 17.
GPS S:37 22.444 E:147 11.197
UTM Zone 55 0516521E 5863617N

▼ 17.7 (0.9)
Track on left and right. CSA on main track.

▲ *4.7 (2.3)*
Track on left and right. CSA.

▼ 20.0 (2.3)
SP Jolly Sailor on right. CSA.

▲ *2.4 (0.7)*
SP Jolly Sailor on left. CSA.

▼ 20.7 (0.7)
SP Grant Cemetery on right. CSA.

▲ *1.7 (1.4)*
SP Grant Cemetery on left. CSA.

▼ 22.1 (1.4)
Y junction. KR. SP Grant. Track on left SP Eldorado Walking Track.

▲ *0.3 (0.3)*
Track junction. CSA.
GPS S:37 20.766 E:147 09.068
UTM Zone 55 0513393E 5866723N

▲ *0.0 (0.0)*
Track junction. KR.

▼ 22.4 (0.3)
Track junction. Track on right leads to Grant Historic Area. Camping, information and walks. Zero trip meter here. Choose either Route Option A (easy/medium) or Route Option B (hard). Route notes for Route Option B commence on page 96.

Route Option A

▼ 0.0 (0.0)
Track junction. KL.

▲ *27.2 (0.6)*
Track junction. Track on left to Grant Historic Area. Route options A and B join here. Zero trip meter here. Route notes continue above at 0.0 (0.0) reading.

▼ 0.6 (0.6)
Track junction. TR. SP Talbotville. This is SP McMillan Rd.

▲ *26.6 (1.3)*
Track junction. VL. SP Grant.

▼ 1.9 (1.3)
Lookout point on right. CSA.

▲ *25.3 (0.3)*
Lookout point on left. CSA.

▼ 2.2 (0.3)
Track junction. KR. SP Talbotville. SP McMillan Rd. Track drops steeply from here with excellent views over the ranges. Track on left SP Collingwood Spur 4x4 Only.

▲ *25.0 (2.8)*
CSA. SP McMillan Rd. Track on right SP Collingwood Spur.

▼ 5.0 (2.8)
Track junction. KL. SP McMillan Rd. Track on right SP Bulltown Spur.

▲ *22.2 (5.3)*
KR. SP McMillan Rd. Track on left SP Bulltown Spur.

▼ 10.3 (5.3)
SP Talbotville Cemetery on left. CSA.
▲ *16.9 (0.2)*
SP Talbotville Cemetery on right. CSA.

▼ 10.5 (0.2)
Track junction. This area was the site of Talbotville township. Excellent camping in this area. Notes TL.
▲ *16.7 (0.1)*
Track junction. TR. SP Dargo 33. SP Grant.
GPS S:37 20.025 E:147 04.059
UTM Zone 55 0505996E 5868103N

▼ 10.6 (0.1)
Y junction. VR and cross river.
▲ *16.6 (0.1)*
Track junction. This area was the site of Talbotville township. Excellent camping in this area. Notes TL.

▼ 10.7 (0.1)
Track junction. KR uphill. SP Brewery Crk Tk. Track on left SP Crooked River Rd.
▲ *16.5 (0.7)*
Track junction. CSA over river. Track on right SP Crooked River Rd.

▼ 11.4 (0.7)
McMillans Walking Track and Bicentennial National Trail cross road here. CSA on main track.
▲ *15.8 (10.6)*
McMillans Walking Track and Bicentennial National Trail cross road here. CSA.

▼ 22.0 (10.6)
Track junction. CSA. Track on left SP Bald Top Tk.
▲ *5.2 (0.9)*
CSA. Track on right SP Bald Top Tk.

▼ 22.9 (0.9)
SP Mad Dog Lookout. Notes CSA.
▲ *4.3 (2.3)*
SP Mad Dog Lookout. Notes CSA.
GPS S:37 16.158 E:147 05.131
UTM Zone 55 0507593E 5875252N

▼ 25.2 (2.3)
Lookout point on right. CSA.
▲ *2.0 (2.0)*
Lookout point on left. CSA.

▼ 27.2 (2.0)
Track junction. TL. SP Ritchie Rd. Track on right SP South Basalt Knob Tk. Route options A and B join here. Zero trip meter here and follow notes continued on page 99 from 0.0 (0.0) reading.
Route Option A
▲ *0.0 (0.0)*
Track junction. TR. SP Talbotville. Track on left SP South Basalt Knob Tk.
GPS S:37 14.997 E:147 06.685
UTM Zone 55 0509878E 5877406N

Route Option B

▼ 0.0 (0.0)
Track junction. KL.
▲ *27.2 (0.6)*
Track junction. Track on left to Grant Historic Area. Route options A and B join here. Zero trip meter here and follow route notes on page 95 at 0.0 (0.0) reading.

▼ 0.6 (0.6)
Track junction. TR. SP Talbotville. This is SP McMillan Rd.
▲ *26.6 (1.3)*
Track junction. VL. SP Grant.

▼ 1.9 (1.3)
Lookout point on right. CSA.
▲ *25.3 (0.3)*
Lookout point on left. CSA.

▼ 2.2 (0.3)
Track junction. KR. SP Talbotville. SP McMillan Rd. Track on left SP Collingwood Spur 4x4 Only.
▲ *25.0 (2.8)*
CSA. SP McMillan Rd. Track on right SP Collingwood Spur.

▼ 5.0 (2.8)
Track junction. TR. SP Bulltown Spur. Track drops steeply. Engage low range. Road SO SP McMillan Rd.
▲ *22.2 (1.5)*
Track junction. TL. SP McMillan Rd.
GPS S:37 19.450 E:147 06.739
UTM Zone 55 0509953E 5869160N

▼ 6.5 (1.5)
Track junction. KL on lower track. Track on right leads to helipad.

▲ *20.7 (1.6)*
Track on left. CSA uphill.

▼ 8.1 (1.6)
Y junction. KL. Track on right leads 200m to SP Stonewall.
▲ *19.1 (0.1)*
Track junction. Track on left leads to SP Stonewall. CSA and KR heading uphill at hairpin bend. SP Bulltown Spur Tk. Track climbs steeply from here. Engage low range.
GPS S:37 18.241 E:147 06.955
UTM Zone 55 0510276E 5871399N

▼ 8.2 (0.1)
CSA. SP Crooked River Tk. Track on right SP Stonewall.
▲ *19.0 (0.6)*
Track junction. KR. Track on left SP Stonewall.

▼ 8.8 (0.6)
Cross Crooked River. Across river tracks on right lead to bush camp sites. You can see a water race cut into the side of the hill here, evidence of mining history. Notes CSA.
▲ *18.4 (0.1)*
Tracks on left lead to bush camp sites. Notes CSA and cross Crooked River.
GPS S:37 18.281 E:147 06.548
UTM Zone 55 0509671E 5871322N

▼ 8.9 (0.1)
Cross river.
▲ *18.3 (0.1)*
Cross river.

▼ 9.0 (0.1)
SP Bulltown on right, site of old township. Bush camp sites in this area. Notes CSA.
▲ *18.2 (0.5)*
SP Bulltown on left. CSA.

▼ 9.5 (0.5)
Cross river.
▲ *17.7 (0.3)*
Cross river.

▼ 9.8 (0.3)
Cross river.
▲ *17.4 (0.1)*
Cross river.

▼ 9.9 (0.1)
SP Hogtown on right, site of old township. Bush camp sites in this area. Notes CSA.
▲ *17.3 (0.4)*
SP Hogtown on left. CSA.

▼ 10.3 (0.4)
Track on right leads to small bush camp sites. *NB:* Numerous mine shafts in this area. Notes CSA.
▲ *16.9 (0.3)*
Track on left. CSA.

▼ 10.6 (0.3)
Cross river.
▲ *16.6 (0.3)*
Cross river.

▼ 10.9 (0.3)
Cross river.
▲ *16.3 (0.4)*
Cross river.

▼ 11.3 (0.4)
Double river crossing.
▲ *15.9 (0.2)*
Double river crossing.

▼ 11.5 (0.2)
Small bush camp site on right. CSA.
▲ *15.7 (0.1)*
Small bush camp site on left. CSA and cross river.

▼ 11.6 (0.1)
Cross river.
▲ *15.6 (0.2)*
Cross river.

▼ 11.8 (0.2)
Cross river. Small bush camp site on right over river.
▲ *15.4 (0.6)*
Small bush camp site on left. CSA and cross river.

▼ 12.4 (0.6)
Cross river.
▲ *14.8 (0.7)*
Cross river.

▼ 13.1 (0.7)
Cross river. Over river track junction. Notes KR. Track on left to SP New Good Hope No. 5 Battery, leads 300m to car park and New Good Hope Mine Walking Track - 15 minute walk.
▲ *14.1 (0.3)*
Track junction. KL and cross river. Track on right SP New Good Hope No 5 Battery.

▼ 13.4 (0.3)
Cross river.
▲ *13.8 (0.2)*
Cross river.

▼ 13.6 (0.2)
Cross river. Over river small bush camp site on left. Notes CSA.
▲ *13.6 (0.2)*
Small bush camp site on right. Notes CSA and cross river.

▼ 13.8 (0.2)
Cross river.
▲ *13.4 (0.5)*
Cross river.

▼ 14.3 (0.5)
Cross river.
▲ *12.9 (0.2)*
Cross river.

▼ 14.5 (0.2)
SP Dry Foot Walking Track to Talbotville 2km on left. This is part of the McMillans Walking Trail. Notes CSA.
▲ *12.7 (0.1)*
SP Dry Foot Walking Track on right. CSA.

▼ 14.6 (0.1)
Cross river.
▲ *12.6 (0.1)*
Cross river.

▼ 14.7 (0.1)
Cross river.
▲ *12.5 (0.4)*
Cross river.

▼ 15.1 (0.4)
Cross river.
▲ *12.1 (0.3)*
Cross river.

▼ 15.4 (0.3)
Cross river.
▲ *11.8 (0.2)*
Cross river.

▼ 15.6 (0.2)
Cross river.
▲ *11.6 (0.1)*
Cross river.

▼ 15.7 (0.1)
Track junction. TR. SP South Basalt Knob Tk. Track has sustained low range climb for 1.5km. Track SO crosses river three more times to Talbotville Camping Area (700m).
▲ *11.5 (2.1)*
Track junction. TL. This is Crooked River Tk. Track on right leads 700m to Talbotville.
GPS S:37 19.745 E:147 04.212
UTM Zone 55 0506218E 5868620N

▼ 17.8 (2.1)
Helipad – good views. Notes CSA.
▲ *9.4 (9.4)*
Helipad. CSA.

▼ 27.2 (9.4)
Track junction. TR onto SP Ritchie Rd. Track on left SP Talbotville. Route options A and B join here. Zero trip meter and follow route notes on page 99 from 0.0 (0.0) reading.

Route Option B
▲ *0.0 (0.0)*
Track junction. TL. SP South Basalt Knob Tk.
GPS S:37 14.997 E:147 06.685
UTM Zone 55 0509878E 5877406N

▼ 0.0 (0.0)
Junction of Ritchie Rd and South Basalt Knob Tk. PSA along Ritchie Rd in northerly direction.
▲ *51.2 (1.2)*
Track junction. Track on right SP Talbotville. Track on left SP South Basalt Knob Tk. Zero trip meter here. Choose either Route Option A notes which commence on page 96 or Route Option B notes which commence on page 98.

▼ 1.2 (1.2)
Track junction. CSA. Track on right SP Tullamarine Tk.
▲ *50.0 (8.3)*
CSA. Track on left SP Tullamarine Tk.

▼ 9.5 (8.3)
Track junction. CSA. Track on left SP Wongungarra Tk.
▲ *41.7 (6.8)*
CSA. Track on right SP Wongungarra Tk.

▼ 16.3 (6.8)
Track junction. TL. SP Basalt Knob Tk. SP Blue Rag. Road SO SP Dargo.
▲ *34.9 (2.6)*
Track junction. TR. SP Basalt Knob Tk. SP Brewery Crk. Road to left SP Dargo.
GPS S:37 09.039 E:147 06.107
UTM Zone 55 0509051E 5888409N

▼ 18.9 (2.6)
Track junction. CSA. SP Blue Rag Tk.
▲ *32.3 (2.3)*
Track junction. CSA. SP Basalt Knob Tk.

▼ 21.2 (2.3)
Minor track on left. KR. SP Blue Rag Tk. Now enter Alpine National Park region.
▲ *30.0 (5.2)*
Minor track on right. KL on main track.

▼ 26.4 (5.2)
Track junction. Sharp TR. Track SO SP Blue Rag Range leads through seasonal closure gate for 3.6km to lookout. Excellent views.

OPPOSITE: *En route to the Blue Rag Range after leaving Talbotville.*

▲ *24.8 (3.0)*
Track junction. Hard TL. SP Basalt North Tk. Track on right SP Blue Rag Range leads 3.6km to lookout.
GPS S:37 05.457 E:147 05.266
UTM Zone 55 0507800E 5895054N

Blue Rag Range

Blue Rag Range Lookout – 1741m.
GPS S:37 05.821 E:147 03.215
UTM Zone 55 0504760E 5894365N

▼ 29.4 (3.0)
Track on right. CSA.
▲ *21.8 (0.5)*
Track on left. CSA.

▼ 29.9 (0.5)
Road junction. TL. This is the Dargo High Plains Road.
▲ *21.3 (11.6)*
Road junction. TR. SP Blue Rag Range. This track is to the right of a large dam.
GPS S:37 05.038 E:147 07.302
UTM Zone 55 0510817E 5895802N

▼ 41.5 (11.6)
Road closure gates. Road junction. This is the Great Alpine Road. Notes TR. SP Mt Hotham 10. TL for SP 45 Bright.
▲ *9.7 (9.7)*
Road junction. TL through road closure gates. SP 62 Dargo. This is Dargo High Plains Road. Road SO SP 45 Bright.
GPS S:37 00.552 E:147 04.831
UTM Zone 55 0507162E 5904106N

▼ 51.2 (9.7)
Hotham Heights.
▲ *0.0 (0.0)*
Zero trip meter on Great Alpine Road at Hotham Heights. Resort management office on left and Hotham Central on right. Head along Great Alpine Road in a northerly direction towards Bright.
GPS S:36 58.945 E:147 08.541
UTM Zone 55 0512663E 5907065N

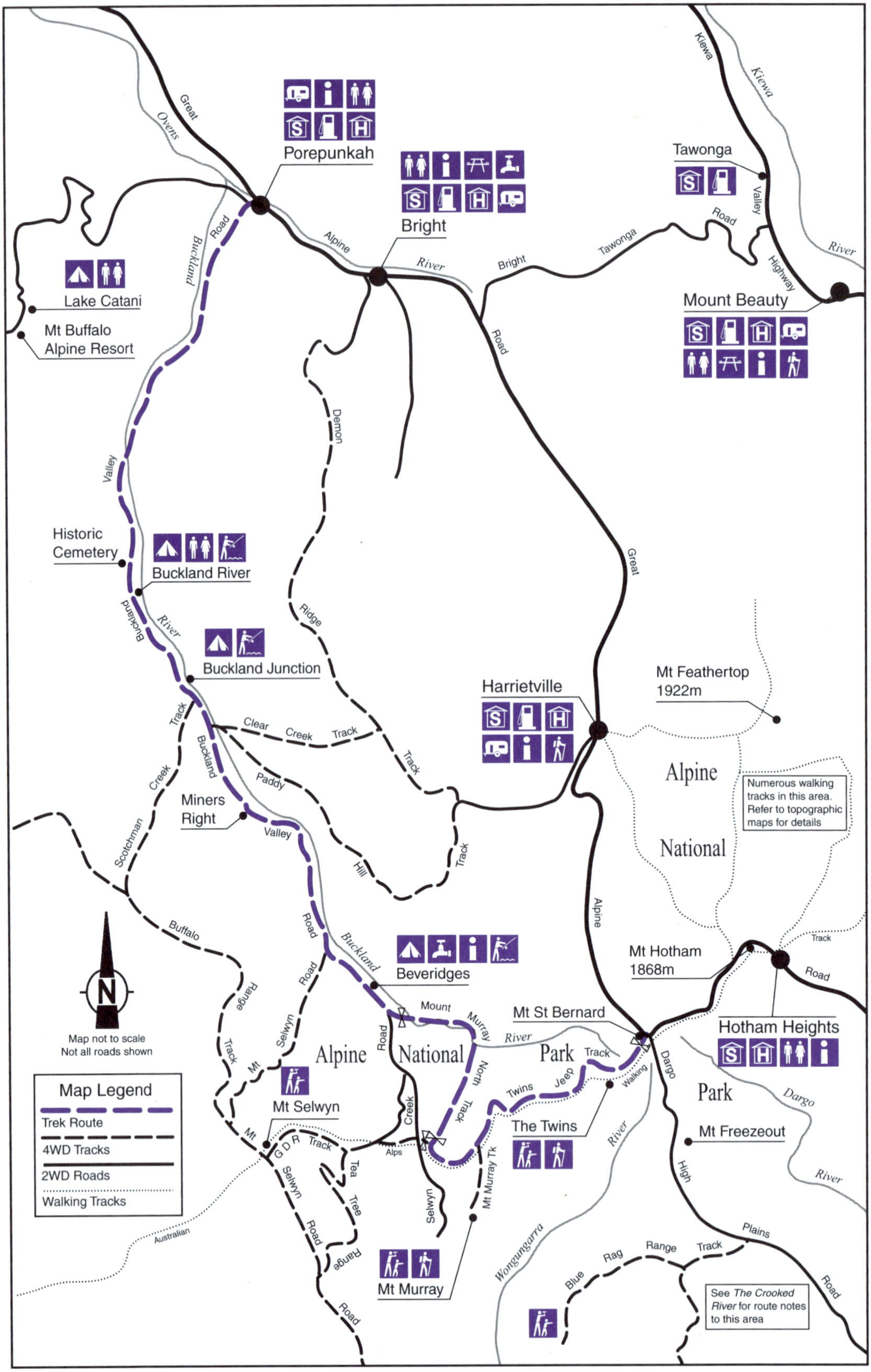
Porepunkah
Bright
Tawonga
Mount Beauty
Lake Catani
Mt Buffalo
Alpine Resort
Historic
Cemetery
Buckland River
Buckland Junction
Miners
Right
Harrietville
Mt Feathertop
1922m
Alpine
National
Park
Numerous walking tracks in this area. Refer to topographic maps for details
Beveridges
Mt Hotham
1868m
Mt St Bernard
Hotham Heights
The Twins
Mt Freezeout
Mt Selwyn
Mt Murray
See The Crooked River for route notes to this area
Map not to scale
Not all roads shown
Map Legend
Trek Route
4WD Tracks
2WD Roads
Walking Tracks
Great Alpine Road
Ovens River
Kiewa Valley Highway
Kiewa River
Tawonga Road
Buckland Valley Road
Buckland River
Demon Ridge Track
Clear Creek Track
Paddy Hill Track
Scotchman Creek Track
Buffalo Range Track
Mt Selwyn Road
Mt Selwyn Road
Mount Murray Track
North Jeep Track
Twins Jeep Track
Walking
Mt Murray Tk
Creek Road
Selwyn Creek
Alps
Mt G D R Track
Tea Tree Range Road
Australian
Wongungarra
Dargo High Plains Road
Dargo River
Blue Rag Range Track
Track
Bright
Road
River

TREK NINE

THE BUCKLAND VALLEY

ALTHOUGH TODAY'S Buckland Valley is a picture of serenity, this has not always been the case. Back in the gold rush years of the 1850s it went by the dubious name of 'The valley of the shadow of death' due to the large number of deaths that occurred in the valley between late 1853 and early 1854 when colonial fever swept through the area.

The valley was also the scene of the infamous Buckland Riot that occurred in 1853 between European and Chinese miners when racial discrimination raised its ugly head. With many Chinese miners arriving on the fields at this time, their mining successes and strange cultural practices (by western European standards of the time) were not appreciated, understood or tolerated by the European settlers, the scene was set for one of our country's first race riots (see *The Buckland Riot* history box on page 103 for details).

Things to Do and See

Visit the historic Buckland Valley Cemetery with its memorial to all those who died and were buried along the valley prior to the cemetery being built in 1863.

Try your luck panning for some 'undiscovered' gold that has been left behind in the Buckland River. If you have no luck with the gold prospecting you could throw in a line or enjoy a dip in the river.

You can set-up camp at one of the many secluded sites beside the Buckland River or at Beveridges Station, once a part of the Beveridge brothers extensive high country grazing runs. The cleared freehold land beside the camping area was once an outstation.

Walk to the summits of either Mt Murray or The Twins to take in the panoramic views.

fast facts

Porepunkah to Mt St Bernard via the Buckland Valley and The Twins

Trek distance: 68km

Standard: Easy (Dry weather only)

Fuel and supplies: Porepunkah and Bright. Limited supplies at Hotham Heights

Trek highlights: Buckland Cemetery, Beveridges Station camping area, Mt Murray and The Twins

Track conditions:
Parks Vic Bright
Ph 03/5755 1577

DNRE Ovens
03/5731 1222

Need help?: RACV Bright
Ph 0500 550 230

Access

The start point for this trek is along the Great Alpine Road at the large roundabout on the Bright side of the village of Porepunkah.

The Trek

Commencing from the Great Alpine Road the trek runs along the east bank of the Buckland River on a well maintained gravel road before crossing to the west side via a small one lane bridge.

Once on the west bank of the river you will note numerous tracks running down to the water's edge, these lead to bush camp sites beside the river. The historic Buckland Valley Cemetery is just 4km after the bridge on the right-hand side and is worth stopping to have a look and reflect on the lives and times of the settlers back in the 1800s.

Leaving the cemetery you will pass the entrance to the Buckland Valley State Forest and large camping area beside the river. Continuing on, the road passes through Buckland Junction, the meeting point of the east and west branches of the Buckland River, before reaching the signposted Miner's Right where a community of about 16 families settled around 1874.

At the large signposted junction the route heads along the East Branch of the Buckland River and enters the Alpine National Park where you arrive shortly afterwards at Beveridges Station. This area offers excellent camping beside the river.

Continuing on from Beveridges Camping Area along Selwyn Creek Road the trek turns into Mt Murray North Track, which after crossing the river a number of times makes its way to the Twins Jeep Track. Follow this track to the next junction where a track leads to a carpark near the summit of Mt Murray. A 2.3km walking track leads from the parking area to the summit. Along The Twins Jeep Track you will notice distinct changes in vegetation from a dry open forest to dense, wet forest as the trek climbs the south side of the mountain.

From The Twins Jeep Track - Mt Murray Track junction our route follows an easterly direction as we make our way to Mt St Bernard. Parts of this track are narrow with steep drops to the side, however it is a beautiful drive through subalpine vegetation. A small cleared area marks the walk to The Twins peak before we emerge out on the Great Alpine Road at Mt St Bernard 10km west of Mt Hotham resort.

Standard

This trek is rated as easy and is suitable for novice four-wheel drivers. Most of the roads and tracks are well maintained and in reasonable condition. Vegetation on some sections of The Twins Jeep Track may encroach over the road and this could cause some minor scratches to your vehicles paintwork.

There are a number of river crossings along Mt Murray Track and under normal conditions should not present any problems.

This is definitely a dry weather only trek. Sections of Mt Murray North Track could be slippery in the wet and travelling this route during wet conditions is not advisable.

Camping

There are a number of tracks along the Buckland Valley Road that lead to bush camp sites beside the river. These are not signposted and have no facilities.

Buckland Valley State Forest camping area is large, grassed and well shaded. Here you will find pit toilets and fireplaces.

Excellent camping is available at Beveridges Station. The sites here are well shaded and have large fire pits. The river runs beside the camping area and you will find a few spots that are a bit deeper to have a splash around in, although the water here can still be chilly over the summer months.

Permits/Restrictions

There are no restrictions on the Buckland Valley Road. Seasonal road closures do apply to Mt Murray North Track and the Twins Jeep Track.

Recommended Maps/Guides

The Hema Maps *High Country - Victoria* map shows the route and is adequate for this trek. Also, the CFA *North East Rural Directory - Regions 23 and 24* (maps 334, 333, 371) cover this route.

Topographic maps in the 1:50 000 series are the *Dargo Plains - Cobungra* and *Howitt - Selwyn* which show greater detail.

Further Information

Parks Victoria
46 Bakers Gully Road, Bright VIC 3741 Ph 03/5755 1577 Fax 03/5755 1176

Dept of Natural Resources and Environment
Great Alpine Road, Ovens VIC 3738 Ph 03/5731 1222 Fax 03/5731 1223

Bright Visitor Centre
119 Gavan Street, Bright Ph 03/5755 2275

Brochures - Parks Victoria: *Alpine National Park – the high country – Feathertop – Hotham Walks*

HISTORY

The Buckland Riot

During the early 1850s gold fever had found its way to the town of Beechworth and from here gold seekers spread out to the Ovens and Buckland Valleys in search of productive mining areas.

By this time there was a growing hostility towards the Chinese miners who had arrived to prospect in the region. However, not all Europeans were anti-Chinese. On the fields there were a number of mixed race marriages and some intermixing between European and Chinese diggers. The 'Celestials', as they were known, were out numbering the Europeans five to one. The Chinese often set up camp at old diggings that the Europeans had left and their hard work was resented as it often resulted in good finds from these abandoned diggings. It was the culmination of their hard work and strange practices (to Europeans) that was the catalyst to the Buckland Riot.

On July 4, 1857 a group of about 50 European miners gathered with intentions to rid the Chinese from the goldfields. Armed with clubs, sticks and some rifles they moved in on the Chinese camp at Lauder's Flat, forcing the Celestials to retreat downriver to other Chinese camps. The rioters looted the camp and set fire to their tents and buildings. What could not be burned was thrown in the river. Not entirely happy with this they then followed the retreating Chinese further downriver to Stoney Point and attacked each camp they came across.

The riot continued downriver to the main camp at Lower Flat where around 200 Chinese miners were camped. Some of the Chinese resisted and were brutally bashed while most fled as fast as they could, some jumping down mine holes to hide. Those slower to escape were also beaten and robbed.

When the retreating Chinese miners reached the only ford across the Buckland River (which was crossed by a large fallen tree), they were helped by a group of diggers who stood in between the Chinese and the rioters. Some Chinese miners returned rifle fire at the ensuing mob, wounding three of the attackers. The total number of casualties was not known but was described as moderate.

Two days later police arrived from Beechworth, led by Inspector Robert O'Hara Burke (of Burke & Wills fame) and tried to enforce some peace. Order was finally restored after reinforcements arrived three weeks later.

Some of the rioters were arrested, charged and gaoled, however most of those involved were not convicted as witnesses, especially the Chinese, were reluctant to give evidence in fear of reprisals. Following the Buckland Riot laws were changed to protect the Chinese from any further instances of discrimination and brutality.

ROUTE NOTES

Trek commences at the roundabout on the Bright side of Porepunkah on the Great Alpine Road.

▼ 0.0 (0.0)
Zero trip meter at roundabout on Great Alpine Road at Porepunkah. Turn into road SP Buckland Valley. This is Buckland Valley Road.
▲ *67.4 (12.4)*
Roundabout on Great Alpine Road. CSA for Myrtleford/Wangaratta. TR for Bright.
GPS S:36 42.033 E:146 54.502
UTM Zone 55 0491813E 5938343N

▼ 12.4 (12.4)
Bridge over Buckland River. CSA.
▲ *55.0 (2.1)*
Bridge.

▼ 14.5 (2.1)
From this point numerous tracks lead off on the left to the river and possible bush camp sites – no facilities.
▲ *52.9 (1.7)*
No camping past this point.

▼ 16.2 (1.7)
Buckland Cemetery on right. CSA.
▲ *51.2 (2.0)*
Buckland Cemetery on left. CSA.
GPS S:36 49.511 E:146 51.140
UTM Zone 55 0486831E 5924509N

▼ 18.2 (2.0)
SP Buckland Valley State Forest on left. Track leads short distance to camp sites. Notes CSA.
▲ *49.2 (1.5)*
Track on right to Buckland Valley State Forest camping area. Notes CSA.

▼ 19.7 (1.5)
Road junction. KR. SP Buckland Valley Rd. Tracks on left to camp sites by river. This area is known as 12 Mile.
▲ *47.7 (3.1)*
CSA. Tracks on right to camp sites by river.

▼ 22.8 (3.1)
SP Buckland Junction. CSA over bridge.
▲ *44.6 (0.2)*
Buckland Junction. CSA over bridge.
GPS S:36 52.478 E:146 52.306
UTM Zone 55 0488566E 5919027N

▼ 23.0 (0.2)
Grid. Track junction over grid. CSA. SP Buckland Rd. Track on right SP Scotchman Ck Tk.
▲ *44.4 (2.0)*
Track junction. CSA over grid. SP Buckland Rd. Track on left SP Scotchman Ck Tk.

▼ 25.0 (2.0)
Track junction. CSA. Track on left SP Clear Ck Tk.
▲ *42.4 (1.5)*
Track on right SP Clear Ck Tk. CSA.

▼ 26.5 (1.5)
KL on main track.
▲ *40.9 (1.0)*
Track on left. CSA.

▼ 27.5 (1.0)
Track on right. CSA.
▲ *39.9 (4.0)*
KR on main track.

▼ 31.5 (4.0)
SP Camping Area on left. CSA.
▲ *35.9 (2.0)*
SP Camping Area on right. CSA.

▼ 33.5 (2.0)
SP Camping Area on left. CSA.
▲ *33.9 (2.9)*
SP Camping Area on right. CSA.

▼ 36.4 (2.9)
Y junction. KL and cross bridge entering Alpine National Park. SP Mt Murray – The Twins via Selwyn Creek Track. SP Beveridges Station. Track on right SP Mount Selwyn via Mount Selwyn Road.
▲ *31.0 (2.7)*
Track junction. CSA. Track on left SP Mount Selwyn via Mount Selwyn Road.
GPS S:36 58.223 E:146 56.098
UTM Zone 55 0494211E 5908411N

TREK 9

▼ 39.1 (2.7)
Track on left SP Beveridges Station. Excellent camping area. Notes CSA.

▲ *28.3 (1.2)*
Track on right SP Beveridges Station. Notes CSA.

▼ 40.3 (1.2)
Track junction. TL. SP Mt Murray North Track.

▲ *27.1 (0.1)*
T junction. TR. This is Selwyn Creek Road.
GPS S:36 59.701 E:146 57.806
UTM Zone 55 0496738E 5905699N

▼ 40.4 (0.1)
Creek crossing. CSA through seasonal closure gate.

▲ *27.0 (1.7)*
Seasonal closure gate. CSA over creek.

▼ 42.1 (1.7)
Cross Buckland River.

▲ *25.3 (0.8)*
Cross Buckland River.

▼ 42.9 (0.8)
Creek crossing.

▲ *24.5 (0.2)*
Creek crossing.

▼ 43.1 (0.2)
Y junction. KL.

▲ *24.3 (1.3)*
Track on left. CSA.

▼ 44.4 (1.3)
Creek crossing.

▲ *23.0 (5.7)*
Creek crossing.

▼ 50.1 (5.7)
Seasonal closure gate.

▲ *17.3 (0.5)*
Seasonal closure gate.

▼ 50.6 (0.5)
Track junction. TL. SP Mt Murray.

▲ *16.8 (1.0)*
Track junction. TR. SP Mt Murray North Tk.
GPS S:37 02.726 E:146 58.653
UTM Zone 55 0498013E 5900085N

▼ 51.6 (1.0)
Seasonal closure gate.

▲ *15.8 (1.4)*
Seasonal closure gate.

ABOVE: *Twins Jeep Track near Mt St Bernard.*

▼ 53.0 (1.4)
T junction. TL. SP Mt St Bernard 14km. Track on right SP Mt Murray car park 2.3km. Mt Murray 2.6km.

▲ *14.4 (10.0)*
Track junction. TR. SP Buckland Valley. SP Porepunkah 53km. Track SO SP Mt Murray 2.6km.
GPS S:37 02.881 E:146 59.666
UTM Zone 55 0499513E 5899803N

▼ 63.0 (10.0)
Walking track to The Twins on right. CSA.

▲ *4.4 (3.1)*
Walking track to The Twins on left. CSA.

▼ 66.1 (3.1)
Seasonal closure gate.

▲ *1.3 (1.3)*
Seasonal closure gate.

▼ 67.4 (1.3)
Road junction with Great Alpine Road at Mt St Bernard. TL for SP 45 Bright. CSA for SP Mt Hotham 10. TR for SP 62 Dargo.

▲ *0.0 (0.0)*
Zero trip meter at Mt St Bernard at junction of Great Alpine Road and Dargo High Plains Road. Turn into track SP Porepunkah 67km. SP Mt Murray 17km. This is Twins Jeep Track.
GPS S:37 00.555 E:147 04.826
UTM Zone 55 0507158E 5904100N

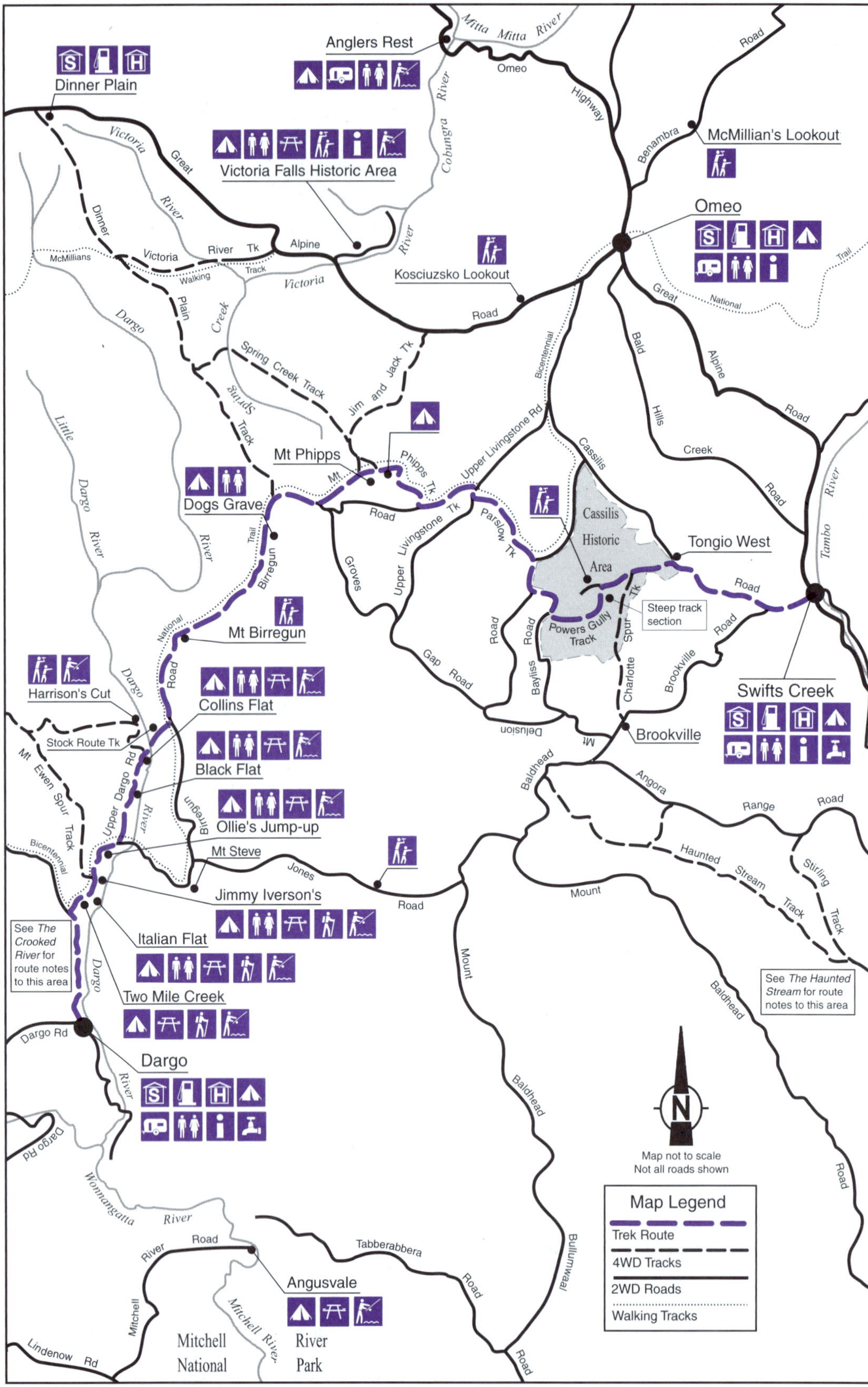
Anglers Rest
Dinner Plain
Mitta Mitta River
Omeo
Omeo Highway
Benambra Road
McMillian's Lookout
Victoria Falls Historic Area
Cobungra River
Victoria Great River
Great Alpine Road
Dinner Plain Track
McMillians Walking Track
Victoria River Tk
Victoria River
Kosciuzsko Lookout
Omeo
Great National Trail
Dargo River
Creek
Spring Creek Track
Spring Track
Jim and Jack Tk
Bald Hills Creek Road
Alpine Road
Bicentennial
Upper Livingstone Rd
Cassilis
Mt Phipps
Mt Phipps Tk
Dogs Grave
Little Dargo River
Dargo River
Birregun Trail
Road
Groves
Upper Livingstone Tk
Parslow Tk
Cassilis Historic Area
Tongio West
Road
Tambo River
Swifts Creek
Steep track section
Powers Gully Track
Spur Tk
Mt Birregun
National
Road
Gap Road
Road
Road
Bayliss
Charlotte
Brookville Road
Harrison's Cut
Dargo
Collins Flat
Black Flat
Ollie's Jump-up
Delusion
Mt
Brookville
Stock Route Tk
Mt Ewen Spur Track
Upper Dargo Rd
River
Birregun
Baldhead
Angora Range Road
Bicentennial
Mt Steve
Jones Road
Haunted Stream Track
Stirling Track
Jimmy Iverson's
Mount
Italian Flat
See The Crooked River for route notes to this area
Mount
See The Haunted Stream for route notes to this area
Baldhead
Dargo
Two Mile Creek
Dargo Rd
Dargo
River
Baldhead
N
Map not to scale
Not all roads shown
Dargo Rd
Road
Wonnangatta River
Road
River
Tabberabbera
Road
Bullumwaal
Map Legend
Trek Route
4WD Tracks
2WD Roads
Walking Tracks
Angusvale
Mitchell
Mitchell River
Mitchell National
River Park
Lindenow Rd
Road

TREK 10

TREK TEN

SWIFTS CREEK TO DARGO

THIS JAUNT ACROSS the Birregun Range from Swifts Creek to Dargo takes in some of the area's best natural features as well as a number of places of historic interest such as Cassilis Historic Area, The Dog's Grave and Harrison's Cut.

Things to Do and See

The Cassilis Historic Area and its rich iron red coloured tailings heap at Powers Gully is visited on this trek. The challenging Powers Gully Track is also traversed and the journey to Mt Phipps makes its way through a forest of gnarled snow gum woodland.

A stopover at the Dog's Grave provides an insight to the special friendships that develop between stockmen and their working dogs.

Down on the Dargo River there are many delightful camping areas and a short side trip to Harrison's Cut—a channel cut through a horseshoe bend on the Dargo River back in the area's gold mining days.

Access

Swifts Creek is the start point of this trek and is situated on the all weather bitumen Great Alpine Road 25km south east of Omeo and 95km north of Bairnsdale.

The Trek

Take the Cassilis Road out of Swifts Creek to Tongio West then turn into Charlotte Spur Track. If you wish to detour around the steep Powers Gully Track continue along Cassilis Road to Mt Delusion Road then to Parslow Track.

Charlotte Spur Track runs through Cassilis Historic Area, the site of a number of large gold mining operations during the early 1900s, and passes the tailings dump of the Cassilis Company's ore crushing plant which is passed in Powers Gully.

Directly after passing the tailings dump turn into the steep Powers Gully Track which climbs for about 600m before levelling out on the ridgeline. Continue on Powers Gully Track, passing Bayliss Spur Track before joining with Mt Delusion Road.

Once on Mt Delusion Road it's only a short distance to Parslow Track which is followed down to the Livingstone River. Follow the river downstream on Upper Livingstone Road for 200m where the trek turns into Birregun Road and then onto Mt Phipps Track for the run up to Mt Phipps through delightful snow gum woodland.

From Mt Phipps stay on Mt Phipps Track, passing Jim and Jack Track (named after the founders of nearby Cobungra Station - the largest cattle station in Victoria) and Spring

fast facts

Swifts Creek to Dargo via Cassilis Historic Area, Dog's Grave and Upper Dargo.

Trek distance: 90km

Standard: Medium/Hard (Dry weather only)

Fuel and supplies: Swifts Creek and Dargo

Trek highlights: Cassilis Historic Area, Dog's Grave, Harrison's Cut, Dargo River

Track conditions:
DNRE Swifts Creek
Ph 03/5159 5100

Need help?: D. Guy Autos, Waterford (4WD Recovery) Ph 03/5140 1265

Creek Track before joining again with Birregun Road. Follow Birregun Road, passing Dinner Plain Track to the Dog's Grave (see *The Dog's Grave* fact box on page 109 for details).

After leaving Dog's Grave continue on Birregun Road, passing over the summit of Mt Birregun before turning down Stock Route Spur Track, a steep 3½km descent to the Dargo River. Once across the river (best to check the crossing on foot before fording) you pick up Upper Dargo Road. An interesting side trip from this point, known as Collins Flat, is to take Matherson Spur Track to Harrison's Cut, a water diversion channel on the Dargo River (see *Harrison's Cut Route Notes* on page 113 for details).

The trek now follows the Dargo River, passing some excellent camp sites before meeting with Dargo High Plains Road at Farm Junction then onto Dargo.

Standard

This trek is rated medium/hard. Powers Gully Track in Cassilis Historic Area is steep and has a loose gravel surface. However, this section can easily be detoured if required by taking the Cassilis Road then the Mt Delusion Road to meet with Parslow Track. The remainder of the trek is of a medium standard.

There is a crossing of the Dargo River at the bottom of Stock Route Spur Track that may be impassable after heavy rain or during the spring snow melt.

Camping

You can camp at the small camping area with facilities near the Dog's Grave on the Birregun Road.

Stretched out along the Upper Dargo Road beside the Dargo River is Collins Flat, Black Flat, Ollie's Jump Up, Jimmy Iverson's, Italian Flat and Two Mile Creek. All of these sites have facilities which include pit toilets.

Permits/Restrictions

This trek is restricted by seasonal road closures which are usually in force from after the Queen's Birthday Long Weekend to just after the Melbourne Cup in November.

Recommended Maps/Guides

The Brookes Bush Maps, Victoria *Omeo and District* map details the route from Swifts Creek to Mt Phipps and the *Crooked River - Dargo Area* map shows the Mt Birregun to Dargo section of the trek. The central section not covered by these two maps is detailed on the *Dargo Plains - Cobungra* 1:50 000 topographic map. The Hema Maps *High Country - Victoria* map shows this route.

Topographic maps for this trek are the *Brookville - Ensay*, *Omeo - Bindi*, *Dargo Plains - Cobungra* and the *Crooked River - Steve* 1:50 000 series.

Further Information

Dept of Natural Resources and Environment
McMillan Ave, Swifts Creek VIC 3896 Ph 03/5159 5100 Fax 03/5159 5111

Parks Victoria and Dept of Natural Resources and Environment
Lind Ave, Dargo VIC 3862 Ph 03/5140 1243 Fax 03/5140 1216

Dargo General Store
16A Lind Ave, Dargo Ph 03/5140 1219

Further Reading - *The Dog's Grave - An Account of Droving Days in Early Gippsland* by Flora John

The Dog's Grave

Throughout time the relationship between man and dog has been strong. Dogs were depended on by early settlers to help catch meat such as kangaroo, farmers to assist with managing cattle and sheep, and drovers to work the end or wings of large mobs of cattle or horses whilst being moved. A drover's dog was reliable and faithful and could work out of sight and hearing distance of its master. The old saying "a man's dog is a man's living" still holds true today.

In the early 1970s while travelling to Omeo to try his luck at some gold prospecting, John Giannarelli was told the story of the Dog's Grave by Jack Treasure, as he knew it. On hearing the story John felt a monument to memorialise the early pioneers and their dogs should be erected. As his father was a monumental mason, when he returned home he commissioned a block of granite to be shaped and engraved. Set into the granite piece are two engravings by a Yugoslavian artist depicting a kelpie dog and a lonely bushman boiling his billy.

The stone monument was unveiled on May 30, 1975 and stands in a small clearing a short distance from Birregun Road.

ABOVE: *Monument at the Dog's Grave*

There are two stories as to the origin of the Dog's Grave. One story is that Peter Meehan, at the time employed by the Gray family who owned a portion of Cobungra Station during the 1860s is the person talked about in this tale. Peter, who only travelled with his horse 'Skinny' and his dog 'Boney' was employed to mind the Gray's cattle on the Wentworth River side of their run.

The story has it that Peter was camped one night at a hut in the bush. In the morning he found Boney dead at the door after eating a poisoned bait. Peter buried his dog not far from the hut and since then the site has been known as the Dog's Grave.

The other story, which has been passed on through generations of the Cobungra story tellers, tells that the dog's name was 'Angus' and was a stumpy tailed Smithfield, not a kelpie. The dog was owned by Johnny Crisp who kept a hotel in Omeo. At the time Johnny was mustering with the Cobungra station men, Peter Meehan, Neddy Gray, Ned Gunn, Tom Worcester and Jack Tolland. Angus died after picking up a bait that had been carried by a dingo. Johnny buried his dog and layered stones over the plot and built a fence out of bush timber. He is said to have written the following verse on a piece of bark:

Once he came across the plain
Wild cattle to surprise
Now he's slain
By strychnine laid
And never more to rise.

No matter which story you suscribe to, the Dog's Grave monument is a lasting tribute to drovers and their dogs and testiment to the area's early pioneers.

ROUTE NOTES

Trek commences in Swifts Creek outside the Albion Hotel.

▼ 0.0 (0.0)
Zero trip meter in Swifts Creek. Albion Hotel on left. PSA across the Great Alpine Road in a south-west direction towards SP Cassilis 13.
▲ *89.4 (2.4)*
Swifts Creek. Junction with Great Alpine Road. Albion Hotel and Oblesik SO.
GPS S:37 15.795 E:147 43.294
UTM Zone 55 0563983E 5875673N

▼ 2.4 (2.4)
Y junction. VR. SP 11 Cassilis. Road on left SP 12 Brookville.
▲ *87.0 (4.3)*
Road junction. VL. SP Swifts Creek 2. Road on right SP 12 Brookville.

▼ 6.7 (4.3)
Road on left SP Rileys Creek Rd. CSA over bridge.
▲ *82.7 (3.2)*
Bridge. CSA over bridge past SP Rileys Creek Rd on right.

▼ 9.9 (3.2)
Track junction. TL. SP Charlotte Spur Tk.
▲ *79.5 (0.3)*
Road junction with bitumen. TR.
GPS S:37 14.755 E:147 37.905
UTM Zone 55 0556027E 5877653N

▼ 10.2 (0.3)
Enter SP Cassilis Historic Area.
▲ *79.2 (0.1)*
Leave SP Cassilis Historic Area.

▼ 10.3 (0.1)
Track on left. CSA.
▲ *79.1 (1.3)*
Track on right. CSA.

▼ 11.6 (1.3)
Track junction. CSA across creek. Track on left SP Charlotte Spur Tk.
▲ *77.8 (0.5)*
Cross creek. At junction over creek CSA. Track on right SP Charlotte Spur Tk.

▼ 12.1 (0.5)
Mine ruins and tailings on right. This is the old Cassilis Mine. CSA.
▲ *77.3 (0.6)*
Mine ruins and tailings on left. CSA.

▼ 12.7 (0.6)
Track junction. TL. SP Powers Gully Tk. *NB:* Track climbs steeply for 600m.
▲ *76.7 (0.6)*
Track junction. TR.

▲ *76.1 (0.4)*
Track drops steeply to next reading.

▼ 13.7 (1.0)
Pass through fence line.
▲ *75.7 (5.2)*
Pass through fence line.

▼ 18.9 (5.2)
Track junction. CSA. SP Powers Gully Tk. Track on left SP Bayliss Spur Road.
▲ *70.5 (2.0)*
Track junction. CSA. SP Powers Gully Tk. Track on right SP Bayliss Spur Road.
GPS S:37 16.068 E:147 33.408
UTM Zone 55 0549377E 5875278N

▼ 20.9 (2.0)
T junction. TR. SP Mt Delusion Road.
▲ *68.5 (2.7)*
Track junction. TL. SP Powers Gully Tk.
GPS S:37 15.702 E:147 32.417
UTM Zone 55 0547907E 5875969N

▼ 23.6 (2.7)
Track junction. TL. This is Parslow Track. This track is not signposted, however there is a Bicentennial Trail triangle marker on a tree a little way down the track.
▲ *65.8 (4.0)*
Track junction. TR. This is Mt Delusion Road.
GPS S:37 14.518 E:147 32.391
UTM Zone 55 0547876E 5878166N

▼ 27.6 (4.0)
Gate in electric dog proof fence. Please shut gate. Once through gate CSA.

OPPOSITE: *Camping at Italian Flat.*

TREK 10

▲ *61.8 (1.6)*
Gate in electric dog proof fence. Please shut gate.

▼ 29.2 (1.6)
T junction. This is Upper Livingstone Road. TR through gate. LAF.
▲ *60.2 (0.2)*
Gate. LAF. Once through gate TL. SP Parslow Tk.
GPS S:37 12.727 E:147 30.565
UTM Zone 55 0545197E 5881466N

▼ 29.4 (0.2)
Gate. LAF. Once through gate TL over bridge. SP Birregun Road.
▲ *60.0 (0.6)*
Bridge. Over bridge junction with Upper Livingstone Road. TR through gate. LAF.

▼ 30.0 (0.6)
Gate. LAF.
▲ *59.4 (0.9)*
Gate. LAF.

▼ 30.9 (0.9)
Gate in electric dog proof fence. Please shut.
▲ *58.5 (2.4)*
Gate in electric dog proof fence. Please shut.

▼ 33.3 (2.4)
Y junction. KR on higher road. SP Zig Zag Tk. Road to left SP Birregun Road.
▲ *56.1 (0.8)*
Track on right. CSA. This is SP Birregun Road.
GPS S:37 13.216 E:147 28.580
UTM Zone 55 0542259E 5880587N

▼ 34.1 (0.8)
Gate. LAF.
▲ *55.3 (2.9)*
Gate. LAF.

▼ 37.0 (2.9)
Track junction near dam. KR.
▲ *52.4 (2.1)*
Track junction near dam. CSA.

▼ 39.1 (2.1)
Track on left leads to possible bush camp site. CSA.
▲ *50.3 (0.4)*
Track on right leads to possible bush camp site. CSA.

▼ 39.5 (0.4)
Track junction. TL. SP Mt Phipps Tk.
▲ *49.9 (1.2)*
TR. SP Zig Zag Tk.

▼ 40.7 (1.2)
Track junction. TL. SP Mt Phipps Tk. Track on right SP Jim & Jack Tk.
▲ *48.7 (0.7)*
TR. Track SO SP Jim & Jack Tk.
GPS S:37 12.143 E:147 26.544
UTM Zone 55 0539259E 5882583N

▼ 41.4 (0.7)
Mt Phipps stone cairn. CSA.
▲ *48.0 (0.1)*
Mt Phipps. CSA.
GPS S:37 12.346 E:147 26.166
UTM Zone 55 0538699E 5882228N

▼ 41.5 (0.1)
Y junction. VL.
▲ *47.9 (2.5)*
Track on left. CSA.

▼ 44.0 (2.5)
T junction. TR. This is Birregun Road.
▲ *45.4 (2.7)*
TL. SP Mt Phipps Tk.
GPS S:37 13.096 E:147 24.924
UTM Zone 55 0536851E 5880827N

▼ 46.7 (2.7)
Track junction. CSA. Track on left SP Carneek Tk.
▲ *42.7 (0.4)*
CSA. Track on right SP Carneek Tk.

▼ 47.1 (0.4)
Track junction. CSA. Track on right SP Dinner Plain Tk.
▲ *42.3 (2.7)*
CSA. SP Birregun Road. Track on left SP Dinner Plain Tk.

▼ 49.8 (2.7)
Track junction. Track on left SP Dogs Grave leads 500m to camping area. Notes CSA.
▲ *39.6 (0.4)*
CSA. SP Dogs Grave on right.

Dogs Grave
GPS S:37 14.024 E:147 22.866
UTM Zone 55 0533806E 5879132N

▼ 50.2 (0.4)
SP Dogs Grave on left. CSA.

▲ *39.2 (2.6)*
Track junction. Track on right SP Dogs Grave leads 500m to camping area. Notes CSA.

▼ 52.8 (2.6)
Track junction. CSA. Track on left is Messmate Spur Track.
▲ *36.6 (3.5)*
CSA. Track on right is Messmate Spur Track.

▼ 56.3 (3.5)
Track junction. CSA. Track on left SP Dane Tk.
▲ *33.1 (2.1)*
CSA. Track on right SP Dane Tk.

▼ 58.4 (2.1)
Mt Birregun.
▲ *31.0 (0.4)*
Mt Birregun.

▼ 58.8 (0.4)
Track junction. CSA. Track on right SP Mt Birregun Spur Tk.
▲ *30.6 (5.6)*
CSA. Track on left SP Mt Birregun Spur Tk.

▼ 64.4 (5.6)
Track junction. TR. SP Stock Route Spur Tk. Track drops steeply for 3.4km to Dargo River.
▲ *25.0 (2.1)*
Track junction. TL. This is Birregun Road.
GPS S:37 19.354 E:147 18.775
UTM Zone 55 0527727E 5869311N

▼ 66.5 (2.1)
Y junction. KL. SP Stock Route S P. Track on right leads to private property.
▲ *22.9 (1.3)*
Track junction. PSA uphill. Track on left to private property.

▼ 67.8 (1.3)
Cross Dargo River. Over river camping in vicinity. Notes CSA on main track past track on right.
▲ *21.6 (0.2)*
Cross Dargo River. Track climbs steeply for 3.4km.
GPS S:37 20.291 E:147 17.969
UTM Zone 55 0526520E 5867591N

▼ 68.0 (0.2)
Track junction. CSA to SP Dargo. SP Collins Flat Camping Area on left. Road to right SP Matherson S.P.
▲ *21.4 (0.3)*
Track junction. KR following river. SP Stock Route Spur. SP Collins Flat Camping Area on right.
GPS S:37 20.360 E:147 17.828
UTM Zone 55 0526318E 5867442N

Harrison's Cut Side Trip

▼ 68.0 TR at junction. SP Matherson S.P.

▲ *21.4 CSA at junction. SP Matherson S.P.*

▼ (0.5) Y junction. KL. SP Matherson S.P. SP Harrisons.

▼ (1.7) Track on right. CSA.

▼ (0.6) Track junction. CSA. SP Harrisons Cut. Track on left SP Matherson Tk.

▼ (0.1) Small parking area. Harrison's Cut opposite.
GPS S:37 19.537 E:147 17.808
UTM Zone 55 0526295E 5868968N

Harrison's Cut on the Dargo River

▼ 68.3 (0.3)
Gate. LAF.
▲ *21.1 (1.8)*
Gate. LAF.

▼ 70.1 (1.8)
Minor tracks on left. CSA on main track.
▲ *19.3 (2.7)*
Tracks on right. CSA on main track.

▼ 72.8 (2.7)
Black Flat Camping Area on left. Notes CSA.
▲ *16.6 (2.0)*
Black Flat Camping Area on right. CSA.

▼ 74.8 (2.0)
Track junction. CSA. Track on right SP Farm Tk.
▲ *14.6 (0.8)*
CSA. Track on left SP Farm Tk.

▼ 75.6 (0.8)
Gate. LAF.
▲ *13.8 (0.1)*
Gate. LAF.

▼ 75.7 (0.1)
Track junction. CSA heading uphill. This is Upper Dargo Road. Track on left SP Swifts Creek/Omeo.
▲ *13.7 (1.2)*
Y junction. KL. SP Upper Dargo.
GPS S:37 22.872 E:147 17.191
UTM Zone 55 0525366E 5862796N

▼ 76.9 (1.2)
Ollie's Jump Up Camping Area on left. CSA.
▲ *12.5 (2.6)*
Camping area on right. CSA.
GPS S:37 23.145 E:147 16.627
UTM Zone 55 0524534E 5862295N

▼ 79.5 (2.6)
Jimmy Iverson's Camping Area on left. SP Mt Ewen Tk on right. Notes CSA.
▲ *9.9 (1.3)*
Camping area on right. SP Mt Ewen Tk on left. Notes CSA.
GPS S:37 23.893 E:147 16.297
UTM Zone 55 0524039E 5860909N

▼ 80.8 (1.3)
Italian Flat Camping Area on left. CSA.
▲ *8.6 (0.9)*
Camping area on right. CSA.
GPS S:37 24.563 E:147 15.912
UTM Zone 55 0523465E 5859684N

▼ 81.7 (0.9)
Two Mile Creek Camping Area on right. CSA on main road.
▲ *7.7 (2.0)*
Camping area on left. CSA over causeway.
GPS S:37 24.557 E:147 15.484
UTM Zone 55 0522828E 5859685N

▼ 83.7 (2.0)
Road junction with bitumen road. TL. This is Dargo High Plains Road.
▲ *5.7 (5.7)*
Road junction. TR. SP Upper Dargo Rd.
GPS S:37 25.347 E:147 15.249
UTM Zone 55 0522490E 5858240N

▼ 89.4 (5.7)
Dargo village. Hotel on left. General Store on right.
▲ *0.0 (0.0)*
Zero trip meter in Dargo village. Hotel on right. General Store on left. Head north along Dargo High Plains Road.
GPS S:37 27.705 E:147 15.067
UTM Zone 55 0522201E 5853864N

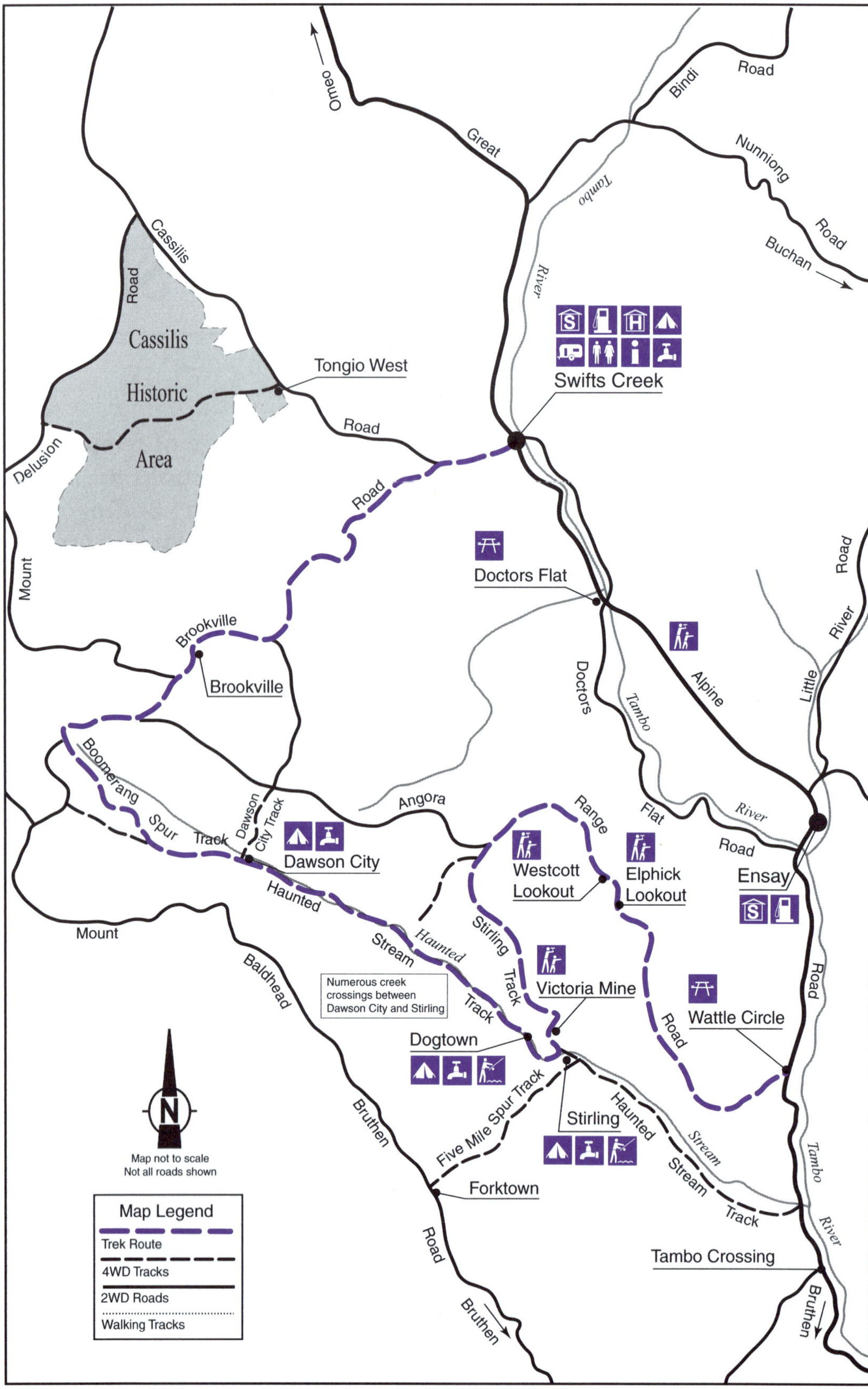
Omeo
Great
Bindi
Road
Nunniong
Road
Buchan
Tambo
River
Cassilis
Road
Cassilis
Historic
Area
Tongio West
Road
Delusion
Swifts Creek
Doctors Flat
Mount
Road
Brookville
Brookville
Doctors
Tambo
Alpine
Little
River
Road
Boomerang
Spur
Track
Dawson City Track
Dawson City
Angora
Range
Flat
River
Road
Ensay
Westcott
Lookout
Elphick
Lookout
Haunted
Stream
Haunted
Track
Stirling
Track
Victoria Mine
Road
Wattle Circle
Road
Mount
Baldhead
Numerous creek crossings between Dawson City and Stirling
Dogtown
Five Mile Spur Track
Stirling
Haunted
Stream
Stream
Track
Tambo
River
Bruthen
Forktown
Road
Bruthen
Tambo Crossing
Bruthen
N
Map not to scale
Not all roads shown
Map Legend
Trek Route
4WD Tracks
2WD Roads
Walking Tracks

TREK ELEVEN

THE HAUNTED STREAM

HAUNTED STREAM IS a major tributary of the Tambo River and like most of the rivers and streams in the Omeo - Swifts Creek area contained gold.

The first finds of alluvial gold were recorded in the late 1850s and from 1865 through to 1885 saw a fevered rush to the valley. It was during the latter part of this time that reef mining prospered.

By the mid 1930s most of the miners had moved on and this once bustling valley reverted to the delightful place it is today.

Things to Do and See

Discover the former gold mining areas along the Haunted Stream, including the sites of Dawson City and Dogtown—home to thousands of prospectors who worked this tributary of the Tambo River during the late 1850s. Observant travellers will notice the relics of mining equipment littered throughout the area.

Apart from the enjoyable four-wheel drive touring and gold mining heritage this area offers, there are a number of lookouts located along Angora Range Road which provide excellent views over the surrounding districts.

Access

This trek commences at Swifts Creek which is 25km south east of Omeo and 95km north of Bairnsdale via the bitumen Great Alpine Road.

The Trek

Commencing at Swifts Creek, take the Cassilis Road out of town where after a few kilometres our route turns into Brookville Road which is then followed to its junction with Mt Delusion Road. From this point the trek follows Dorothy Cutting Forest Drive, passing Angora Range Road before turning into Boomerang Spur Road.

fast facts

Swifts Creek to Wattle Circle via Dawson City and Dogtown

Trek distance: 86km

Standard: Medium (Dry weather only)

Fuel and supplies: Swifts Creek and Ensay

Trek highlights: Travelling Boomerang Spur Track, Haunted Stream, old mining relics, lookouts on Angora Range Road

Track conditions:
DNRE Swifts Creek
Ph 03/5159 5100

About 8km along Boomerang Spur Road becomes Boomerang Spur Track after passing through the seasonal closure gate. From the gate the track drops steeply to Haunted Stream at Dawson City—the site of a long abandoned mining village. Dawson City Track, which climbs out of the valley from Dawson City to Angora Range Road is an alternative route used to access this area.

From Dawson City the trek now follows Haunted Stream downriver, crossing and recrossing the stream around 45 times before arriving at the Haunted Stream Track - Stirling Track junction.

Turn into Stirling Track, where after a few hundred metres you pass the remains of the Victoria Mine before climbing out of the valley to meet with Angora Range Road. From here take the well maintained Angora Range Road, from which there are good views from a number of lookouts, out to the Great Alpine Road and the conclusion of the trek at Wattle Circle—a little to the north of Tambo Crossing.

Standard

We have rated this trek as medium under normal conditions, however wet weather will see the standard jump from medium to hard to downright impossible. Boomerang Spur Track is steep in sections with a soil base that would become very slippery in the wet.

Recent heavy rain can cause problems at the 40 or so crossings of the Haunted Stream. Generally most of these crossings are little more than knee deep but the areas steep catchment can bring a rise to the stream in a short period of time.

Stirling Track climbs steeply in places from Haunted Stream to Angora Range Road, however the challenging sections have been bypassed and should pose little concern to most drivers.

Camping

All the camp sites on this trek are bush camping areas and as such have no facilities, so you will need to be fully self-sufficient.

There are camping areas at the sites of the former mining villages of Dawson City, Dogtown and Stirling as well as a few possible bush camp sites scattered along the Haunted Stream Track, mostly near the stream crossings. All camp sites are detailed in the route notes.

Permits/Restrictions

Seasonal road closures apply to this trek and are usually in force from after the Queen's Birthday Long Weekend to just after the Melbourne Cup in November.

Recommended Maps/Guides

The Hema Maps *High Country - Victoria* map shows the route described in this trek.

Topographic map covering this trek is the *Brookville - Ensay* 1:50 000 series.

Further Information

Dept of Natural Resources and Environment
McMillan Ave, Swifts Creek VIC 3896 Ph 03/5159 5100 Fax 03/5159 5111

HANDY TIP

Wood for camp fires

Most of the established camping areas throughout the High Country, and especially the more popular ones are usually devoid of firewood. If you plan on having a camp fire for cooking or socialising by, then it is best to collect wood for your fire well before reaching your camp site or bring some from home. If you have a roof-rack then this is a good place to store the wood you have collected or if you do a bit of camping then a small rooftop basket for this purpose may be more practical.

Please, do not cut down any vegetation either living or dead from around camping areas.

What's in a Name? - The Haunted Stream

When gold was first discovered in the rugged mountains around Omeo in the early 1850s, the region was a rough and lawless frontier. And as the prospectors began to flood the area so too did an assorted collection of villans and outlaws. According to Rolf Boldrewood, author of the 1888 Australian classic *Robbery Under Arms* '... Omeo has the worst reputation of any goldfield ever discovered...'

One of the more sinister of these new arrivals was one Tom Toke, who within a short time of coming to Omeo had struck up an acquaintance with a young prospector named 'Ballarat Harry'. One day in 1857 Ballarat Harry confided to Toke that he was in possession of around £400 (roughly $1300), which was a sizeable sum of money for the time. Ever watchful for an opportunity, Toke decided to invite Ballarat Harry on a prospecting trip to an area that is now known as The Haunted Stream. Toke is said to have murdered Ballarat Harry on this trip, taken his possessions—including the large stash of cash—and disposed of his body.

Some weeks later Toke returned to Omeo wearing Ballarat Harry's clothes, leading his horse and dog. Flush with cash, Toke offered no explanation to the whereabouts of his prospecting companion. After a time when Ballarat Harry failed to return to Omeo suspicion was levelled at Toke, who was subsequently arrested for the murder of Ballarat Harry. However, in a strange twist, Toke was acquitted at his trial—for lack of evidence!

Toke then set himself up as a somewhat respectable storekeeper in Omeo where things went pretty much trouble free for the next few years. However, in 1859 two local misfits were arrested by police, with the help of Toke, for the brutal murder of gold buyer Cornelius Green. One of those arrested, William Armstrong was keen to revenge Toke's part in his capture by revealing to police that Toke had offered him a part in helping to murder Ballarat Harry a few years earlier in exchange for some of the £400 booty. Armstrong said he wanted nothing to do with the murder so Toke pledged him £100 to keep quiet. As promised, Toke paid Armstrong the cash shortly on returning to Omeo after murdering Ballarat Harry, boasting how he had butchered his victim with a tomahawk while he slept, then burned his body and scattered the crushed remains along the creek.

Armstrong was hanged for the murder of Green and Tom Toke fled the area without a trace.

However, the name Ballarat Harry was to continue on in the public arena as one of the characters in Rolf Boldrewood's 1889 novel *Nevermore*, which was inspired by the 1865 *Tichborne Affair*. It is said that Lady Tichborne of Hampshire in England advertised in newspapers throughout Australia for information as to the whereabouts of her missing son Roger, who had supposedly come to the Australian goldfields and was the heir to an estate worth one million pounds (about 2.3 million dollars). Scores of unlikely imposters came forward but the real Roger Tichborne was never found.

In *Nevermore*, Boldrewood's character Lance Trevanion, alias Ballarat Harry draws a likely coincidence to Roger Tichborne. Did Boldrewood draw on his own account of the murder of Ballarat Harry by Tom Toke for his novel and did he suspect the well-heeled Ballarat Harry to really be Roger Tichborne in disguise?

Whatever the case, the legend of Ballarat Harry was not to rest peacefully. When gold was found in the creek, where some years earlier the murder of Ballarat Harry had taken place, prospectors camped along its bank would be woken in the dead of night by bloodcurdling screams piercing the silence of the bush. Some of the less suspicious believed the noise to be that of the barking owl which is found in the area, but others stood firm that the terrifying noises where made by the ghost of Ballarat Harry who had meet his brutal end there. From that time on the picturesque watercourse which winds its way through this secluded valley has been known as Haunted Stream.

ROUTE NOTES

Zero trip meter in Swifts Creek with Albion Hotel on left.

▼ 0.0 (0.0)
Zero trip meter in Swifts Creek. Albion Hotel on left. PSA across the Great Alpine Road in a south-west direction towards SP Cassilis 13.
▲ *86.4 (2.4)*
Swifts Creek. Junction with Great Alpine Road. Albion Hotel and Oblesik SO.
GPS S:37 15.795 E:147 43.294
UTM Zone 55 0563983E 5875673N

▼ 2.4 (2.4)
Y junction. VL. SP 12 Brookville. Road to right SP 11 Cassilis.
▲ *84.0 (12.1)*
CSA. SP Swifts Creek 2. Road to left SP 11 Cassilis.

▼ 14.5 (12.1)
Road junction. CSA. Road on left SP Burwood Road.
▲ *71.9 (1.5)*
CSA. Road on right SP Burwood Road.

▼ 16.0 (1.5)
Track junction. CSA. Track on left SP Gordans Tk.
▲ *70.4 (1.6)*
CSA. Track on right SP Gordans Tk.

▼ 17.6 (1.6)
Track junction. CSA. Track on right SP Charlotte Spur.
▲ *68.8 (0.3)*
CSA. Track on left SP Charlotte Spur.

▼ 17.9 (0.3)
Y junction. VL. SP Dorothy Cutting Forest Drive. Road to right SP Mt Delusion Road.
▲ *68.5 (2.2)*
TR. SP Swifts Creek 18km.
GPS S:37 19.581 E:147 35.913
UTM Zone 55 0553029E 5868757N

▼ 20.1 (2.2)
Track on left. CSA.
▲ *66.3 (0.6)*
Track on right. CSA downhill.

▼ 20.7 (0.6)
Track junction. CSA. Track on right SP Ezard Tk.
▲ *65.7 (1.2)*
CSA. Track on left SP Ezard Tk.

▼ 21.9 (1.2)
Track junction. CSA. SP Dorothy Cutting. Track on left SP Angora Range Road. Track on right SP Notch Hill Tk.
▲ *64.5 (2.1)*
CSA. SP Swifts Creek 22km.

▼ 24.0 (2.1)
Track junction. CSA. SP Dorothy Cutting. Track on right SP Grassy Ridge Tk.
▲ *62.4 (1.5)*
CSA. Track on left SP Grassy Ridge Tk.

▼ 25.5 (1.5)
Track junction. TL. This is Boomerang Spur Road.
▲ *60.9 (5.2)*
TR. SP Dorothy Cutting.
GPS S:37 21.286 E:147 33.095
UTM Zone 55 0548867E 5865642N

▼ 30.7 (5.2)
Y junction. KL on lower track.
▲ *55.7 (2.8)*
Track on left. CSA.

▼ 33.5 (2.8)
Track on right. CSA through Seasonal closure gate. This is Boomerang Spur Track. *NB:* Steep descent from here to next reading.
▲ *52.9 (2.0)*
Seasonal closure gate and track on left. CSA.
GPS S:37 23.132 E:147 35.973
UTM Zone 55 0553084E 5862192N

▼ 35.5 (2.0)
Log bridge. PSA over bridge to intersection. At intersection TR SP Haunted Stream Tk and proceed over wooden bridge. Track on left SP Dawson City Tk. This is Dawson City. Possible bush camp sites in this vicinity.

OPPOSITE: *Haunted Stream Track at Dawson City.*

▲ *50.9 (0.1)*
Track junction. TL and cross log bridge. SP Boomerang Spur Tk. NB: *Steep climb from here to next reading.*
GPS S:37 23.271 E:147 37.094
UTM Zone 55 0554735E 5861927N

▼ 35.6 (0.1)
Track on right just over wooden bridge. CSA.
▲ *50.8 (1.1)*
Track on left. CSA over wooden bridge.

▼ 36.7 (1.1)
Track junction. CSA. SP Haunted Stream Tk. Track on right SP Dawson City Tk.
▲ *49.7 (0.2)*
CSA. Track on left SP Dawson City Tk.

▼ 36.9 (0.2)
Track junction. CSA. Track on right SP Joes Tk.
▲ *49.5 (0.4)*
CSA. Track on left SP Joes Tk.

▼ 37.3 (0.4)
Track junction. CSA. Track on right SP Valentines Tk.
▲ *49.1 (0.3)*
CSA. Track on left SP Valentines Tk.

▼ 37.6 (0.3)
First crossing of Haunted Stream.
▲ *48.8 (1.3)*
Last crossing of Haunted Stream.

▼ 38.9 (1.3)
Track junction. CSA. SP Haunted Stream Tk. Track on right SP Turntable Tk.
▲ *47.5 (4.6)*
CSA. Track on left SP Turntable Tk.

▼ 43.5 (4.6)
Track on left. CSA.
▲ *42.9 (1.1)*
Track on right. CSA.

▼ 44.6 (1.1)
Bush camp site on left. CSA.
▲ *41.8 (4.9)*
Bush camp site on right. CSA.
GPS S:37 24.664 E:147 41.231
UTM Zone 55 0560813E 5859307N

▼ 49.5 (4.9)
Remains of old battery stamp on right. CSA.
▲ *36.9 (0.2)*
Ruins on left. CSA.

▼ 49.7 (0.2)
Camp site on left. This is Dog Town. Remains of boiler and mine equipment in this area and across river. Notes PSA across Haunted Stream.
▲ *36.7 (0.1)*
Camp site on right. CSA.
GPS S:37 25.921 E:147 43.280
UTM Zone 55 0563809E 5856918N

▼ 49.8 (0.1)
Minor track on left leads to ruins. CSA.

▲ *36.6 (0.1)*
Minor track on right. CSA over Haunted Stream.

▼ 49.9 (0.1)
Seasonal closure gate. CSA.
▲ *36.5 (0.2)*
Seasonal closure gate. CSA over Haunted Stream.

▼ 50.1 (0.2)
Track on left leads to old mining sites. Notes CSA over Haunted Stream.
▲ *36.3 (0.4)*
Track on right leads to old mining sites. CSA.

▼ 50.5 (0.4)
Last crossing of Haunted Stream.
▲ *35.9 (2.5)*
First crossing of Haunted Stream.
GPS S:37 26.180 E:147 43.584
UTM Zone 55 0564274E 5856486N

▼ 53.0 (2.5)
Track passes through cutting with glimpses of Haunted Stream below. This cutting displays good examples of stone retaining walls.
▲ *33.4 (0.3)*
Track passes through cutting.

▼ 53.3 (0.3)
Track junction. TL. SP Stirling Tk. Along the first 200m of Stirling Tk are chimney and fireplace ruins which can be seen on the lower side of the track. Track on right is SP Haunted Stream Tk which crosses the stream then leads 300m to the old Stirling Town site. There is a small camping area on left just prior to crossing Haunted Stream.
▲ *33.1 (0.6)*
Track junction. Sharp TR. SP Haunted Stream Tk. Track SO crosses Haunted Stream and leads 300m to old Stirling Town site.
GPS S:37 26.470 E:147 44.667
UTM Zone 55 0565857E 5855917N

▼ 53.9 (0.6)
Track on left. CSA on lower track.
▲ *32.5 (0.1)*
Track on right. CSA.

▼ 54.0 (0.1)
Victoria Mine Tunnel on left. PSA. *NB:* Track climbs steeply for the next 2km.

▲ *32.4 (2.0)*
Victora Mine Tunnel on right.

▲ *30.4 (7.6)*
Track declines steeply from here to next reading.

▼ 63.6 (9.6)
Track junction. TR. SP Angora Range Road. Track on immediate left is SP Sunshine Wattle Tk.
▲ *22.8 (3.8)*
Track junction. TL. SP Stirling Tk. NB: *SP Sunshine Wattle Tk is on right immediately after turning.*
GPS S:37 23.210 E:147 42.477
UTM Zone 55 0562683E 5861971N

▼ 67.4 (3.8)
Track junction. CSA. SP Angora Range Road. Track on left SP Boonabirrah Tk.
▲ *19.0 (4.7)*
CSA. Track on right SP Boonabirrah Tk.

▼ 72.1 (4.7)
SP Westcott Lookout on left. CSA.
▲ *14.3 (1.8)*
SP Westcott Lookout on right. CSA.

▼ 73.9 (1.8)
SP Elphick Lookout on right. CSA.
▲ *12.5 (5.1)*
SP Elphick Lookout on left. CSA.

▼ 79.0 (5.1)
SP Kelty Lookout on right. CSA.
▲ *7.4 (7.4)*
SP Kelty Lookout on left. CSA.

▼ 86.4 (7.4)
Intersection with bitumen. This is the Omeo Highway. SP Wattle Circle. TL for Ensay 10km and Swifts Creek 27km. TR for Bruthen 43km.
▲ *0.0 (0.0)*
Zero trip meter on Omeo Highway at SP Wattle Circle. This is 10km south of Ensay and 43km north of Bruthen. Notes turn into SP Angora Range Rd Forest Drive.
GPS S:37 26.987 E:147 49.566
UTM Zone 55 0573069E 5854909N

OPPOSITE: *Crossing Haunted Stream at Dogtown.*

ShippShape

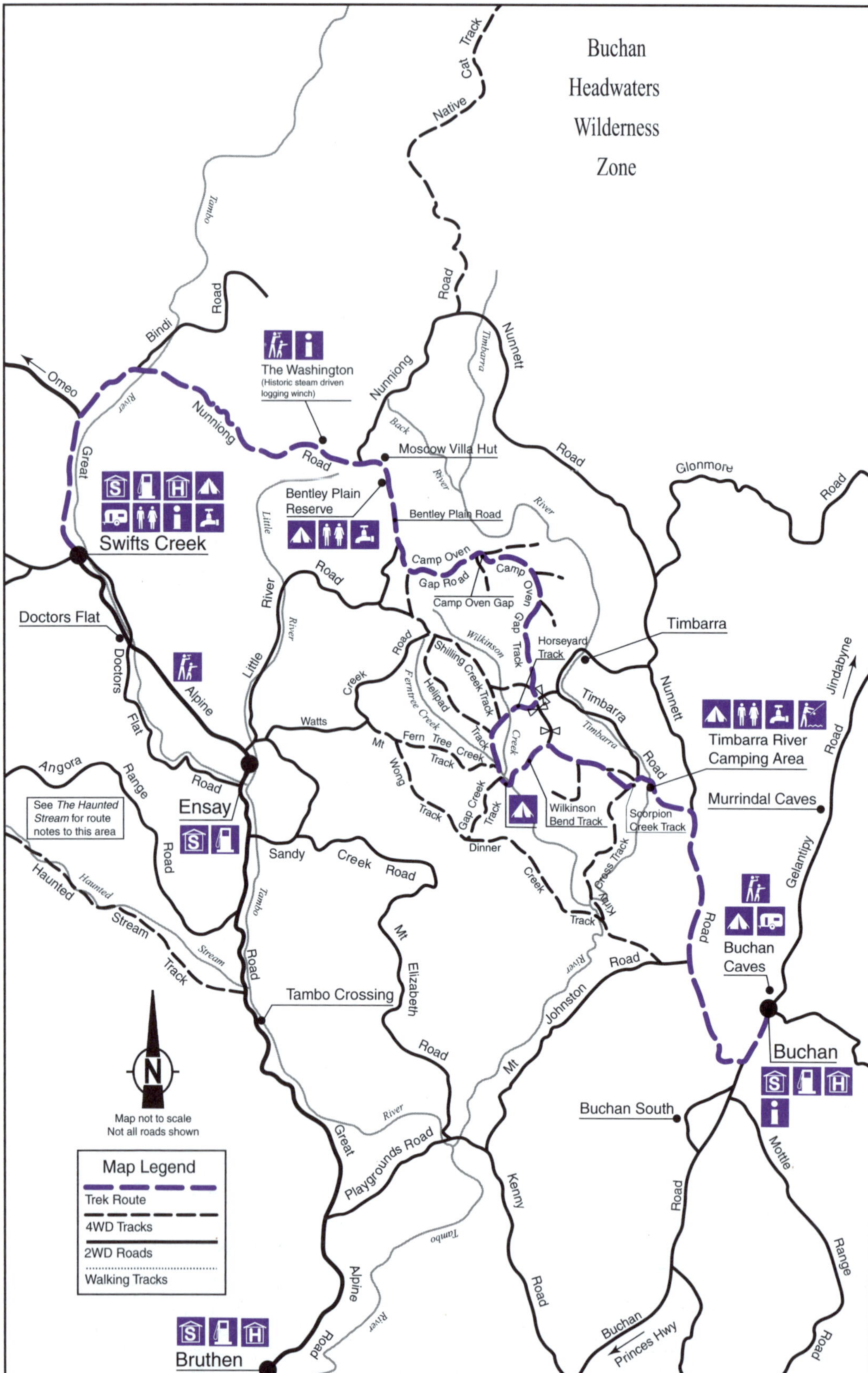
Buchan Headwaters Wilderness Zone
Native Cat Track
Road
Nunnett Road
Nunniong
Timbarra
Tambo
Bindi Road
Omeo
Great
River
Nunniong Road
The Washington
(Historic steam driven logging winch)
Moscow Villa Hut
Back River
Bentley Plain Reserve
Bentley Plain Road
Glonmore Road
Swifts Creek
Little River Road
Camp Oven Gap Road
Camp Oven Gap
Camp Oven Gap Track
Horseyard Track
Timbarra
Doctors Flat
Doctors Flat Road
Alpine
Creek Road
Wilkinson
Shilling Creek Track
Helipad Track
Ferntree Creek
Watts
Fern Tree Creek Track
Timbarra Road
Jindabyne
Timbarra River Camping Area
Angora Range Road
Ensay
Mt Wong Track
Gap Creek Track
Wilkinson Bend Track
Scorpion Creek Track
Murrindal Caves
See The Haunted Stream for route notes to this area
Sandy Creek Road
Dinner Creek Track
Cross Track
Kiley
Gelantipy Road
Haunted Stream Track
Mt Elizabeth Road
Johnston Road
Buchan Caves
Tambo Crossing
Buchan
Mt
Map not to scale
Not all roads shown
Buchan South
Playgrounds Road
Kenny Road
Mottle Range Road
Map Legend
Trek Route
4WD Tracks
2WD Roads
Walking Tracks
Alpine Road
Buchan
Princes Hwy
Bruthen

TREK TWELVE

CAMP OVEN GAP

ON THIS SHORT SORTIE from Buchan to Swifts Creek we take in some interesting, and little known High Country plains, as well as facets of the area's history as we travel between the Snowy and Tambo Rivers.

Things to Do and See

At Buchan there are the spectacular Buchan Caves which are well worth taking a guided tour to inspect.

Once on the trek proper there is reputedly excellent fishing to be had in the Timbarra River and surrounding streams of the district.

Up on Bentley Plain, which is so named after Richard Bentley who used the area as part of his cattle duffing exploits, there are some good camping areas and you can also visit Moscow Villa Hut, built as a summer retreat by local bushman Bill Ah Chow in the early 1940s.

On Nunniong Road is the historic 'Washington', a steam driven winch used during the 1960s to haul timber out of the surrounding gullies.

Access

Buchan, a small East Gippsland village, situated on the all weather bitumen Buchan Road is the start point for this trek. Buchan can be reached from the south from Orbost (via the mostly gravel Orbost - Buchan Road) or Nowa Nowa (35km) on the Princes Highway or from Bruthen (48km) on the Great Alpine Road. From the north Buchan can be accessed via the mostly gravel Barry Way and Snowy River Roads from Jindabyne (180km).

The Trek

From Buchan township head towards South Buchan where the route notes turn into Timbarra Road. Follow Timbarra Road to the camping area beside the Timbarra River, passing Gillingal Road along the way.

fast facts

Buchan to Swifts Creek via Camp Oven Gap and Bentley Plain

Trek distance: 109km

Standard: Easy/Medium (Dry weather only)

Fuel and supplies: Buchan and Swifts Creek

Trek highlights: Buchan Caves (guided tours), Bentley Plain Reserve, Moscow Villa and the Washington Winch

Track conditions:
DNRE Swifts Creek
Ph 03/5159 5100

Cross the bridge over the Timbarra River and after 500m or so turn into Scorpion Creek Track which climbs steeply from Timbarra Road to the junction with Timbarra Bridge Track. Stay on Scorpion Creek Track, passing Kirby Cross Track and Raccoon Track before joining again with Timbarra Bridge Track.

Follow Timbarra Bridge Track to Wilkinson Bend Track and follow this to a good bush camp site at Wilkinson Bend. Cross the creek then take Helipad Track to Shilling Creek Track then onto Horseyard Track which is followed to its junction with Watts Creek Track.

A short way along Watts Creek Track turn into Camp Oven Track, passing Paling Spur Track and Surveyors Track before descending to Camp Oven Gap Road at Camp Oven Gap.

From Camp Oven Gap follow the well maintained Camp Oven Gap Road out to Bentley Plain Road, passing a number of signposted tracks branching off on both the left and right. Once on Bentley Plain Road its only 3½km to the pleasant camping areas of Bentley Plain and Moscow Villa Hut.

Leaving Bentley Plain the trek joins with Nunniong Road which will take you past the historic Washington Steam Winch (see fact box on page 127 *'The Washington' Steam Winch*) before meeting with the Great Alpine Road about 8km north of Swifts Creek.

The route notes conclude in Swifts Creek township.

Standard

Easy/medium. This trek takes in some interesting and rarely visited country between the Snowy River Valley to the east and the Tambo River to the west.

Under normal conditions this trek would be suitable for those with limited four-wheel drive experience with only a couple of moderately steep track sections having to be negotiated. This area is best avoided during wet weather.

Camping

You can camp at the Buchan Caves Campground (fees apply) at the start of the trek. Bush camp sites with limited or no facilities detailed in the route notes are at the Timbarra River at Timbarra and at Wilkinson Bend beside Wilkinson Creek.

Up on Bentley Plain there is very good camping at Bentley Plain Reserve which has pit toilets, picnic tables, fireplaces and a shelter hut. You can also stay in the vicinity of Moscow Villa Hut which is located on the edge of Bentley Plain.

Permits/Restrictions

Seasonal road closures affect this trek and are usually in force from after the Queen's Birthday Long Weekend to just after the Melbourne Cup in November.

Recommended Maps/Guides

The Hema Maps *High Country - Victoria* map shows an overview of the trek route, however not all tracks and roads are shown in detail.

Topographic maps covering this trek are the *Brookville - Ensay* and *Murrindal - Yalmy* 1:50 000 series.

Further Information

Dept of Natural Resources and Environment
McMillan Ave, Swifts Creek VIC 3896 Ph 03/5159 5100 Fax 03/5159 5111

Parks Victoria
Buchan Caves, Buchan VIC 3885 Ph 03/5155 9264 Fax 03/5155 9490

Bairnsdale Visitor Information Centre
240 Main St, Bairnsdale Ph 03/5152 3444

'The Washington' Steam Winch

The Washington Winch, which is located beside Nunniong Forest Road was one of two of its type to be brought to Australia from America in the early 1920s for use at the Karri Timber Mills in Western Australia. Both winches where used there until around 1940.

After serving their time in Western Australia both winches were relocated to Victoria and used in the Powelltown and Noojee areas before one was purchased in 1959 by the Ezard's Sawmill in Swifts Creek.

The winch was brought to Swifts Creek by low loader and on its arrival a considerable amount of time was spent rebuilding and repairing it for its new location in the mountains.

'Washington' Steam Winch

After all work was completed the winch was moved to the bush and positioned on the topside of Nunniong Forest Road beside a permanent spring fed stream. The water from the stream was used to feed the boiler.

Once the winch was in place an area on the opposite side of the road was clear fell, leaving only a couple of 'spar trees' for the overhead rigging.

A spar tree is a large tree opposite the winch from which 'skyline' rigging is attached to pull logs out of the gully below up to the road for loading onto log trucks. To prepare a spar tree one man was required to climb the selected tree and cut off every branch, leaving the tree as a straight pole. This was done by the 'rigger' wearing a special belt around his waist which held pieces of rope plus a one man crosscut saw. A spare belt was also carried just in case! In addition to the belt, the climber had special leggings strapped to his legs that had a steel bar on the inside with a sharp steel spike.

Spar tree

The belt was placed around the tree trunk and the climber would then lift the belt as high as possible and slowly 'walk' up the tree, pushing the leg spikes into the tree to hold him. Once he had cut all the branches up to the desired height (which was usually about 45m or 150 feet) he would then descend the tree in the same fashion. It was then necessary to climb back up the spar tree and attach the necessary pulleys and ropes.

The Washington was only used for a short period of time due to the snig tracks becoming too deep and the logs being hauled often jamming on rocks in the gully below. In this short time however, the 'Washington' hauled just over 9000 cubic metres or three million super feet of timber from the forest.

The Washington Winch has been placed on the heritage list and is now in the process of being restored by the DNRE. Recent renovations include the erection of new spar trees along with the associated rigging.

ROUTE NOTES

Zero trip meter in Buchan on Buchan Road in front of the Caves Hotel. Head in southerly direction towards Buchan South.

▼ 0.0 (0.0)
Caves Hotel on right. PSA along Buchan Road towards South Buchan.
▲ *108.8 (4.2)*
Buchan township. Caves Hotel on left.
GPS S:37 29.950 E:148 10.321
UTM Zone 55 0603594E 5849108N

▼ 4.2 (4.2)
Road junction. TR. SP Timbarra Rd. SP Timbarra 35.
▲ *104.6 (1.9)*
Road junction. TL. SP Buchan 5. Road to right SP Bairnsdale 69.

▼ 6.1 (1.9)
Road junction. VR. SP Timbarra Rd.
▲ *102.7 (17.6)*
KL. SP Buchan.

▼ 23.7 (17.6)
Y junction. KL. SP Timbarra Rd. Road to right SP Gillingal Rd.
▲ *85.1 (4.5)*
Road junction. CSA. SP Timbarra Rd. Road to left SP Gillingal Rd.
GPS S:37 23.531 E:148 07.384
UTM Zone 55 0599411E 5861040N

▼ 28.2 (4.5)
Bush camping area on left and on right over bridge. CSA over bridge.
▲ *80.6 (0.6)*
Bush camping area on left and on right over bridge. CSA over bridge.

▼ 28.8 (0.6)
Track junction. TL. SP Scorpion Crk Tk. Road SO leads 4.9km to more camp sites beside river.
▲ *80.0 (1.1)*
Track junction. TR. This is Timbarra Road. Road to left leads 4.9km to camp sites.
GPS S:37 22.838 E:148 05.413
UTM Zone 55 0596520E 5862360N

▼ 29.9 (1.1)
Track junction. CSA. SP Scorpion Ck Tk. Track on right SP Timbarra Bridge Tk.
▲ *78.9 (0.7)*
Track junction. CSA downhill. SP Scorpion Ck Tk. Track on left SP Timbarra Bridge Tk.

▼ 30.6 (0.7)
Bridge over Scorpion Creek.
▲ *78.2 (0.1)*
Bridge over Scorpion Creek.

▼ 30.7 (0.1)
Track junction. CSA. Track on left SP Kirby Cross Tk.
▲ *78.1 (0.2)*
CSA. Track on right SP Kirby Cross Tk.

▼ 30.9 (0.2)
Bridge.
▲ *77.9 (1.8)*
Bridge.

▼ 32.7 (1.8)
Track junction. TR. Track on left SP Raccoon Tk.
▲ *76.1 (1.4)*
TL. Track SO SP Raccoon Tk.

▼ 34.1 (1.4)
Track junction. TL. SP Timbarra Bridge Tk.
▲ *74.7 (1.9)*
TR. SP Scorpion Ck Tk.

▼ 36.0 (1.9)
Track junction. TL. SP Wilkinson Bend Tk.
▲ *72.8 (3.6)*
TR.

▼ 39.6 (3.6)
Wilkinson Bend. Good bush camping in this vicinity. CSA across river.
▲ *69.2 (0.2)*
River crossing. Good bush camping on opposite side of river.

▼ 39.8 (0.2)
Track junction. TR. SP Helipad Tk. Track on left. SP Gap Creek Tk.
▲ *69.0 (0.2)*
TL. SP Bend in Wilkinson Tk.
GPS S:37 22.788 E:148 00.123
UTM Zone 55 0588709E 5862523N

RIGHT: *There are magic views over the Howqua River Valley from near Bluff Hut (Trek 2)*

BELOW: *'Eric' the emu and Dave at Seldom Seen Service Station (Trek 16)*

BOTTOM: *Crossing the Swampy Plains River at Geehi near Commission Hut (Trek 17)*

TOP: *Travelling on the Mt Murray North Track as it winds from the Buckland River to the Twins Jeep Track* (Trek 9)

ABOVE: *The climb from Craig's Hut to Mt Stirling has wonderful vistas over the Alpine National Park* (Trek 3)

RIGHT: *Ryan with a nice pan size rainbow trout taken from* Paddys River Dam (Trek 19)

ABOVE: *Cave Creek cuts its way through Clarke Gorge at Blue Waterholes (Trek 20)*

TOP: *Looking over the site of the former township of Ravine or Lobbs Hole. The Yarrangobilly River meanders through the valley before flowing into Talbingo Reservoir not far from here (Trek 18)*

ABOVE: *Wombat PO camping area with Wombat PO Hut in the background. Around 200 hardy souls worked the surrounding area for gold during the late 1860s (Trek 13)*

RIGHT: *Summer wildflowers on Mt Stirling (Trek 3)*

TOP: *Davies Plain Hut (Trek 15)*

ABOVE RIGHT: *Old mine workings beside the Yarrangobilly River at Ravine (Trek 18)*

ABOVE: *Camp site at Italian Flat beside the Dargo River (Trek 10)*

LEFT: *Limestone formation in one of the self-guided caves near Blue Waterholes (Trek 20)*

ABOVE: *Gold fossicking at Parson's Gully* (Trek 19)

ABOVE: *Camping at Beveridges* (Trek 9)

ABOVE: *Cattle grazing on the lush pastures of Tom Groggin Station* (Trek 14)

TOP: *Driving the Mt Wellington Track near the Mt Wellington summit (Trek 7)*

ABOVE LEFT: *Craig's Hut was originally built for 'The Man from Snowy River' movie (Trek 3)*

ABOVE RIGHT: *Camping at Three Mile Dam in Kosciuszko National Park (Trek 18)*

LEFT: *'The Staircase' on Speculation Road (Trek 4)*

TOP: *Crossing Broken Cart Creek (Trek 20)*

ABOVE: *Remains of an oven along the Crooked River Track. The Crooked River Goldfields were discovered by Alfred Howitt and his party in 1860 and were at the time probably the most remote goldfields in Victoria (Trek 8)*

RIGHT: *Ruins of Jounama Homestead in Kosciuszko National Park (Trek 18)*

▼ 40.0 (0.2)
Track junction. VR. SP Helipad Tk. Track on left SP Fern Tree Creek.
▲ *68.8 (0.4)*
CSA. SP Gap Creek Tk.

▼ 40.4 (0.4)
Creek crossing. *NB:* avoid using bridge.
▲ *68.4 (2.2)*
Creek crossing.

▼ 42.6 (2.2)
Track junction. TR. SP Shilling Creek Tk.
▲ *66.2 (0.6)*
TL. SP Helipad Tk.

▼ 43.2 (0.6)
Track junction. TR. SP Horseyard Tk.
▲ *65.6 (0.1)*
TL uphill. SP Shilling Creek Tk.

▼ 43.3 (0.1)
Creek crossing.
▲ *65.5 (3.1)*
Creek crossing.

▼ 46.4 (3.1)
Track junction. TL.
▲ *62.4 (0.1)*
TR. SP Horse Yard Tk.

▼ 46.5 (0.1)
Track junction. TL. SP Watts Ck Tk. Track on right SP Locked gate.
▲ *62.3 (0.7)*
TR. SP Timbarra Bridge Tk.

▼ 47.2 (0.7)
Track junction. TR. SP Camp Oven Tk.
▲ *61.6 (6.3)*
KL. SP Watts Ck Tk.
GPS S:37 20.277 E:148 01.136
UTM Zone 55 0590257E 5867137N

▼ 53.5 (6.3)
Track junction. CSA. SP Camp Oven Gap Tk. Track on right SP Paling Spur Tk.
▲ *55.3 (1.7)*
VR. SP Camp Oven Gap Tk. Track on left SP Paling Spur Tk.

▼ 55.2 (1.7)
Track junction. CSA. SP Camp Oven Gap Tk. Track on right SP Surveyors Tk.
▲ *53.6 (3.9)*
CSA. SP Camp Oven Gap Tk. Track on left SP Surveyors Tk.

▼ 59.1 (3.9)
Track junction. This is SP Camp Oven Gap. TL onto main track, keeping SP on left. PSA past good gravel track on left.
▲ *49.7 (0.1)*
TR. This track is just after SP Camp Oven Gap.
GPS S:37 16.032 E:147 59.189
UTM Zone 55 0587469E 5875029N

▼ 59.2 (0.1)
Tracks on right. KL on main track.
▲ *49.6 (3.6)*
Tracks on left. KR on main track. PSA past good gravel track on right and past SP Camp Oven Gap on right.

▼ 62.8 (3.6)
Track junction. CSA. SP Camp Oven Gap Road. Road on left SP FDA Road.
▲ *46.0 (1.2)*
CSA. SP Camp Oven Gap Road. Road on right SP FDA Road.

▼ 64.0 (1.2)
Track junction. CSA. SP Camp Oven Gap Road. Track on right SP Long Spur Tk.
▲ *44.8 (1.3)*
CSA. SP Camp Oven Gap Road. Track on left SP Long Spur Tk.

▼ 65.3 (1.3)
Track junction. CSA. SP Camp Oven Gap Road. Track on left SP Mt Tom Tk.
▲ *43.5 (1.8)*
CSA. SP Camp Oven Gap Road. Track on right SP Mt Tom Tk.

▼ 67.1 (1.8)
Track junction. CSA. SP Camp Oven Gap Road. Track on right SP Woodhouse Creek Tk.
▲ *41.7 (0.4)*
CSA. SP Camp Oven Gap Road. Track on left SP Woodhouse Creek Tk.

▼ 67.5 (0.4)
Track junction. TR. SP Bentley Plain Road.
▲ *41.3 (1.3)*
TL. SP Camp Oven Gap Road.
GPS S:37 15.466 E:147 55.961
UTM Zone 55 0582708E 5876127N

▼ 68.8 (1.3)
Track junction. CSA. SP Bentley Plain Road. Track on left SP South Escarpment Tk.

▲ *40.0 (0.2)*
CSA. SP Bentley Plain Road.

▼ 69.0 (0.2)
Track junction. CSA. SP Bentley Plain Road. Road on right SP Winter Road.
▲ *39.8 (1.6)*
CSA. Road on left SP Winter Road.

▼ 70.6 (1.6)
Track junction. CSA. SP Bentley Plain Road. Road on right SP Flynns Road.
▲ *38.2 (0.6)*
CSA. Road on left SP Flynns Road.

▼ 71.2 (0.6)
Bentley Plain Reserve. Camping area. Notes CSA over Bentley Creek.
▲ *37.6 (0.2)*
Bentley Plain Reserve. CSA.
GPS S:37 13.681 E:147 55.398
UTM Zone 55 0581905E 5879435N

Moscow Villa Hut

Moscow Villa Hut, located on the edge of Bentley Plain was originally built in the early 1940s as a summer retreat by local bushman and master of the 'tall story' Bill Ah Chow.

The story goes that Ah Chow most probably named his log style cabin 'Moscow Villa' at the time of Hitler's advance towards Moscow during the second World War. At this time Russia were our allies.

However, at the height of the Cold War in 1957 Bill was paid a visit by high ranking officials from the Forestry Commission along with the Governor who were not at all pleased with the cabins title. As quick as a flash Ah Chow devised the acronym 'My Own Summer Cottage Officially Welcomes Visitors Inside Light Lunch Available'.

▼ 71.4 (0.2)
Moscow Villa Hut. Camping area. Notes CSA.
▲ *37.4 (0.5)*
Moscow Villa Hut. Camping area. Notes CSA over Bentley Creek.
GPS S:37 13.585 E:147 55.329
UTM Zone 55 0581807E 5879611N

▼ 71.9 (0.5)
Track on left. CSA.
▲ *36.9 (1.5)*
Track on right. CSA.

▼ 73.4 (1.5)
Track junction. CSA. SP Bentley Plain Road. Track on right SP Dobbys Tk.
▲ *35.4 (1.3)*
CSA. Track on left SP Dobbys Tk.

▼ 74.7 (1.3)
Track on left. CSA on main track.
▲ *34.1 (0.1)*
CSA on main track.

▼ 74.8 (0.1)
Track junction. CSA. This is Nunniong Road.
▲ *34.0 (0.5)*
Track junction. CSA. This is Bentley Plain Road. Road on left is Nunniong Road.

▼ 75.3 (0.5)
Cross roads. CSA. SP Nunniong Road. Track on left SP South Escarpment Tk. Track on right SP Escarpment Tk.
▲ *33.5 (1.9)*
Cross roads. CSA. SP Nunniong Road.

▼ 77.2 (1.9)
Washington Winch on right. CSA.
▲ *31.6 (5.1)*
Washington Winch on left. CSA.
GPS S:37 12.714 E:147 53.037
UTM Zone 55 0578425E 5881254N

▼ 82.3 (5.1)
Track junction. CSA. SP Nunniong Road. Road on left SP No Through Road.
▲ *26.5 (1.7)*
CSA. SP Nunniong Road.

▼ 84.0 (1.7)
Track junction. CSA. SP Nunniong Road. Road on left SP Windy Ridge Rd.
▲ *24.8 (0.4)*
CSA. Road on right SP Windy Ridge Rd.

▼ 84.4 (0.4)
Track junction. CSA on main track crossing grid. Track on left SP Low Saddle Tk.
▲ *24.4 (6.7)*
CSA. Track on right SP Low Saddle Tk.

▼ 91.1 (6.7)
CSA.
▲ *17.7 (2.5)*
Y junction. KR.

▼ 93.6 (2.5)
CSA onto bitumen. SP Golf Course on right.
▲ *15.2 (1.0)*
CSA onto gravel. SP Golf Course on left.

▼ 94.6 (1.0)
KL on bitumen road.
▲ *14.2 (0.6)*
KR on bitumen road.

▼ 95.2 (0.6)
Bridge over Tambo River.
▲ *13.6 (0.4)*
Bridge over Tambo River.
GPS S:37 10.202 E:147 45.773
UTM Zone 55 0567723E 5885989N

▼ 95.6 (0.4)
Road junction. TL.
▲ *13.2 (4.6)*
Road junction. VR. SP Nunniong Rd Forest Drive.
GPS S:37 10.105 E:147 45.551
UTM Zone 55 0567396E 5886176N

▼ 100.2 (4.6)
Road junction. Give Way sign. CSA.
▲ *8.6 (8.6)*
Y junction. TR. SP Tambo Valley Golf Club 8. SP Bindi.

▼ 108.8 (8.6)
Swifts Creek. Albion Hotel on left.
▲ *0.0 (0.0)*
Zero trip meter in Swifts Creek on the Great Alpine Road with the Albion Hotel on the right. PSA on the Great Alpine Road in a northerly direction.
GPS S:37 15.795 E:147 43.294
UTM Zone 55 0563983E 5875673N

THINGS TO SEE AND DO

Buchan Caves

First explored by Europeans in the early 1900s, the Buchan Caves are an underground world of beauty and colour.

The caves and their formations were formed some 300-400 million years ago when the sea covered the land. Deposits of coral and shell formed limestone on the ocean floor and when the sea waters recessed, causing the earth to move, the land crumpled into its existing formation. Water moving through the earth's surface layers over thousands of years carved the caves and their chambers where the limestone formations are found.

Like many caves, the spectacular formations at Buchan Caves are created when water, which has acids from the soil and carbon dioxide from air dissolves the limestone. Water seeping through the roof of the caves at different speeds and angles cause the variety of formations which occur throughout the caves. Stalactites form from the ceiling, whilst stalagmites grow from the floor and columns occur when both meet. When the water follows the line of a sloping roof, blankets are formed and waterfall formations occur from where the water has flowed over rock ledges. Many of the formations within Buchan Caves are tinted red, orange and brown caused by the iron oxide within soils.

Guided tours of the Fairy and Royal Caves are available each day except Christmas Day. From October to March there are five tours daily and from April to September three tours daily. During the warmer months and at Easter and school holidays bookings are essential. Ph 03/5155 9264

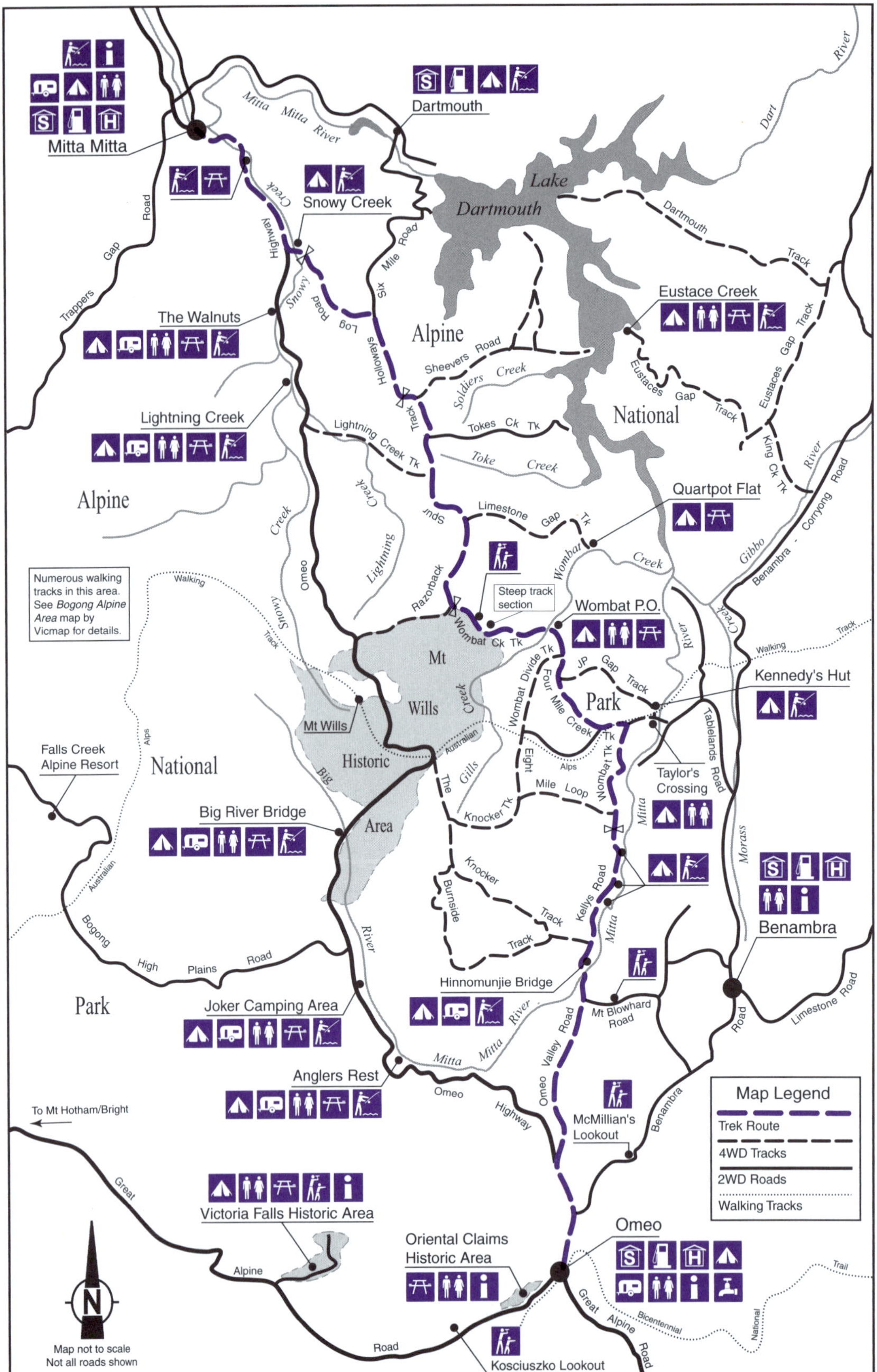
Mitta Mitta
Dartmouth
Mitta Mitta River
Lake Dartmouth
Snowy Creek
Highway
Creek
Trappers Gap Road
Six Mile Road
Log Road
Snowy
The Walnuts
Alpine
Hollowleys Track
Sheevers Road
Soldiers Creek
Dartmouth Track
Eustace Creek
Eustaces Gap Track
Eustaces Gap Track
National
Lightning Creek
Lightning Creek Tk
Tokes Ck Tk
Toke Creek
King Ck Tk
River
Dart River
Alpine
Quartpot Flat
Limestone Gap Tk
Spur
Creek
Lightning
Omeo
Creek
Wombat Creek
Gibbo Creek
Benambra - Corryong Road
Numerous walking tracks in this area. See Bogong Alpine Area map by Vicmap for details.
Walking
Snowy Track
Razorback
Steep track section
Wombat P.O.
Wombat Ck Tk
Mt Wills
Creek
Wombat Divide Tk
JP Gap Track
Four Mile Creek Tk
Park
River
Kennedy's Hut
Walking Track
Mt Wills
Historic
Area
Australian Alps
Tablelands Road
Taylor's Crossing
Falls Creek Alpine Resort
National
Alps
Big
The Gills
Eight Mile Loop
Wombat Tk
Knocker Tk
Big River Bridge
Mitta
Morass
Knocker Track
Burnside Track
Kellys Road
Mitta
Australian
Bogong High Plains Road
River
Benambra
Hinnomunjie Bridge
Mt Blowhard Road
Limestone Road
Road
Park
Joker Camping Area
Mitta Mitta River
Omeo Valley Road
Anglers Rest
Omeo Highway
Benambra Road
McMillian's Lookout
To Mt Hotham/Bright
Map Legend
Trek Route
4WD Tracks
2WD Roads
Walking Tracks
Great Alpine Road
Victoria Falls Historic Area
Omeo
Oriental Claims Historic Area
Bicentennial National Trail
Great Alpine Road
Kosciuszko Lookout
N
Map not to scale
Not all roads shown

TREK THIRTEEN

WOMBAT AMBLE

IT'S HARD TO IMAGINE Wombat Creek, or Township Flat as it was originally known, was once home to a butcher shop, hotel, post office, blacksmith and two general stores with a population peaking at 500.

The town sprung to life in the latter part of 1865 when gold was found beside nearby Peg Leg Creek, however the gold rush didn't last for long and by the early 1870s the majority of the people had left the area. Wombat PO - a post office and accommodation house of sorts was the only remaining business in town come 1890, serving travellers and the few remaining hopefuls that stayed on after the rush.

Things to Do and See

Omeo has many historic sites that are worthwhile visiting. A.M. Pearson Historical Park in the centre of town contains the original courthouse along with other buildings, a waterwheel and a small indoor museum.

Along the Great Alpine Road towards Mt Hotham is the Oriental Claims where the Chinese used hydraulic water pressure to successfully mine the area and a little further west is Victoria Falls where the ruins of the state's first hydro-electric scheme to power the Cassilis mine 23km away can be seen.

The Mitta Mitta River is popular for fishing, white water rafting and camping. Fishing and camping is also popular on Snowy Creek.

In the vicinity of Wombat PO there are some good camp sites as well as views east over the Alpine National Park from Wombat Creek Track.

There are views across to Lake Dartmouth from Razorback Spur Track and Holloways Log Road. The lake, which dams the Mitta Mitta and Dart Rivers, was built in the 1970s to regulate the Hume Weir and also contributes to the Murray Valley Irrigation System. For the keen fisherman the lake contains brown and rainbow trout as well as Macquarie perch.

fast facts

Omeo to Mitta Mitta via Wombat PO Hut

Trek distance: 96km

Standard: Easy/Medium (Dry weather only)

Fuel and supplies: Omeo and Mitta Mitta

Trek highlights: Mitta Mitta River, Wombat PO site and hut, Wombat Creek Track and views, Lake Dartmouth

Track conditions:
Parks Vic Omeo
Ph 03/5159 1660
DNRE Mitta Mitta
Ph 02/6072 3410

Access

The start point for this trek is at the historic township of Omeo. Omeo is easily accessible via the Great Alpine Road from Bairnsdale in the south (130km) or from Bright via Mt Hotham (107km) and via the part gravel Omeo Highway from Mitta Mitta (107km) from the north.

The Trek

The trek commences opposite the Golden Age Hotel in Omeo, once one of the most exquisite buildings in the East Gippsland region. Heading north out of Omeo on the Omeo Highway the route turns onto Omeo Valley Road to cross Hinnomunjie Bridge, the site of the Hinnomunjie Pastoral Station.

Continuing along the well maintained Kellys Road the

route runs on the western side of the Mitta Mitta River and enters Alpine National Park. At the Wombat Track Junction our route heads in a north-westerly direction towards Mitta Mitta. It is possible to turn east at this junction and travel for 5km to Kennedy Hut and Taylors Crossing on the Mitta Mitta River.

The route continues on Wombat Track, which is a relatively easy jaunt until it reaches Wombat PO Hut. From Wombat PO Hut the track climbs steeply to Razorback Ridge with its breathtaking views over the Alpine National Park.

Once on Razorback Spur Track, the route leaves the national park and enters state forest, passing Limestone Gap Track which leads to Quart Pot Flat Hut and some bush camping areas. Not long after this the junction with Holloways Log Road is met where to the east you will see glimpses of the massive expanse of Lake Dartmouth.

Continue on Holloways Log Road, which crosses Snowy Creek, a popular fishing and camping spot, before meeting with the bitumen Omeo Highway where it's only a short run to Mitta Mitta.

Standard

This trek is given an easy/medium rating. The roads and tracks travelled on this trek are mostly gravel based and in good condition. The steep climb from Wombat PO on Wombat Creek Track has some loose gravel sections and will require low range 4WD.

Holloways Log Road is the exception with its clay base and is a dry weather route. In the wet this road would be extremely slippery. Razorback Spur Track and Holloways Log Road are both used by logging trucks and it would be wise to check on any logging activities in this area prior to your trip.

Camping

At the beginning of the trek there is camping at Victoria Falls, just west of Omeo. This delightful shaded spot has tables, fire pits and toilets.

Bush camping beside the Mitta Mitta River is possible at Hinnomunjie Bridge and along Kellys Road where you will find numerous tracks leading to riverside camp sites.

A short detour at the Wombat Track junction will take you to Taylors Crossing on the Mitta Mitta River where you will find grassy camping spots with tables and fireplaces and at Kennedys Hut you can camp in the hut's vicinity. Facilities here include toilets, tables and fireplaces.

There are pleasant camp sites in the vicinity of Wombat PO Hut and facilities here include a pit toilet and picnic table. You can also bunk down in the hut.

Towards the end of the trek at Snowy Creek you will find bush camp sites on either side of the bridge. Also beside Snowy Creek is the Walnuts camping area which is located 2km south on the Omeo Highway. At the Walnuts you will find tables, fireplaces and toilets.

Permits/Restriction

Seasonal closures apply to this trek. Seasonal closure gates are located at the start of Wombat Track, at the junction of Wombat Track and Razorback Spur Track and along Holloways Log Road.

Recommended Maps/Guides

The Hema Maps *High Country - Victoria* map and *The Upper Murray Touring Map & Visitors Guide* both show this trek route as does the CFA *North East Rural Directory - Regions 23 and 24* (maps 337, 336, 301).

Further Information

Parks Victoria
Day Avenue, Omeo VIC 3898 Ph 03/5159 1660 Fax 03/5159 1665

Dept of Natural Resources and Environment
Omeo Highway, Mitta Mitta VIC 3701 Ph 02/6072 3410 Fax 02/6072 3524

Brochures - Parks Victoria: *Alpine National Park – source of the rivers around Mitta Mitta, Benambra and Corryong*

ROUTE NOTES

Trek commences in Omeo on Great Alpine Road opposite Golden Age Hotel.

▼ 0.0 (0.0)
Zero trip meter at junction of Great Alpine Road and Tongio Road in Omeo, Golden Age Hotel on the right. Proceed along Great Alpine Road in northerly direction.
▲ *95.6 (4.3)*
Omeo township. Golden Age Hotel on left.
GPS S:37 06.049 E:147 35.457
UTM Zone 55 0552510E 5893786N

▼ 4.3 (4.3)
Road junction. CSA. SP Falls Creek. Road on right SP Benambra.
▲ *91.3 (2.8)*
Road junction. CSA over bridge. SP Omeo. Road on left SP Benambra.

▼ 7.1 (2.8)
Road junction. TR. SP Omeo Valley. Road SO SP Tallangatta/Mitta Mitta.
▲ *88.5 (3.4)*
Road junction. TL. SP Omeo. Road on right SP Tallangatta.

▼ 10.5 (3.4)
Road junction. CSA. Road on right SP Parish Boundary La.
▲ *85.1 (6.7)*
CSA. Road on left SP Parish Boundary La.

▼ 17.2 (6.7)
Road junction. CSA. Road on right SP Benambra via Mt Blowhard.
▲ *78.4 (1.7)*
Road junction. CSA. Road on left SP Benambra via Mt Blowhard.

▼ 18.9 (1.7)
Hinnomunjie Bridge.
▲ *76.7 (0.1)*
Hinnomunjie Bridge.

▼ 19.0 (0.1)
Track on right leads to bush camp sites. Notes CSA on bitumen.
▲ *76.6 (1.6)*
Track on left leads to bush camp sites. Notes CSA over bridge.

▼ 20.6 (1.6)
Track junction. CSA. SP Kellys Rd. Track on left SP The Knocker Tk.
▲ *75.0 (0.8)*
CSA onto bitumen. Track on right SP The Knocker Tk.

▼ 21.4 (0.8)
Gate. LAF.
▲ *74.2 (0.6)*
Gate. LAF.

▼ 22.0 (0.6)
Gate. LAF.
▲ *73.6 (0.7)*
Gate. LAF.

▼ 22.7 (0.7)
Enter SP Alpine National Park. CSA.
▲ *72.9 (0.4)*
Now leaving Alpine National Park.
GPS S:36 55.020 E:147 37.045
UTM Zone 55 0554987E 5914155N

▼ 23.1 (0.4)
Track on right leads to bush camp sites beside river. CSA.
▲ *72.5 (0.3)*
Track on left leads to bush camp sites. CSA.

▼ 23.4 (0.3)
Track on right leads to bush camp sites. CSA.
▲ *72.2 (0.5)*
Track on left leads to bush camp sites. CSA.

▼ 23.9 (0.5)
Track on right. KL.
▲ *71.7 (1.8)*
Track on left. CSA.

▼ 25.7 (1.8)
Numerous bush camp sites beside river here. CSA.
▲ *69.9 (0.9)*
Bush camp sites beside river. CSA.

▼ 26.6 (0.9)
Track on right leads to river. CSA.
▲ *69.0 (2.0)*
Track on left. CSA.

▼ 28.6 (2.0)
Bridge.
▲ *67.0 (0.3)*
Bridge.

ABOVE: *Wombat Creek.*

▼ 28.9 (0.3)
Track junction. CSA. SP Kellys Rd. Track on left SP Eight Mile Loop Tk.
▲ *66.7 (1.8)*
CSA. SP Kellys Rd. Track on right SP Eight Mile Loop Tk.

▼ 30.7 (1.8)
Track on right. KL on main track.
▲ *64.9 (1.0)*
Track on left. CSA.

▼ 31.7 (1.0)
Causeway.
▲ *63.9 (0.1)*
Causeway.

▼ 31.8 (0.1)
Seasonal closure gate.
▲ *63.8 (1.5)*
Seasonal closure gates.

▼ 33.3 (1.5)
Track junction. KR. SP Wombat Tk. Track SO SP Eight Mile Loop Tk.
▲ *62.3 (1.2)*
Track junction. KL. Track on right SP Eight Mile Loop Tk.

▼ 34.5 (1.2)
Track junction. CSA. SP Wombat Tk. Track on left SP Toms Link Tk.
▲ *61.1 (0.5)*
CSA. SP Wombat Tk. Track on left SP Toms Link Tk.

▼ 35.0 (0.5)
Track junction. TL uphill. SP Wombat Tk. Track on right SP Four Mile Creek Tk leads approx. 5km to Taylors Crossing and Kennedy Hut.
▲ *60.6 (4.2)*
Y junction. VR. SP Wombat Tk. Track on left SP 4 Mile Creek Tk.
GPS S:36 49.413 E:147 37.177
UTM Zone 55 0555269E 5924522N

▼ 39.2 (4.2)
Track junction. CSA. SP Four Mile Crk Tk. Track on right SP J P Gap Trk.
▲ *56.4 (2.7)*
CSA. SP 4 Mile Crk Tk. Track on left SP J P Gap Trk.

▼ 41.9 (2.7)
Track on left. CSA. SP Four Mile Crk Tk.
▲ *53.7 (1.0)*
Track on right. CSA. SP Four Mile Crk Tk.

▼ 42.9 (1.0)
Y junction. KR on lower track.
▲ *52.7 (0.3)*
Track on right. KL.

▼ 43.2 (0.3)
Track junction. TL. SP Wombat Ck Tk. Road SO leads short distance to Wombat Hut and camping area.
▲ *52.4 (0.4)*
Track junction. TR. SP Four Mile Crk Trk. Track on left leads to Wombat Hut and camping area.
GPS S:36 46.348 E:147 35.693
UTM Zone 55 0553075E 5930211N

▼ 43.6 (0.4)
Track on left. CSA.
▲ *52.0 (1.2)*
Track on right. CSA.

▼ 44.8 (1.2)
Minor track on left. KR and cross Wombat Creek. From here track climbs steeply for 1.5km.
▲ *50.8 (1.8)*
Cross Wombat Creek. Over creek minor track on right, KL uphill.

▲ *49.0 (4.4)*
Track drops steeply from here to Wombat Creek.

▼ 51.0 (6.2)
Spectacular views over Alpine National Park on right. CSA.
▲ *44.6 (1.0)*
Spectacular views on left. CSA.
GPS S:36 46.162 E:147 32.115
UTM Zone 55 0547770E 5930579N

▼ 52.0 (1.0)
Seasonal closure gate. CSA to track junction and PSA. This is Razorback Spur Track.
▲ *43.6 (2.6)*
Track junction. CSA through seasonal closure gate. This is Wombat Crk Trk.
GPS S:36 45.763 E:147 31.885
UTM Zone 55 0547433E 5931310N

▼ 54.6 (2.6)
Track junction. CSA. Track on right SP Pegleg Tk.
▲ *41.0 (2.8)*
CSA. Track on left SP Pegleg Tk.

▼ 57.4 (2.8)
Y junction. KL. Track on right is Limestone Gap Track, leads to Quart Pot Flat Hut and camping area.
▲ *38.2 (4.4)*
Track junction. CSA. Track on left is Limestone Gap Track.
GPS S:36 43.704 E:147 32.447
UTM Zone 55 0548282E 5935126N

▼ 61.8 (4.4)
Track junction. KR. Track on left SP Lightning Ck Tk.
▲ *33.8 (4.2)*
Track junction. KL. Track on right SP Lightning Ck Tk.

▼ 66.0 (4.2)
Track junction. CSA. Track on right SP Tokes Ck Tk.
▲ *29.6 (1.7)*
Y junction. KR. Track on left SP Tokes Ck Tk.

▼ 67.7 (1.7)
Track junction. TL. SP Holloways Log Road. Track on right SP Sheevers Road. Glimpses of Lake Dartmouth on right.
▲ *27.9 (0.5)*
Track junction. TR heading uphill. SP Razorback Spur Tk. Road SO SP Sheevers Road. Glimpses of Lake Dartmouth on left.
GPS S:36 39.994 E:147 30.617
UTM Zone 55 0545595E 5941995N

▼ 68.2 (0.5)
Seasonal closure gate.
▲ *27.4 (5.5)*
Seasonal closure gate.

▼ 73.7 (5.5)
T junction. TL. SP Holloways Log Road. Road to right SP Six Mile Rd.
▲ *21.9 (9.4)*
Track junction. TR. SP Holloways Log Road. Road SO SP Six Mile Rd.
GPS S:36 37.805 E:147 29.135
UTM Zone 55 0543411E 5946049N

▼ 83.1 (9.4)
Seasonal closure gate.
▲ *12.5 (0.1)*
Seasonal closure gate.

▼ 83.2 (0.1)
Bridge. Snowy Creek Camping Area on both sides of creek.
▲ *12.4 (0.6)*
Bridge.

▼ 83.8 (0.6)
T junction with bitumen. This is the Omeo Highway. Notes TR. Road on left leads 2km to the Walnuts Camping Area and 95km to Omeo.
▲ *11.8 (2.9)*
Road junction. TL. SP Holloways Log Rd.
GPS S:36 35.925 E:147 26.046
UTM Zone 55 0538824E 5949539N

▼ 86.7 (2.9)
Track junction. CSA. SP Mitta Mitta 9. Road on right SP Walshs Rd.
▲ *8.9 (8.9)*
CSA. SP 98 Omeo. Road on left SP Walshs Rd.

▼ 95.6 (8.9)
Mitta Mitta village. Laurel Hotel and road to Dartmouth on right.
▲ *0.0 (0.0)*
Zero trip meter in village of Mitta Mitta. Laurel Hotel on left. Head in southerly direction SP 107 Omeo.
GPS S:36 32.212 E:147 22.696
UTM Zone 55 0533860E 5956415N

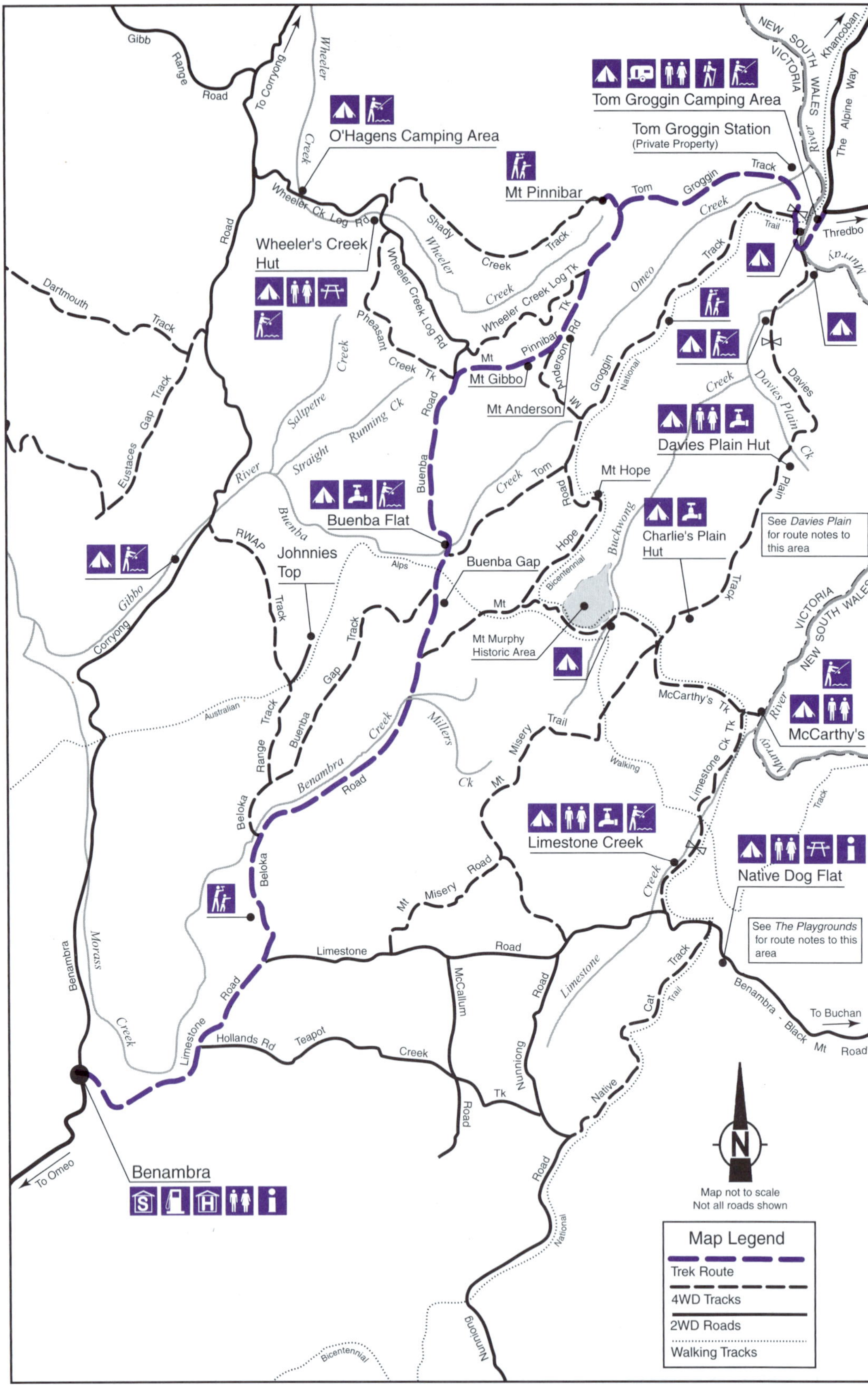

Tom Groggin Camping Area
Tom Groggin Station
(Private Property)
O'Hagens Camping Area
Mt Pinnibar
Wheeler's Creek Hut
Mt Gibbo
Mt Anderson
Davies Plain Hut
Mt Hope
Buenba Flat
Johnnies Top
Buenba Gap
Charlie's Plain Hut
See Davies Plain for route notes to this area
Mt Murphy Historic Area
McCarthy's
Limestone Creek
Native Dog Flat
See The Playgrounds for route notes to this area
Benambra
NEW SOUTH WALES
VICTORIA
Khancoban
The Alpine Way
Thredbo
To Corryong
To Omeo
To Buchan
Gibb Range Road
Dartmouth Track
Eustaces Gap Track
Wheeler Ck Log Rd
Shady Creek Track
Wheeler Creek Log Rd
Wheeler Creek Log Tk
Pheasant Creek Tk
Mt Pinnibar Rd
Mt Anderson Rd
Tom Groggin Track
Groggin Creek
Omeo Trail Track
Groggin Track
Davies Plain Track
Davies Plain Ck
Buenba Road
Tom Creek
Hope Road
Buckwong
Bicentennial
National
Alps
RWAP Track
Gap Track
Buenba Range Track
Gibbo River
Corryong
Saltpetre Creek
Running Ck
Straight Creek
Australian
Benambra Creek Road
Millers Ck
Mt Misery Trail
Walking
McCarthy's Tk
Limestone Ck Tk
Murray River
Beloka Road
Mt Misery Road
Limestone Road
McCallum Road
Nunniong Road
Limestone
Cat Track
Trail
Benambra - Black Mt Road
Morass Creek
Benambra
Limestone Road
Hollands Rd
Teapot Creek Tk
Native
National
Bicentennial
Nunniong
N
Map not to scale
Not all roads shown
Map Legend
Trek Route
4WD Tracks
2WD Roads
Walking Tracks

TREK 14

Choose the right option

Rental type	Linkup pass	CityLink pass	Access account	Everyday/ Commercial account
Business or tourist traveller	✓	✓	✓	
General car hire	✓	✓	✓	✓
Light commercial vehicle rental	✓	✓	✓	✓
Heavy commercial vehicle rental	✓	✓	✓	✓

BRO_RENTAL_PAD 10-05

CityLink

CityLink travel options
when renting a vehicle

CityLink is the 22 kilometre automated tollway that makes getting around Melbourne quick and easy. Just look for the blue and yellow signs. There are no cash booths. To pay is simple – just choose the option below that best suits your needs.

Option 1 Linkup pass

For unlimited use of CityLink, you can pay your car rental company an additional charge for each day you are renting a vehicle. Just ask the rental company about the Linkup pass when you pick up your vehicle.

Option 2 CityLink pass

To purchase your own CityLink pass:

- visit citylink.com.au
- go to a participating Australia Post office
- use the Touch machines at major Coles Express outlets and the Melbourne airport carpark (see overleaf)
- look for the Touch logo at participating newsagents
- call into our CityLink Customer Centre at 67 Lorimer Street (see overleaf)
- or phone CityLink on 13 26 29.

You can purchase a CityLink pass up to midnight on the third day after your nominated day of travel. 24 Hour or Tulla passes are valid for 24 hours from the time of your first trip on CityLink, on your nominated day. A Weekend pass is valid from midday Friday to midnight Sunday. When buying a Weekend pass, your nominated day will be a Saturday.

The CityLink pass you purchase must match the class of vehicle you are renting. All passes are available for cars and light commercial vehicles. Heavy commercial vehicles may only purchase a 24 hour pass.

- **Car:** includes cars towing a trailer or caravan and small buses with 12 or less seats
- **LCV:** any cab chassis, 1.5 – 4.5 tonnes GVM, two axles
- **HCV:** includes rigid trucks with three or more axles or over 4.5 tonnes GVM; buses with 13 or more seats including driver; articulated trucks

Option 3 Use your own CityLink account

If you are already a CityLink customer you can use your own Everyday, Access or Commercial account. (Just remember that if you are using an e-TAG device it must match the vehicle class you are renting.)

All you need to do is call CityLink on 13 26 29 prior to travelling on the road. We will then transfer the primary account status of the rental vehicle and link the licence plate number to your account.

To avoid having to pay future CityLink charges incurred by the rental vehicle, it is important that you contact CityLink again once your rental is completed to remove the licence plate number and primary account status of the vehicle from your account.

TREK FOURTEEN

MOUNT PINNIBAR

On a fine, clear day the magnificent panoramas that unfold from the summit of Mt Pinnibar are breathtaking. Named by Strzelecki on his expedition to Mt Kosciuszko in March 1840, the 1772 metre peak affords vistas over Alpine National Park and across the border to the Kosciuszko Main Range and surrounding ranges.

Things to Do and See

The highlights of this trek are the secluded bush camp sites at Buenba Flat, the enjoyable four-wheel driving over Mt Gibbo and Mt Anderson to Mt Pinnibar and the stunning views across to Mt Kosciuszko from Mt Pinnibar.

Drive through the lush paddocks (please do not trespass by deviating from the signposted route) of the famous High Country Tom Groggin Station and relax on the banks of the mighty Murray River.

Access

Benambra, located 23km north of Omeo is the start point of this trek. Benambra can be reached via the Omeo Highway and Benambra Road from Omeo, the mostly gravel Corryong - Benambra Road from Corryong (128km) or the winding gravel Benambra - Black Mountain Road and Barry Way from Jindabyne (195km).

The Trek

From Benambra head out along the Limestone Road to Beloka Gap where we turn into Beloka Road. From here follow Beloka Road to Buenba Flat, passing Mt Hope Road on the right at Buenba Gap.

Leaving Buenba Flat, the route climbs Smiths Logging Road, passing areas of alpine ash logging and Pheasant Creek Track before meeting at a four way track junction with Wheelers Creek Log Road and Wild Boar Track. Our route turns east into the signposted Pinnibar Track which climbs steeply in sections along a narrow, and in places rocky ridge to the summits of Mt Gibbo and Mt Anderson.

From Mt Anderson continue on Pinnibar Track, where you will notice areas of alpine ash logging at the head of Wheelers Creek until the route joins with the Pinnibar - Tom Groggin Track. At this junction it is a short drive to the summit of Mt Pinnibar with its stunning 360° views.

Leaving Mt Pinnibar, backtrack to the Pinnibar Track junction. This time however, take the Tom Groggin Track which descends steeply through towering ash forest to the lush pastures of Tom Groggin Station on the Murray, or Indi River as it is also known. Follow the signposted track through the property until it joins with the Tom Groggin Track which is then followed to the Murray River crossing, passing Dogmans Hut Camping Area on the way.

fast facts

Benambra to Tom Groggin Camping Area (NSW) via Buenba Flat and Mt Pinnibar

Trek distance: 97km

Standard: Medium (Dry weather only)

Fuel and supplies: Omeo/Benambra and Thredbo/Khancoban

Trek highlights: Buenba Flat, Mt's Gibbo, Anderson and Pinnibar, views from Mt Pinnibar, Tom Groggin Station, Murray River

Track conditions:
Parks Vic Omeo
Ph 03/5159 1660

NPWS Khancoban (NSW)
Ph 02/6076 9373

At this point you have the option of crossing the Murray River into New South Wales or joining with Trek 15 - *Davies Plain* and following Davies Plain Track out to the Black Mountain Road and (if fuel reserves permit - around 270km with a lot of low range 4WD work between fuel stops) picking up Trek 16 - *The Playgrounds* to eventually finish on the Snowy River Road near Willis.

At the ford the route notes cross the Murray River into New South Wales and pass through Tom Groggin Camping Area before concluding on the Alpine Way. Another option here is to travel along the Alpine Way towards Khancoban where at Geehi you can join with Trek 17 - *Geehi Walls*.

Standard

This trek is rated as medium. From Benambra to the start of the Pinnibar Track it is easy going along the well maintained Limestone Creek, Beloka and Buenba Roads. Once on the rocky Pinnibar Track the route climbs steeply in places as it approaches Mt Gibbo and Mt Anderson along a razorback ridge line.

The climb to Mt Pinnibar is moderately steep and the descent from here to Tom Groggin Station on the Tom Groggin Track is also steep in sections.

Tom Groggin Station is private property and a working cattle station. Please do the right thing by obeying all signs (the route is signposted) and do not trespass by deviating from the track, leaving all gates as found.

The crossing of the Murray River at Tom Groggin into New South Wales can be very deep at times (especially during the spring snow melt) and carries a considerable volume of water. Treat this crossing with caution. It is best checked first on foot as the most direct way across is not always the shallowest.

Camping

There is good camping at Buenba Flat with water from Buenba Creek. There are no facilities here.

A number of small clearings exist along Pinnibar Track around the Mt Gibbo and Mt Anderson areas which could be used for an overnight camp.

Towards the end of the trek there is a camping area with facilities at Dogmans Hut on the Victorian side and the very large Tom Groggin Camping Area over the border in New South Wales. Camping is also available at Buckwong Creek, located a few kilometres along Davies Plain Track (see Trek 15 - *Davies Plain*).

Permits/Restriction

Seasonal closures apply to this trek. Seasonal closure gates are located at the start of Pinnibar Track and on the Victorian side of the Murray River crossing at Tom Groggin.

Recommended Maps/Guides

The Hema Maps *High Country - Victoria* map and *The Upper Murray Touring Map & Visitors Guide* both show this trek route. The CFA *North East Rural Directory - Regions 23 and 24* (maps 337, 303, 304) details the route from Buenba Flat to Tom Groggin.

Further Information

Parks Victoria
Day Avenue, Omeo VIC 3898 Ph 03/5159 1660 Fax 03/5159 1665

National Parks and Wildlife Service
Cnr Mitchell Ave and Scott St, Khancoban NSW 2642 Ph 02/6076 9373 Fax 02/6076 9567

Jack Riley - 'The Man From Snowy River'?

Jack Riley is considered by many to be the main contender as 'The Man from Snowy River', the now famous verse written by AB 'Banjo' Paterson. Born in Ireland in 1841, Riley arrived in Australia in 1854 at age 13 where he moved to Omeo and lived with his widowed sister. In Omeo Riley worked for a time as a tailor, a trade he learnt from his father.

Riley eventually left Omeo to pursue his love of horses and riding. His reputation as a bushman, horse breaker and brumby hunter soon grew amongst the riders of the Gippsland and Snowy regions.

In 1884 Riley was employed as manager of Tom Groggin, an area of 20 000 acres situated some 60km upstream of Khancoban on the Murray River, by John Pierce of Greg Greg station in Cooryong. Jack was to drive cattle to Tom Groggin in the summer to graze in the High Country and then return them to Greg Greg as two year olds.

Riley lived a solitary life for some 30 years in a small hut on Tom Groggin Station and became known as the 'Hermit of Tom Groggin'. However, there were times that Pierce employed men to travel to Tom Groggin and assist with clearing and fencing.

One time during the mid 1880s, legend has it Riley joined a party of stockmen trying to capture a thoroughbred stallion that was running with a mob of wild horses near Mt Leatherhead. The stockmen built a yard at the foot of the mountain and Riley predicted the mob would be found on a high ridge, which they were. The riders moved in on the mob and the stallion broke away heading down a frightening slope covered with low scrub, loose stones and wombat holes, with Riley in pursuit. Both the stallion and Riley's pony literally slid down the mountainside to the bottom where the stallion blundered into the stockyard. Riley lifted the sliprails of the yards and waited for the stockmen to join him who had followed a much easier route down.

Jack Riley

The Man From Snowy River legend is said to have begun when a Walter Mitchell introduced Riley to AB 'Banjo' Paterson, when he and Paterson went on a camping trip in the mountains. During the night that they spent at Riley's hut, Jack told his visitors of his adventures in the mountain areas and of his ride and the capture of the thoroughbred running with the wild horses. 'Banjo' Paterson admired the mountain riders and was impressed with Jack's story. It was shortly after that Banjo penned his famous poem, 'The Man From Snowy River'.

The rough mountain life eventually took its toll on Riley's physical condition. When Will Findlay, a local resident and mountain guide, visited him during a muster, he found Riley quite ill and suggested he would take Jack to the doctor in Corryong, but Riley refused his offer.

Will and his companions continued on with their muster and a couple of days later returned to find Jack lying on the floor totally worn out. Quickly making a stretcher out of tree saplings and hessian they set out to carry Riley to the doctor. They left Jack's hut early in the morning on Tuesday July 14, 1914.

The going was rough at Hermit Hill and the snow thick on the ground. They reached the junction of The Hermit and Surveyors Creeks just before dark and camped the night in a deserted miner's hut. Riley's strength seemed to return with one of the party saying "Now he'll be OK", however as they sat by the fire that night Riley quietly passed away in his sleep.

Jack Riley, 'The Man From Snowy River' was buried in the Corryong Cemetery on July 16, 1914.

ROUTE NOTES

Trek starts in the town of Benambra.

▼ 0.0 (0.0)
Zero trip meter in town of Benambra in front of Benambra Hotel. Turn into SP Limestone Rd. SP Black Mountain. Continue on bitumen.
▲ *77.9 (15.8)*
Benambra. TL SP Omeo 22. TR Corryong 122.
GPS S:36 57.311 E:147 42.187
UTM Zone 55 0562594E 5909870N

▼ 15.8 (15.8)
Y junction. VL. SP Beloka Rd. Gravel road commences. Road on right SP Limestone Rd.
▲ *62.1 (1.3)*
Road junction with bitumen. TR. This is Limestone Rd.
GPS S:36 54.011 E:147 48.782
UTM Zone 55 0572437E 5915896N

▼ 17.1 (1.3)
Cross roads. CSA.
▲ *60.8 (0.1)*
Cross roads. CSA.

▼ 17.2 (0.1)
Track on right. CSA.
▲ *60.7 (2.0)*
Track on left. CSA.

▼ 19.2 (2.0)
Track junction. CSA. Track on right SP Heaneys La.
▲ *58.7 (4.1)*
Track on left SP Heaneys La. KR.

▼ 23.3 (4.1)
Track junction. CSA uphill. Track on left SP Beloka Range Tk.
▲ *54.6 (13.7)*
Track on right SP Beloka Range Tk. CSA.

▼ 37.0 (13.7)
Enter SP Alpine National Park.
▲ *40.9 (0.6)*
Exit SP Alpine National Park.

▼ 37.6 (0.6)
Y junction. VL. SP Buenba Rd. Road on right SP Mt Hope Rd.
▲ *40.3 (4.8)*
Road junction. CSA. SP Beloka Rd. Road on left SP Mt Hope Rd.
GPS S:36 45.278 E:147 54.188
UTM Zone 55 0580615E 5931961N

▼ 42.4 (4.8)
Track junction. CSA. Track on left SP Buenba Gap Tk.
▲ *35.5 (1.7)*
Track on right SP Buenba Gap Tk. CSA.

▼ 44.1 (1.7)
Track junction. CSA. Track on right SP Tom Groggin Tk.
▲ *33.8 (0.4)*
Track on left SP Tom Groggin Tk. CSA.

▼ 44.5 (0.4)
Bridge over Buenba Creek. Notes CSA. This is Buenba Flat. Tracks on right before and after bridge lead to camp sites beside the creek. The track on left before the bridge leads to camp sites.
▲ *33.4 (6.2)*
Bridge over Buenba Creek. CSA.
GPS S:36 42.018 E:147 55.264
UTM Zone 55 0582278E 5937981N

▼ 50.7 (6.2)
Track on right. CSA.
▲ *27.2 (2.1)*
Track on left. CSA.

▼ 52.8 (2.1)
Track on left. KR.
▲ *25.1 (2.9)*
Track on right. KL.

▼ 55.7 (2.9)
Track junction. KR on main track. Track on left SP Pheasant Ck Tk.
▲ *22.2 (0.9)*
SP Pheasant Ck Tk on right. KL.

▼ 56.6 (0.9)
Track junction. TR uphill. SP Pinnibar Tk. Track on left SP Wild Boar Tk.

ABOVE: Dogman's Hut and camping area beside the Murray River near Tom Groggin Station.

▲ *21.3 (1.4)*
Track junction. TL. SP Buenba Log Rd. Track SO SP Wild Boar Tk.
GPS S:36 37.527 E:147 54.037
UTM Zone 55 0580521E 5946300N

▼ 58.0 (1.4)
Track junction. CSA uphill. Track on right SP Buenba Tk.
▲ *19.9 (6.2)*
Track junction. CSA downhill. SP To Corryong. SP Benambra Rd. Track on left SP Buenba Tk.

▼ 63.5 (5.5)
Track climbs steeply to Mt Gibbo summit.

▼ 64.2 (0.7)
Summit of Mt Gibbo.
▲ *13.7 (1.8)*
Summit of Mt Gibbo. Track declines steeply from here for next 700m.
GPS S:36 36.753 E:147 57.617
UTM Zone 55 0585876E 5947679N

▼ 66.0 (1.8)
Track junction. CSA. Track on right SP Mt Anderson Tk.
▲ *11.9 (0.1)*
Track junction. KR. SP Pinnibar Gibbo Tk. Track on left SP Mt Anderson Tk.

▼ 66.1 (0.1)
Mt Anderson summit and helipad.
▲ *11.8 (1.8)*
Mt Anderson summit and helipad.

▼ 67.9 (1.8)
Track on left. CSA.
▲ *10.0 (0.2)*
Track on right. CSA.

▼ 68.1 (0.2)
Track on left. CSA.
▲ *9.8 (0.5)*
Track on right. CSA.

▼ 68.6 (0.5)
Track on left. CSA.
▲ *9.3 (0.7)*
Track on right. CSA.

▼ 69.3 (0.7)
Track on left. CSA.
▲ *8.6 (2.4)*
Track on right. CSA.

▼ 71.7 (2.4)
Track junction. CSA. SP Pinnibar Tk. Track on left SP Wheelers Ck Log Rd.
▲ *6.2 (1.8)*
Track junction. CSA. SP Pinnibar Tk. Track on right SP Wheelers Ck Log Rd.
GPS S:36 34.104 E:148 00.032
UTM Zone 55 0589527E 5952537N

▼ 73.5 (1.8)
Track junction. VR.
▲ *4.4 (0.3)*
Track on right. CSA.

▼ 73.8 (0.3)
Track junction. VR uphill. Keeping area of recent logging on left.
▲ *4.1 (0.8)*
Track on right to logging area. CSA.

▼ 74.6 (0.8)
Track on left to logging area. CSA.
▲ *3.3 (1.8)*
Track junction. KL uphill. Keeping area of recent logging on right.

▼ 76.4 (1.8)
Track junction. TL. SP Pinnibar Gibbo Tk. Track on right SP Tom Groggin Tk.
▲ 1.5 (1.5)
Track junction. CSA. SP Pinnibar Gibbo Tk. Track on left SP Tom Groggin Tk.
GPS S:36 32.253 E:148 01.103
UTM Zone 55 0591160E 5955944N

▼ 77.9 (1.5)
Mt Pinnibar Summit. Zero trip meter here and return from way you came.
▲ *0.0 (0.0)*
Mt Pinnibar Summit. Returning way you came.
GPS S:36 32.135 E:148 00.209
UTM Zone 55 0589827E 5956178N

▼ 0.0 (0.0)
Mt Pinnibar Summit. Return way you came. The cleared area directly below is Tom Groggin Station.
▲ *19.6 (1.5)*
Mt Pinnibar Summit. Zero trip meter here and return from way you came.

▼ 1.5 (1.5)
Track junction. TL. SP Tom Groggin Tk. Track drops steeply from here.
▲ 18.1 (10.3)
Track junction. TR uphill SP Pinnibar Gibbo Tk.
GPS S:36 32.253 E:148 01.103
UTM Zone 55 0591160E 5955944N

▼ 11.8 (10.3)
Exit Alpine National Park. Track now passes through Tom Groggin Station. This is private property and all vehicles must keep to signposted route.
▲ *7.8 (0.3)*
Leave private property and enter Alpine National Park. Track climbs steeply in sections from here.

▼ 12.1 (0.3)
CSA. SP To Tom Groggin Tck. To Davies Plain Tck. To Alpine Way.
▲ *7.5 (0.2)*
CSA. SP Mt Pinnibar Tck.

▼ 12.3 (0.2)
Gate. LAF. At junction TR. SP To Tom Groggin Tck.
▲ *7.3 (0.4)*
Track junction. TL through gate. LAF. SP To Mt Pinnibar Tck.

▼ 12.7 (0.4)
Grid. Over grid TR. SP To Tom Groggin Tck.
▲ *6.9 (0.1)*
Track junction. TL over grid. SP To Mt Pinnibar Tck.

▼ 12.8 (0.1)
CSA.
▲ *6.8 (0.5)*
CSA.

▼ 13.3 (0.5)
CSA uphill. Track on right to fence and gate.
▲ *6.3 (0.5)*
CSA. Track on left to fence and gate.

▼ 13.8 (0.5)
Gate. LAF. CSA to T junction. At junction TL. This is Tom Groggin Track. SP To Alpine Way. To Davies Plain Tck.
▲ *5.8 (0.4)*
Track junction. TL. SP To Mt Pinnibar Tck and CSA through gate. LAF. Track now passes through Tom Groggin Station. This is private property and all vehicles must keep to signposted route.
GPS S:36 32.085 E:148 06.514
UTM Zone 55 0599234E 5956165N

▼ 14.2 (0.4)
Track junction. TR uphill. SP Tom Groggin Tck. To Alpine Way. Track SO SP No Through Road.

▲ *5.4 (1.4)*
Track junction. TL. SP Tom Groggin Tck. To Mt Pinnibar Tck. Track on right SP No Through Road.

▼ 15.6 (1.4)
CSA.
▲ *4.0 (0.2)*
CSA.

▼ 15.8 (0.2)
Track junction. CSA. SP To Alpine Way. Track on left SP Camping Area. Leads short distance to Dogmans Hut and camping area.
▲ *3.8 (1.2)*
Track junction. CSA. SP To Mt Pinnibar Tck. Track on right SP Camping Area.

▼ 17.0 (1.2)
Creek crossing.
▲ *2.6 (0.6)*
Creek crossing.

▼ 17.5 (0.5)
Track junction. Hard TL over grid and cross Murray River. SP To Alpine Way. Once over the Murray River enter Kosciuszko National Park. *NB:* Use turning circle short distance up track on right. *NB:* Trek 15 - Davies Plain joins here.
▲ *2.0 (1.0)*
Cross Murray River. Over river track junction. At junction hard TR. SP Tom Groggin Tck. SP To Mt Pinnibar Tck.
GPS S:36 33.124 E:148 07.464
UTM Zone 55 0600630E 5954226N

▼ 18.6 (1.1)
Track on left to camping areas. Notes CSA.
▲ *1.0 (0.6)*
Track on right to camping areas. Notes CSA. SP To Alpine National Park via Davies Plain Trail.

▼ 19.2 (0.6)
Track on left to camping area. CSA.
▲ *0.4 (0.4)*
Track on right to camping area. CSA.

▼ 19.6 (0.4)
T junction with bitumen. This is the Alpine Way. TL for Khancoban and Trek 17 - Geehi Walls 21km. TR for Thredbo/Jindabyne.
▲ *0.0 (0.0)*
Zero trip meter at junction of Alpine Way and SP Tom Groggin Picnic Area. Proceed through picnic area.
GPS S:36 32.303 E:148 08.100
UTM Zone 55 0601597E 5955736N

ABOVE: *Approaching the Summit of Mt Pinnibar with Mt Kosciuszko and the Main Range in the background.*

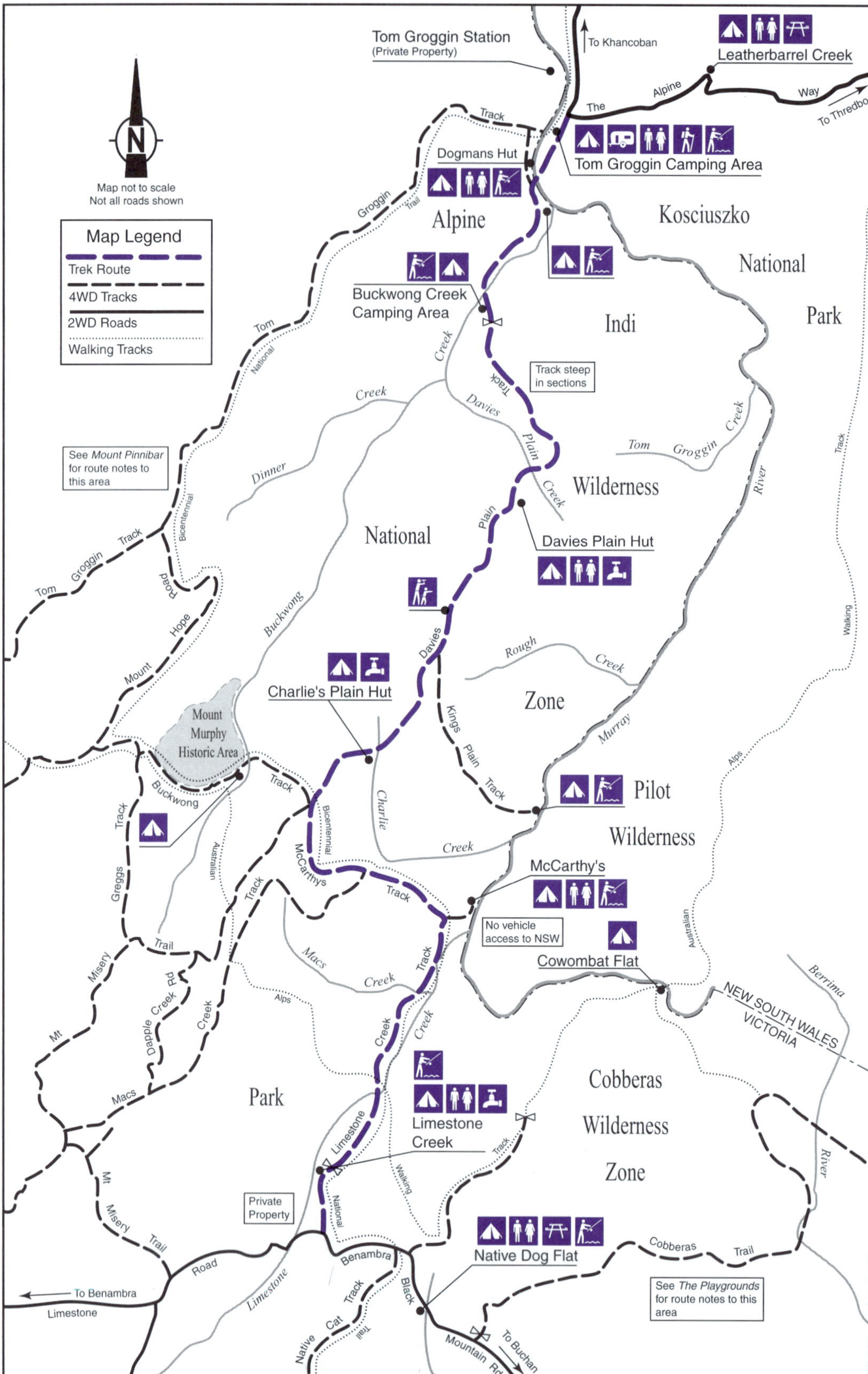
Tom Groggin Station
(Private Property)
To Khancoban
Leatherbarrel Creek
The Alpine Way
To Thredbo
Tom Groggin Camping Area
Dogmans Hut
Map not to scale
Not all roads shown
Map Legend
Trek Route
4WD Tracks
2WD Roads
Walking Tracks
Alpine
Kosciuszko
National
Park
Indi
Buckwong Creek
Camping Area
Track steep
in sections
See Mount Pinnibar
for route notes to
this area
Wilderness
Davies Plain Hut
National
Zone
Charlie's Plain Hut
Mount
Murphy
Historic Area
Pilot
Wilderness
McCarthy's
No vehicle
access to NSW
Cowombat Flat
NEW SOUTH WALES
VICTORIA
Cobberas
Wilderness
Zone
Park
Limestone
Creek
Private
Property
Native Dog Flat
See The Playgrounds
for route notes to this
area
To Benambra
To Buchan

TREK FIFTEEN

DAVIES PLAIN

THE FABLED DAVIES High Plain is one of the most popular four-wheel drive touring destinations in the northern part of the Victorian High Country.

Still used as a summer grazing area for the cattle of Tom Groggin Station, the Davies Plain and Charlie's Plain areas have that wonderful High Country appeal of history, ruggedness and remoteness.

Things to Do and See

Visit Davies Plain Hut, an historic cattlemen's hut built by the Gibson family in 1939. The hut has been largely rebuilt in recent times using traditional construction methods and with its new lease on life it is sure to survive a few more of those freezing alpine winters.

By taking a short detour you can also visit Charlie's Plain Hut on the edge of Charlie's Plain. The area around Charlie's Plain is a good place to catch a glimpse of wild brumbies.

The Murray River and surrounding creeks are popular with trout fisherfolk over the summer months.

Access

This trek commences at the NPWS Tom Groggin Picnic and Camping Area just off the all weather bitumen Alpine Way. Tom Groggin is situated 52km south of Khancoban and 17km west of Thredbo.

The Trek

Starting at the camping area at Tom Groggin on the Alpine Way, our route takes us across the deep ford of the Murray River into Victoria. From here it is a gradual, and at times challenging climb up through towering ash forests and snow gums onto Davies Plain and to Davies Plain Hut with its pleasant camping area. Leaving Davies Plain the route passes through some spectacular mountain scenery, including the picturesque Charlie's Plain, again with good camping before dropping down to the Murray River on McCarthy's Track with its secluded camping. From McCarthy's it's a little over 15 kilometres via the well maintained Limestone Creek Track to the Benambra - Black Mountain Road.

fast facts

Tom Groggin Camping Area (NSW) to Native Dog Flat via Davies High Plain

Trek distance: 59km

Standard: Medium/Hard (Dry weather only)

Fuel and supplies: Thredbo/Khancoban and Omeo/Benambra

Trek highlights: Murray River, Davies High Plain and Hut, Charlie's Plain, McCarthy's

Track conditions:
Parks Vic Omeo
Ph 03/5159 1660

NPWS Khancoban (NSW)
Ph 02/6076 9373

Standard

This route is given a medium/hard rating. The Murray River crossing is impassable at high water and at all times requires caution.

There are a couple of steep climbs up to Davies Plain after crossing Buckwong Creek. Depending on track maintenance careful wheel placement may be needed on this section due to wash-outs.

Keep an eye on the weather as rain makes these tracks very slippery and dangerous and will cause problems at river crossings. This is definitely a dry weather only trek.

Please note, this is remote country and it is advisable to travel in the company of at least one other vehicle. Be prepared for all types of weather conditions—even snow storms in summer.

Camping

Camping is available at the beginning of the trek at the large Tom Groggin Camping Area beside the Murray River. Facilities here include picnic tables, fireplaces and composting toilets.

Once across the river and into Victoria you will find a number of secluded bush camp sites beside the Murray River along the first few kilometres of Davies Plain Track.

There is a large bush camp site at the Buckwong Creek crossing and once up on Davies Plain there is good camping in the vicinity of the hut as well as at a number of secluded sites scattered around the plain. There is a pit toilet near the hut.

After Davies Plain good camping is available at Charlie's Plain, which has a toilet and fireplaces and then down on the Murray River at McCarthy's, which also has limited facilities.

Permits/Restrictions

Seasonal closures apply to this route with winter barriers at the Murray River Crossing, Buckwong Creek and Limestone Creek Track being closed from mid June through to October/November.

Recommended Maps/Guides

The maps covering this route are *The Upper Murray Touring Map and Visitors Guide*, Hema Maps *High Country - Victoria* and the CFA *North East Rural Directory - Regions 23 and 24* (maps 304 and 339).

Topographic map for this trek is the *Jacobs River* 1:100 000 series map.

Further Information

Parks Victoria
Day Avenue, Omeo VIC 3898 Ph 03/5159 1660 Fax 03/5159 1665

National Parks and Wildlife Service
Cnr Mitchell Avenue and Scott Street, Khancoban NSW 2642 Ph 02/6076 9373 Fax 02/6076 9567

Snowy Region Visitors Centre
Kosciuszko Road, Jindabyne Ph 02/6450 5600

Brochures - Parks Victoria: *Alpine National Park - Wilderness and the Snowy around Benambra, Buchan and Bonang*

BELOW: *Amongst the snow gums on Davies Plain Track.*

ROUTE NOTES

Trek commences along the Alpine Way at junction with SP Tom Groggin Picnic Area. This is 17km west of Thredbo.

▼ 0.0 (0.0)
Zero trip meter on the Alpine Way at junction with SP Tom Groggin Picnic Area. PSA through the picnic area. SP To Alpine National Park via Davies Plain Trail.
▲ *59.0 (0.4)*
Road junction. This is the Alpine Way. TR for Thredbo. TL for Khancoban and Trek 17 - Geehi Walls 21km.
GPS S:36 32.303 E:148 08.100
UTM Zone 55 0601597E 5955736N

▼ 0.4 (0.4)
Track on right to camping areas. Notes CSA.
▲ *58.6 (0.6)*
Track on left to camping areas. Notes CSA.

▼ 1.0 (0.6)
Track on right. CSA. SP To Alpine National Park via Davies Plain Trail. Four Wheel Drive Dry Weather Road Only.
▲ *58.0 (1.1)*
Track on left to camping areas. Notes CSA.

▼ 2.0 (1.0)
Cross Murray River.

▼ 2.1 (0.1)
Track junction. CSA SP Davies Plain Tk and enter Alpine National Park. Track on right SP Tom Groggin Tk.
▲ *56.9 (1.1)*
Track junction. VR and cross Murray River. SP Alpine Way. Track on left SP Tom Groggin Tk.
GPS S:36 33.124 E:148 07.464
UTM Zone 55 0600630E 5954226N

▼ 3.2 (1.1)
Minor track on left leads to camping area by river. Notes CSA.
▲ *55.8 (0.6)*
Minor track on right. CSA.

▼ 3.8 (0.6)
Track on left. CSA.
▲ *55.2 (1.2)*
Track on right. KL.

▼ 5.0 (1.2)
Creek crossing. This is Buckwong Creek. Bush camp sites across creek.
▲ *54.0 (1.0)*
Bush camp sites in this area. CSA and cross creek. This is Buckwong Creek.

▼ 6.0 (1.0)
Seasonal closure barrier. Track climbs steeply from here.
▲ *53.0 (12.1)*
Seasonal closure barrier.

▼ 18.1 (12.1)
Enter snow plain.
▲ *40.9 (0.3)*
Enter forest. Track drops steely from forest.

▼ 18.4 (0.3)
Cross creek.
▲ *40.6 (0.3)*
Cross creek.

▼ 18.7 (0.3)
Track junction. KR past horse/cattle yards on left. Track on left to Davies Hut and camping areas.
▲ *40.3 (7.1)*
Track junction. KL. Horseyards on right. Track on right to Davies Hut.
GPS S:36 39.030 E:148 07.534
UTM Zone 55 0600605E 5943301N

▼ 25.8 (7.1)
Enter snow plain.
▲ *33.2 (1.2)*
Enter snow plain.

▼ 27.0 (1.2)
Track junction. CSA. SP Davies Plain Tk. Track on left SP Kings Plain Tk.
▲ *32.0 (4.8)*
Track junction. CSA. SP Davies Plain Tk. Track on right SP Kings Plain Tk.

▼ 31.8 (4.8)
Cross Charlie's Creek and enter Charlie's Plain. Camping on right over creek.
▲ *27.2 (0.3)*
Cross Charlie's Creek.
GPS S:36 43.943 E:148 03.871
UTM Zone 55 0595055E 5934286N

▼ 32.1 (0.3)
Track junction. KR. Track on left leads 300m to Charlie's Hut.
▲ *26.9 (2.5)*
Track junction. KL and cross Charlie's Creek.

▼ 34.6 (2.5)
Cross roads. TL. SP McCarthy Tk. Track on right SP Buckwong Tk leads 4.4km to hut. Track SO SP Misery Trail.
▲ *24.4 (5.7)*
Cross roads. TR. SP Davies Plain Tk. Track on left SP Misery Trail. Track SO SP Buckwong Tk.
GPS S:36 44.675 E:148 02.649
UTM Zone 55 0593215E 5932966N

▼ 40.3 (5.7)
Track junction. CSA. SP McCarthys Tk. Track on right SP Mac's Creek Tk.
▲ *18.7 (3.4)*
Track junction. CSA. SP McCarthys Tk. Track climbs steeply from here. Track on left SP Mac's Creek Tk.

▼ 43.7 (3.4)
Track junction. TR. SP Limestone Creek Tk. Track SO SP McCarthys Tk leads 1.1km to camping areas.
▲ *15.3 (0.7)*
Track junction. TL. SP McCarthys Tk. Track on right leads 1.1km to camping areas.
GPS S:36 46.761 E:148 05.847
UTM Zone 55 0597927E 5929046N

▼ 44.4 (0.7)
Creek crossing.
▲ *14.6 (3.5)*
Creek crossing.

▼ 47.7 (3.3)
Steep rutted climb.
▲ *11.1 (1.6)*
Steep rutted descent.

▼ 49.5 (1.8)
Creek crossing. Small bush camp sites over creek. Track now climbs steeply.
▲ *9.5 (1.1)*
Creek crossing.

▲ *8.4 (1.7)*
Track drops steeply to creek.

▼ 52.3 (2.8)
Bush camp site on left. CSA and cross creek.
▲ *6.7 (0.7)*
Creek crossing.

▼ 53.0 (0.7)
Creek crossing.
▲ *6.0 (0.9)*
Creek crossing.

▼ 53.9 (0.9)
Minor track on right leads to camping on creek flats. Notes CSA.
▲ *5.1 (0.5)*
Minor track on left. CSA.

▼ 54.4 (0.5)
Track junction. TL. Track on right to bush camp sites.
▲ *4.6 (0.8)*
Track junction. TR. Track SO to camping areas.
GPS S:36 50.535 E:148 03.964
UTM Zone 55 0595051E 5922099N

▼ 55.2 (0.8)
Seasonal closure barrier.
▲ *3.8 (1.3)*
Seasonal closure barrier.

▼ 56.5 (1.3)
SP Limestone Creek Camping Area on right. Notes CSA.
▲ *2.5 (1.0)*
SP Limestone Creek Camping Area on left. Notes CSA.
GPS S:36 51.319 E:148 03.307
UTM Zone 55 0594060E 5920660N

▼ 57.5 (1.0)
Exit Alpine National Park.
▲ *1.5 (1.5)*
Enter Alpine National Park.

▼ 59.0 (1.5)
Track junction. This is the Limestone-Black Mountain Road. TR for Benambra. TL for Jindabyne and Buchan or TL to join Trek 16 - The Playgrounds at Native Dog Flat 6.7km.
▲ *0.0 (0.0)*
Zero trip meter on the Limestone-Black Mountain Road at junction with SP Limestone Ck Tk. PSA along Limestone Ck Tk.
GPS S:36 52.366 E:148 03.117
UTM Zone 55 0593755E 5918727N

OPPOSITE: *Crossing Davies Plain Creek.*

BBP 001
Boiling Billy Publications

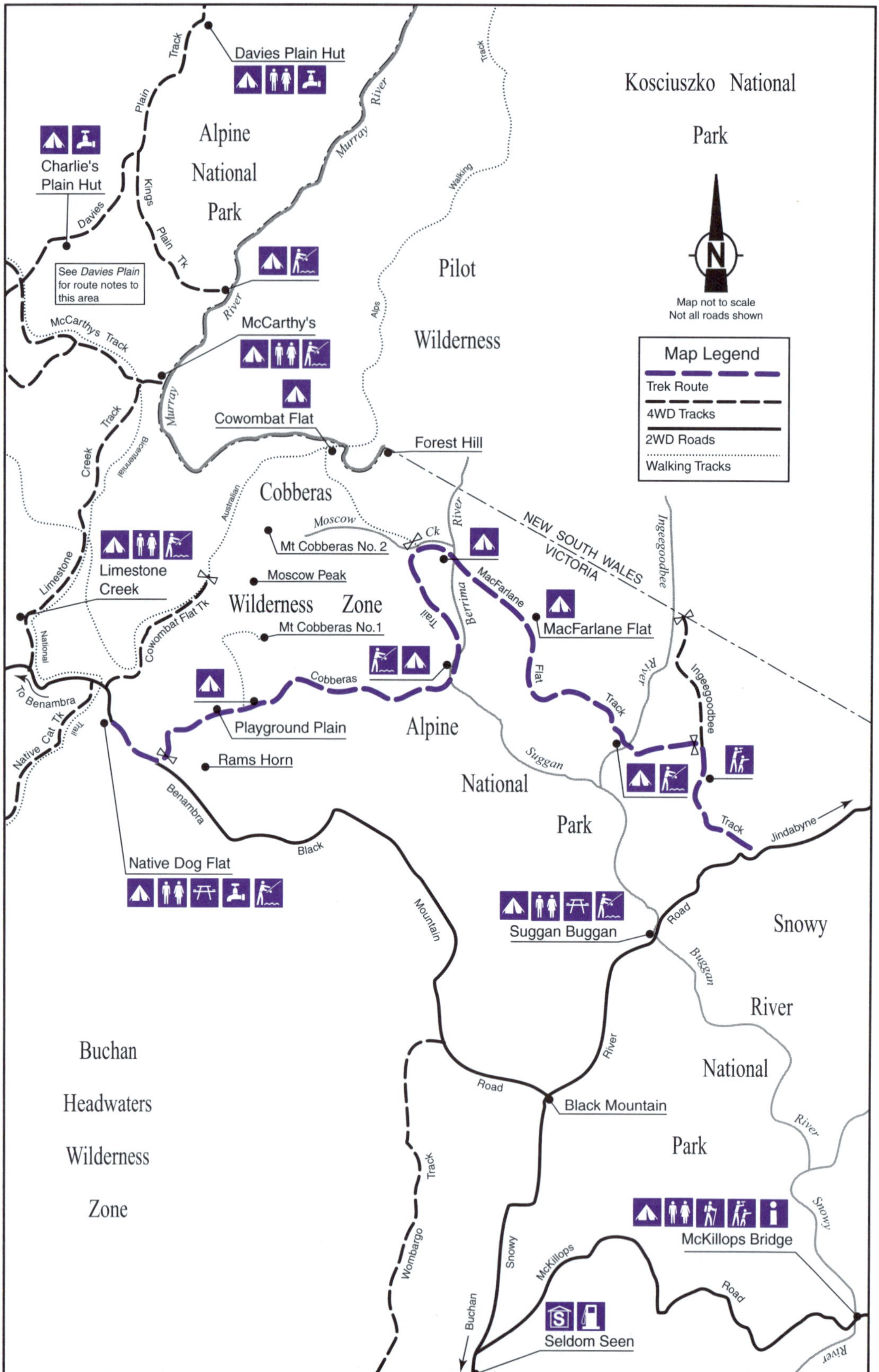
Davies Plain Hut
Charlie's Plain Hut
Davies
Plain
Track
Kings Plain Tk
Alpine National Park
Murray River
See *Davies Plain* for route notes to this area
McCarthys Track
McCarthy's
Cowombat Flat
Forest Hill
Kosciuszko National Park
Pilot Wilderness
Walking
Alps
Track
Map not to scale
Not all roads shown
Map Legend
Trek Route
4WD Tracks
2WD Roads
Walking Tracks
Limestone Creek Track
Bicentennial
Cobberas
Australian
Moscow Ck
Mt Cobberas No. 2
River
NEW SOUTH WALES
VICTORIA
Ingeegoodbee
Limestone Creek
Moscow Peak
Wilderness Zone
MacFarlane
MacFarlane Flat
Cowombat Flat Tk
Mt Cobberas No.1
Trail
Berrima
Flat
National
To Benambra
Cobberas
Playground Plain
Alpine
Track
Ingeegoodbee
Native Cat Tk
Trail
Rams Horn
Suggan
National
Benambra
Park
Track
Jindabyne
Black
Native Dog Flat
Mountain
Suggan Buggan
Road
Snowy
Buggan
River
Buchan Headwaters Wilderness Zone
Road
River
Black Mountain
National
River
Park
Track
Wombargo
Snowy
McKillops
Road
McKillops Bridge
Snowy
Buchan
Seldom Seen
River

TREK 16

TREK SIXTEEN

THE PLAYGROUNDS

THE AREA EXPLORED on this trek was part of the original route used by early pioneers travelling from the Monaro area in New South Wales to Omeo. First opened up by George MacKillop, George Livingstone and James MacFarlane in 1835, this area is some of the most remote in the High Country. In times past weary travellers, upon reaching 'The Playground', would have appreciated the parklike snow plain after their climb through the Snowy and Ingeegoodbee Rivers and through the Cobberas.

MacFarlane Flat, which is also visited on this trek, is named after James MacFarlane who had established his cattle run here on the Victorian side of the border. MacFarlane is believed to have been the first settler in this part of the state and he helped establish the stock route from the Monaro Plains to Omeo.

Things to Do and See

You can walk to Cowombat Flat, a large grassy plain where the Murray River springs as a tiny mountain stream. Here it becomes the NSW/Vic border as surveyed in 1870 by Alexander Black from Victoria and Alexander Allen from New South Wales. Access to Cowombat Flat from this trek is from the locked gate at Moscow Creek from MacFarlane's Flat Track .

Both the Australian Alps Walking Trail and the Bicentennial National Trail pass close to this trek and you could join these and walk a short section. There is a walk to the summit of Mount Cobberas No. 1 that is for experienced walkers only.

Along Cobberas Trail there are excellent views to the craggy Mt Cobberas and above Ingeegoodbee River there are some magnificent views to be had over the surrounding wilderness areas and over the border to the NSW ranges.

fast facts

Native Dog Flat to Willis (VIC/NSW Border) via The Playground Plain and MacFarlane Flat

Trek distance: 50km

Standard: Medium/Hard (Dry weather only)

Fuel and supplies: Omeo/Benambra and Seldom Seen/Buchan and Jindabyne

Trek highlights: The Playgrounds and MacFarlane Flat, enjoyable four-wheel driving and scenic views

Track conditions:
Parks Vic Omeo
Ph 03/5159 1660

Access

Native Dog Flat, which is the start point for this trek is located on the gravel Benambra - Black Mountain Road, 45km east of Benambra.

The Trek

Starting from Native Dog Flat our route continues along the Benambra - Black Mountain Road until the signposted turn for Cobberas Trail. Heading north towards the Cobberas on Cobberas Trail, it's a slow and bumpy ride until The Playground plain is reached. The track then skirts the southern side of the plain and around to the eastern face of Mount Cobberas No. 1.

Once past the Cobberas the track crosses a few creeks before reaching the large open grassy plain of MacFarlane Flat which runs parallel with the border. From here the track makes its way down to the Ingeegoodbee River crossing. Once across the river there is a long steep climb to the top of the ridge then an easy run to the Mt Mennak Trig and the Alpine National Park boundary. From here the track drops down to meet the Snowy River Road and the conclusion of the trek, 12km south of the Vic/NSW border.

Standard

This route is rated medium/hard due the long and steep climb from the Ingeegoodbee River on McFarlane's Flat Track. This track has a loose gravelly surface where wheel spin and loss of traction is likely.

The Cobberas Trail is slow going with numerous large rocks, however, once on MacFarlane's Flat Track the going is a little easier until the Ingeegoodbee River crossing.

Camping

Native Dog Flat is a large grassy area beside the Buchan River. Here you will find picnic tables, a composting toilet and an information board. There is bush camping at The Playgrounds and at MacFarlane Flat. Neither of these sites have facilities. In addition there are a few other bush camp sites detailed in the route notes.

Permits/Restrictions

Seasonal closures apply to this trek. Also, the Benambra - Black Mountain Road may be closed at times during the winter months due to snow coverage.

Recommended Maps/Guides

The best map for this trek is the *Jacobs Creek* 1:100 000 topographic map.

The Hema *High Country - Victoria* map also shows this trek and the CFA *North East Rural Directory Regions 23 and 24* (Map 339) shows part.

Further Information

Parks Victoria
Day Avenue, Omeo VIC 3898 Ph 03/5159 1660 Fax 03/5159 1665

BELOW: *High up on a ridge looking over the Ingeegoodbee River.*

ROUTE NOTES

Trek commences at Native Dog Flat along the Limestone-Black Mountain Road.

▼ 0.0 (0.0)
Zero trip meter on Limestone-Black Mountain Road at Native Dog Flat. This is 48km east of Benambra and 49km north west of Seldom Seen. Parks information board on right. Proceed along Limestone-Black Mountain Road in south-east direction towards Black Mountain.
▲ *49.9 (2.1)*
Native Dog Flat. Parks information board on left.
GPS S:36 53.741 E:148 05.392
UTM Zone 55 0597104E 5916146N

▼ 2.1 (2.1)
Track junction. VL through seasonal closure gate. SP Cobberas Trail. SP Playgrounds Plain.
▲ *47.8 (3.4)*
Seasonal closure gate. CSA to intersection with Limestone-Black Mountain Rd. TL for Jindabyne/Buchan. Notes TR for Native Dog Flat and Benambra.
GPS S:36 54.223 E:148 06.390
UTM Zone 55 0598578E 5915236N

▼ 5.5 (3.4)
Bush camp site on left. CSA.
▲ *44.4 (0.3)*
Bush camp site on right. CSA.

▼ 5.8 (0.3)
Creek crossing.
▲ *44.1 (0.2)*
Creek crossing.

▼ 6.0 (0.2)
KR. The Playgrounds Plain and camp sites on left. Views across to Mt Cobberas No 1 along this section of track.
▲ *43.9 (2.3)*
The Playgrounds Plain and camping on right. CSA.

▼ 8.3 (2.3)
Minor track on left to snow plain. CSA.
▲ *41.6 (2.8)*
Minor track on right. CSA. Views across to Mt Cobberas No 1 along this section of track.

▼ 11.0 (2.7)
Small creek crossing. Track climbs steeply from creek.
▲ *38.8 (7.7)*
Steep descent to small creek crossing.

▼ 18.8 (7.8)
River crossing. Good camp site on left over river.
▲ *31.1 (0.1)*
Camp site on right. CSA and cross river.
GPS S:36 51.987 E:148 14.086
UTM Zone 55 0610064E 5919238N

▼ 18.9 (0.1)
River crossing. Exit is very rocky. Track climbs steeply from here.
▲ *31.0 (5.8)*
River crossing. Very rocky entry.

▼ 24.7 (5.8)
Track junction. CSA. SP McFarlane's Flat Tk. Track on left leads 500m to Wilderness Boundary and locked gate at Moscow Creek. Cowombat Flat walking trail leads from gate.
▲ *25.2 (0.8)*
Track junction. TL. SP Cobberas Tk. Track SO leads 500m to Wilderness Boundary.
GPS S:36 49.726 E:148 13.135
UTM Zone 55 0608700E 5923430N

▼ 25.5 (0.8)
Possible bush camping in this area.
▲ *24.4 (2.1)*
Possible bush camping in this area.

▼ 27.6 (2.1)
Creek crossing. Over creek minor track on left. KR. Possible bush camp sites in this area.
▲ *22.3 (2.1)*
Minor track on right. CSA and cross creek. SP MacFarlane Flat Tk.

▼ 29.7 (2.1)
Gate. LAF.
▲ *20.2 (0.4)*
Gate. LAF.

Boiling Billy Publications

▼ 30.1 (0.4)
MacFarlane's Flat. Possible camping in this vicinity.
▲ *19.8 (0.8)*
MacFarlane's Flat.
GPS S:36 51.177 E:148 15.546
UTM Zone 55 0612247E 5920708N

▼ 30.9 (0.8)
Minor track on left. CSA.
▲ *19.0 (0.4)*
Minor track on right. CSA.

▼ 31.3 (0.4)
Gate. LAF.
▲ *18.6 (3.2)*
Gate. LAF.

▼ 34.5 (3.2)
Small creek crossing – normally dry.
▲ *15.4 (0.6)*
Small creek crossing – normally dry.

▼ 35.1 (0.6)
Small creek crossing.
▲ *14.8 (0.4)*
Small creek crossing.

▼ 35.5 (0.4)
Small creek crossing – normally dry. Track climbs steeply from here.
▲ *14.4 (3.2)*
Small creek crossing – normally dry.

▼ 38.7 (3.2)
Cross Ingeegoodbee River. Camp sites on right prior to river. Track climbs steeply from river.
▲ *11.2 (0.3)*
Cross Ingeegoodbee River.
GPS S:36 53.760 E:148 18.470
UTM Zone 55 0616527E 5915862N

▲ *10.9 (0.3)*
Steep descent to river crossing.

▼ 39.3 (0.6)
Minor tracks on right. CSA on main track. From here track begins to climb steeply with a number of short steep climbs for 1.2km.
▲ *10.6 (1.2)*
Minor tracks on left. CSA on main track.

OPPOSITE: *Lunch and a Cuppa along McFarlane's Flat Track.*

▲ *9.4 (1.7)*
Track declines steeply from here with a number of short steep sections.

▼ 42.2 (2.9)
Seasonal closure gates. CSA to track junction. TR. SP Ingeegoodbee Tk.
▲ *7.7 (1.5)*
Track junction. TL. SP MacFarlanes Flat Tk. CSA through seasonal closure gate.
GPS S:36 53.592 E:148 20.231
UTM Zone 55 0619147E 5916141N

▼ 43.7 (1.5)
Mt Menaak Trig.
▲ *6.2 (1.2)*
Mt Menaak Trig.

▼ 44.9 (1.2)
Helipad. Spectacular views.
▲ *5.0 (1.8)*
Helipad.
GPS S:38 54.655 E:148 20.186
UTM Zone 55 0619066E 5914176N

▼ 46.7 (1.8)
Exit Alpine National Park.
▲ *3.2 (1.5)*
Enter Alpine National Park.

▼ 48.2 (1.5)
Minor track on right. CSA.
▲ *1.7 (0.4)*
Minor track on left. CSA.

▼ 48.6 (0.4)
Minor track on right. CSA.
▲ *1.3 (0.2)*
Minor track on left. CSA.

▼ 48.8 (0.2)
Minor track on right. CSA.
▲ *1.1 (1.1)*
Minor track on left. CSA.

▼ 49.9 (1.1)
T junction. This is the Snowy River Road. TL for Willis and NSW/Vic border 12km and Jindabyne 85km via The Barry Way. TR for Buchan 87km/Benambra.
▲ *0.0 (0.0)*
Zero trip meter on Snowy River Road at junction of SP Ingeegoodbee Tk. Turn into Ingeegoodbee Tk and climb uphill.
GPS S:36 56.137 E:148 21.884
UTM Zone 55 0621535E 5911399N

4WD TREKS IN THE NEW SOUTH WALES HIGH COUNTRY

Murrumbidgee River at Tantangara Dam

KEY MAP 2 - NEW SOUTH WALES

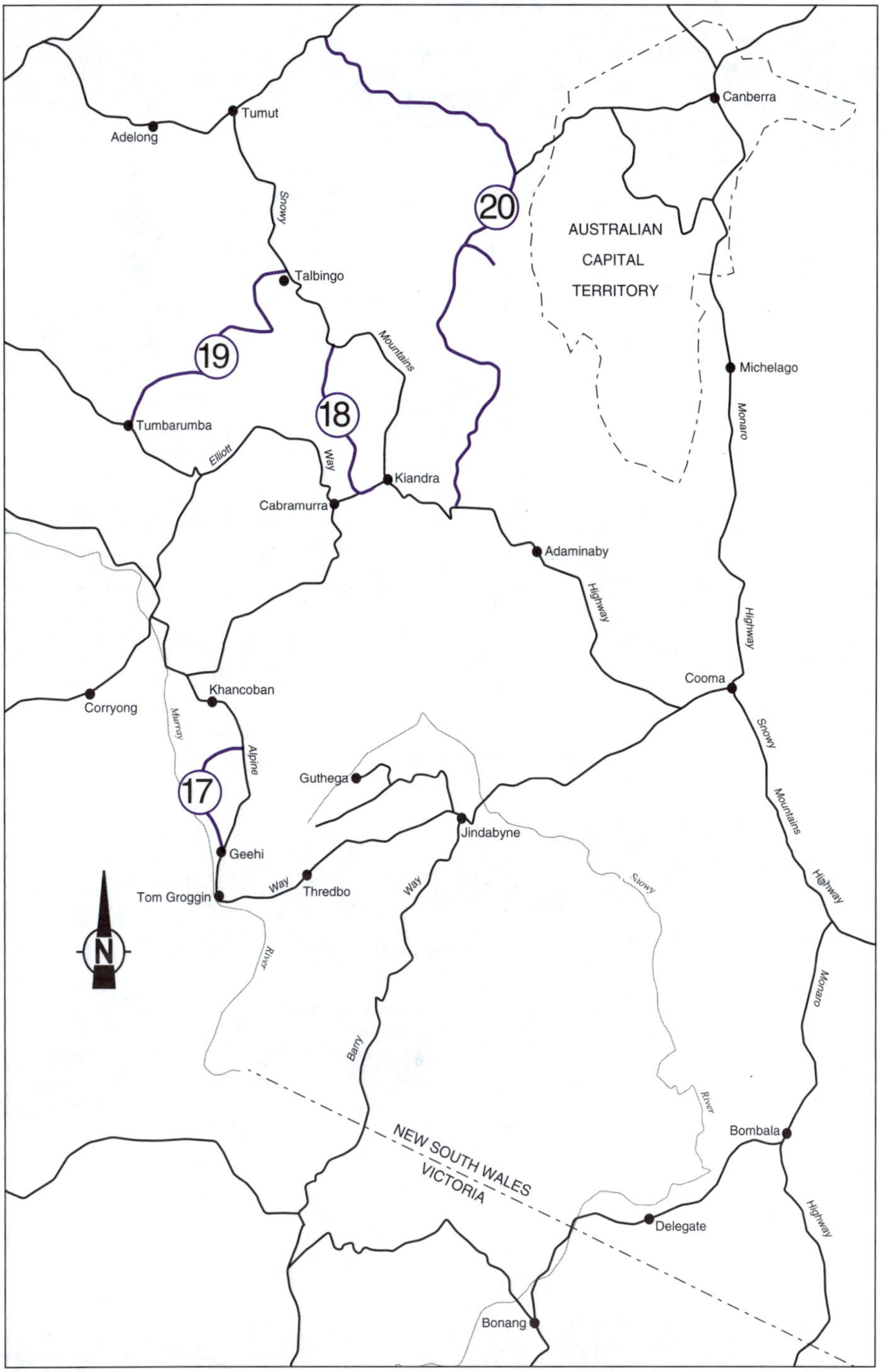

17. Geehi Walls
18. Ravine - Hidden Valley
19. Best of Bago
20. Broken Cart Trail

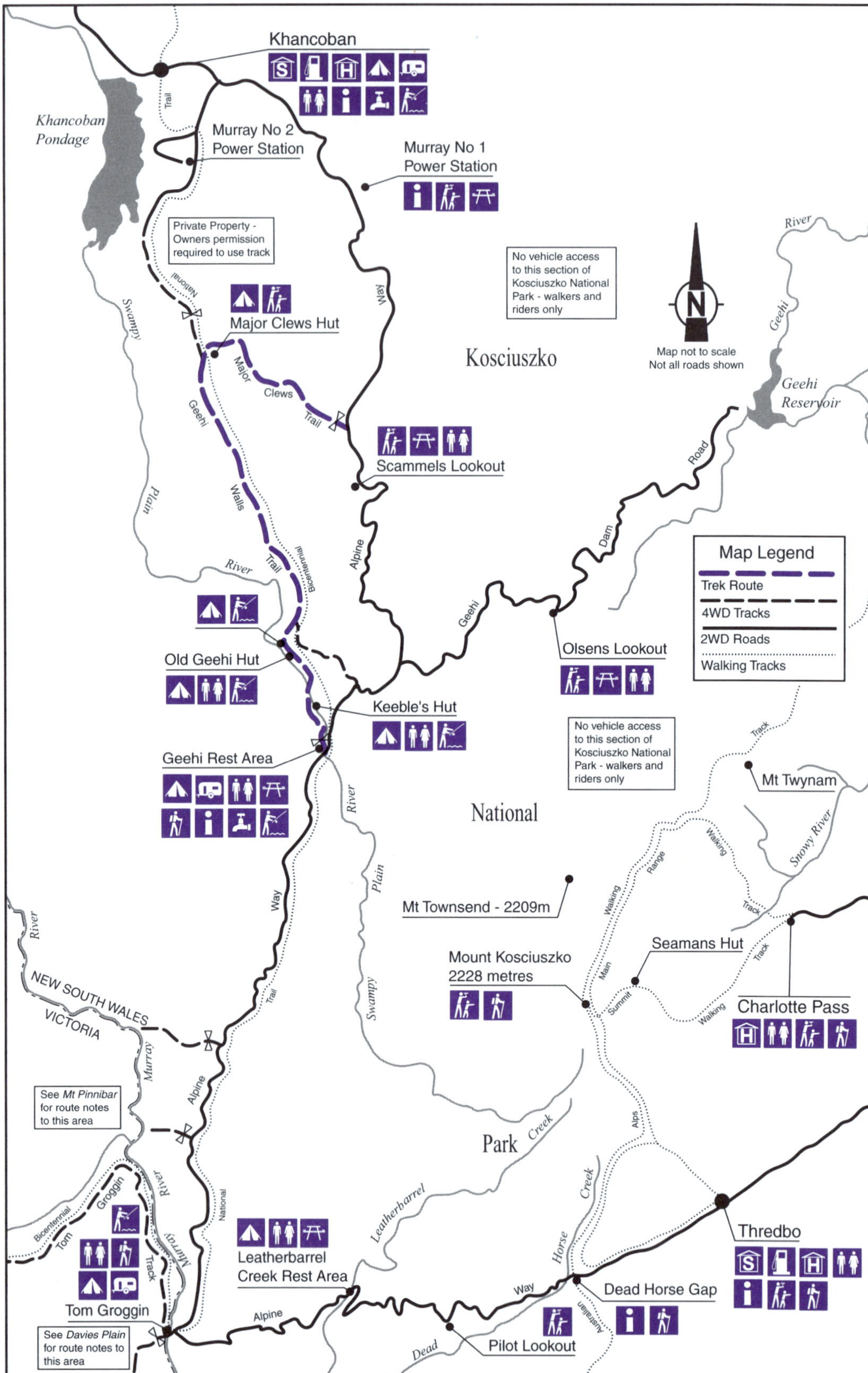
Khancoban
Khancoban Pondage
Trail
Murray No 2 Power Station
Murray No 1 Power Station
Private Property - Owners permission required to use track
No vehicle access to this section of Kosciuszko National Park - walkers and riders only
Map not to scale
Not all roads shown
Major Clews Hut
Major Clews Trail
Kosciuszko
National
Park
Geehi Reservoir
River
Geehi
Swampy Plain River
Geehi Walls Trail
Bicentennial
Alpine Way
Scammels Lookout
Geehi Dam Road
Map Legend
Trek Route
4WD Tracks
2WD Roads
Walking Tracks
Old Geehi Hut
Keeble's Hut
Olsens Lookout
Geehi Rest Area
Mt Twynam
Snowy River
Walking Track
Main Range
Mt Townsend - 2209m
Mount Kosciuszko 2228 metres
Seamans Hut
Summit Walking Track
Charlotte Pass
NEW SOUTH WALES
VICTORIA
Murray River
See Mt Pinnibar for route notes to this area
Creek
Tom Groggin Track
Bicentennial
National
Leatherbarrel Creek Rest Area
Leatherbarrel
Horse Creek
Alps
Thredbo
Dead Horse Gap
Australian Alps
Tom Groggin
See Davies Plain for route notes to this area
Pilot Lookout
Dead

TREK 17

TREK SEVENTEEN

GEEHI WALLS

SITTING IN THE SHADOW of the craggy western side of the towering Main Range is Geehi—a one time Snowy Mountains Hydro-electric Authority worker's camp during the late 1950s and early 1960s.

Before the Snowy Mountains Scheme, the Geehi Valley was considered a hidden paradise. The local farmers saw the river flats as excellent grazing country, and the well-to-do professionals of Sydney and Melbourne saw the area as a fishing retreat where they built their impressive huts from local river stone.

These days this area is a haven for recreation with campers and fisherfolk taking advantage of delightful Geehi. During late afternoons numerous mobs of kangaroos graze on the flats.

Things to Do and See

There's plenty to see and do at Geehi. Besides taking in the awe inspiring rocky outcrops of the Main Range that towers over the camping area you can watch the wildlife feed in the late afternoon or take a walk along the Bicentennial National Trail.

There are five huts built of river stone on Geehi Flats and this trek visits three of them, namely Geehi, Keebles and Old Geehi Huts. Both Doctors Hut and Dr Forbes Hut are walk-in only access.

Visit Major Clews Hut, which he hand built himself from mud brick. Its isolated site typifies the Major's love of the bush and his dislike for modern society.

Swampy Plain River contains trout for those who wish to try their luck, or in the hotter months it's a great spot for a cooling dip.

Access

The trek commences at Geehi Rest Area which is signposted from the Alpine Way, an all weather bitumen road. Geehi is located 31km south of Khancoban and 21km north of Tom Groggin.

fast facts

Geehi Rest Area to The Alpine Way via Geehi Walls Fire Trail and Major Clews Hut

Trek distance: 22km

Standard: Easy (Dry weather only)

Fuel and supplies: Thredbo/Jindabyne and Khancoban

Trek highlights: Views of the Main Range, Swampy Plain River, Numerous stone huts, Major Clews Hut

Track conditions:
NPWS Khancoban
Ph 02/6076 9373

The Trek

Leaving the bitumen at Geehi Rest Area the trek travels through the camping area to the crossing of Swampy Plain River. This crossing, although wide is generally easy in low water, however do check water depth and river flow prior to crossing.

Once across Swampy Plain River you enter the vast expanse of Bears Flat where you pass Keebles Hut before making your way to the next river crossing. Just prior to this crossing there is a cleared area to the right from where you can wade across to Doctors Hut on the opposite bank. Be aware, this second crossing of Swampy Plain River is much wider and at times it is difficult to judge the water depth here.

Our route now follows the river to the next hut, Old Geehi Hut at Round Flat beside the Swampy Plain River, prior to heading north along the scenic Geehi Walls Fire Trail to the junction of Walls Creek and Bogong Creek. There is a small bridge at this crossing with the track just before the bridge leading to the Swampy Plain River.

The track now climbs the steep and winding southern end of Geehi Walls, passing through forests of wonderful manna gums and eurabbie blue gums.

Once on top of the Geehi Walls the route meets with Major Clews Fire Trail, where it is only a short detour to Major Clews Hut. From Major Clews Hut the trail drops to a small crossing of Back Creek before climbing up Clews Ridge to the conclusion of the trek on the Alpine Way near Scammels Lookout.

Standard

This trek is rated easy and is an ideal trek for those new to four-wheel drive touring, although old hands will enjoy the area's history and scenery.

As previously mentioned, the crossings of Swampy Plain River are wide and the water is quite clear, making it difficult to judge the water depth. If in doubt it is best to check the crossings on foot before plunging in.

Camping

At Geehi Rest Area you will find plenty of shaded, grassy spots beside Swampy Plain River. Facilities here include fireplaces, picnic tables and toilets with wheelchair access. There is also an information board with details on the area. This area can become very crowded during holiday periods.

Once on the Geehi Plains you will find camping in the vicinity of Keebles Hut and Old Geehi Hut; both areas have a toilet. There is camping in the vicinity of Major Clews Hut, although there are no facilities.

In addition to the established camping areas there are a number of bush camp sites beside Swampy Plain River, notably at the second river crossing and at the junction of Swampy Plain River and Bogong Creek. These are detailed in the route notes.

Permits/Restrictions

This route is restricted by seasonal road closures at the crossing of Swampy Plain River and on Major Clews Trail during the winter months. During the spring snow melt the route may be impassable at the river crossings.

Recommended Maps/Guides

The CMA Tourist Map, *The Snowy Mountains* shows this trek as does the CMA *The Snowy Mountains Tourist Atlas* and the CFA *North East Rural Directory Regions 23 and 24* (Map 269).

The topographic map for this route is the *Mount Kosciusko* 1:50 000 series map.

Further Information

National Parks and Wildlife Service
Cnr Mitchell Avenue and Scott Street, Khancoban NSW 2642 Ph 02/6076 9373 Fax 02/6076 9567

Snowy Region Visitors Centre
Kosciuszko Road, Jindabyne Ph 02/6450 5600

The 'Major'

When the Snowy Mountains Hydro-electric Scheme was first mooted in the early 1900s much of Australia's mountain country hadn't been mapped and it wasn't until the late 1940s when the scheme came to fruition that teams of surveyors began to comb the Snowy Mountains to gather information for this engineering wonder.

Lieutenant Colonel Hugh Powell Clews

The man in charge of all this was an ex-army surveyor Hugh Powell Clews. Born in Yorkshire in 1890, Clews trained there as a surveyor before immigrating to Western Australia in 1910 where he worked surveying the wheat belt.

After 37 years and a distinguished career as a surveyor in the Australian Army he retired in 1949 as a lieutenant colonel.

In January of 1950 at the age of sixty, 'The Major', a name that stuck with him until his death, came out of retirement to join the Snowy Mountains project. He was in charge of the first survey party beginning work at Tumut Pond.

From their base camp at Cabramurra the survey teams crisscrossed the mountain ranges on horseback, using packhorses to carry equipment and supplies. However the Major disliked riding horses, so he walked.

The party were to use information gained in 1874 by surveyors who had marked the New South Wales/ Victorian boundary. However, they had trouble finding the original blazed trees and stone cairns of seventy five years previous with the survey teams only locating two of the original cairns. Using these two cairns along with other information the whole Kosciuszko region was remapped for engineering requirements. Their job was to cut the first tracks around the steep slopes and map the region. The mapping of the mountains and the trails that Clews and his party blazed helped the realisation of the Snowy Scheme.

The Major was renowned for his hard work and those who surveyed with him often said that the work was exhausting and done at a cracking pace, with many miles of track cleared and levelled each day.

ABOVE: *Major Clews Hut*

Seldom seen without his trademark pipe, the Major would, apparently, turn it upside down when it rained and keep puffing away. He was also fond of a tot of rum and carried a hip flask with him during his wanderings throughout the mountains.

His love was the bush and he hated the intrusions of modern society. When the Major retired from the Snowy Scheme in 1958 he built a mud brick cottage in the bush in the Indi region that he so loved. Here he lived a quiet life until his death in 1980.

ROUTE NOTES

Trek commences on the Alpine Way at the signposted entrance to Geehi Rest Area.

▼ 0.0 (0.0)
Zero trip meter on Alpine Way at entrance to SP Geehi Rest Area. This is beside Swampy Plains River, 31km south of Khancoban and 21km north of Tom Groggin. Proceed through rest area and camping area.
▲ *21.7 (0.9)*
T junction with bitumen. This is the Alpine Way. TL for Khancoban 31km. TR for Tom Groggin (21km) and Treks 14 and 15.
GPS S:36 23.112 E:148 10.893
UTM Zone 55 0605970E 5972678N

▼ 0.9 (0.9)
Geehi Hut on right. VL.
▲ *20.8 (0.1)*
Geehi Hut on left. TR.

▼ 1.0 (0.1)
Cross Swampy Plains River and CSA through seasonal closure gate.
▲ *20.7 (0.9)*
Cross Swampy Plains River.

▼ 1.9 (0.9)
Track junction. TL. Track SO leads short distance to Kebbles Hut and camping area.
▲ *19.8 (0.8)*
Track junction. TR. Track on left to hut and camping area.

▼ 2.7 (0.8)
Minor track on right to camp site. CSA.
▲ *19.0 (0.3)*
Minor track on left to camp site. CSA.

▼ 2.9 (0.2)
Track on left to camping sites. CSA and cross river. This is a wide crossing.
▲ *18.7 (0.3)*
Cross river. Over river track on right. CSA.

▼ 3.3 (0.4)
Track junction. TR. Track on left leads 200m to camp sites and Old Geehi Hut.
▲ *18.4 (0.8)*
Track junction. TL. Track SO to camp site and hut.
GPS S:36 21.656 E:148 09.962
UTM Zone 55 0604617E 5975384N

▼ 4.1 (0.8)
Track junction. TL downhill. SP Geehi Walls Fire Trail.
▲ *17.6 (1.0)*
Track junction. TR.

▼ 5.1 (1.0)
Track on left to small bush camp site by river. CSA over bridge.
▲ *16.6 (8.1)*
Bridge. Over bridge KL. Track on right.

▼ 13.2 (8.1)
Minor track on left. CSA.
▲ *8.5 (0.2)*
Minor track on right. CSA.

▼ 13.4 (0.2)
Track junction. TR. SP Major Clews Fire Trail. Track SO SP No through road.
▲ *8.3 (0.3)*
Track junction. TL. Track on right SP No through road.
GPS S:36 17.575 E:148 08.373
UTM Zone 55 0602330E 5982965N

▼ 13.7 (0.3)
Track on right leads short distance to Major Clews Hut and camping area. Notes KL.
▲ *8.0 (0.2)*
Track on left leads short distance to Major Clews Hut and camping area. Notes KR.
Hut – GPS S:36 17.566 E:148 08.576
UTM Zone 55 0602629E 5982968N

▼ 13.9 (0.2)
Cross Back Creek.
▲ *7.8 (7.8)*
Cross Back Creek.

▼ 21.7 (7.8)
T junction with bitumen road. This is the Alpine Way. TL for Khancoban 17km. TR for Geehi 13km, Thredbo and Jindabyne 96km.
▲ *0.0 (0.0)*
Zero trip meter on Alpine Way at junction with SP Major Clews Fire Trail. This is 17km south of Khancoban and 13km north of Geehi. Proceed along Major Clews Fire Trail SP 4 Wheel Drive Dry Weather Road Only.
GPS S:36 18.543 E:148 11.262
UTM Zone 55 0606617E 5981105N

THIS PAGE: *Major Clews Fire Trail near the junction with the Alpine Way.*

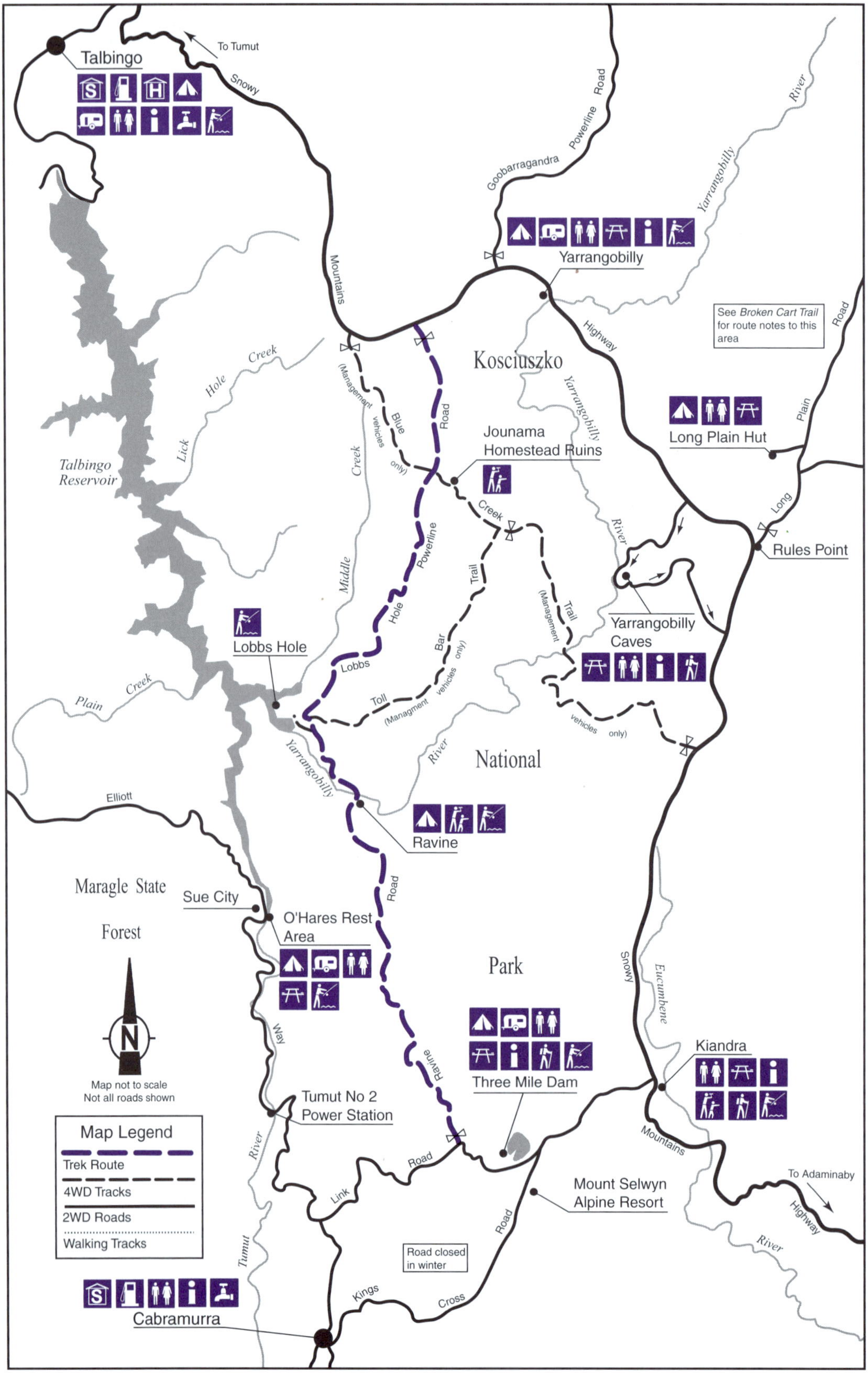
Talbingo
To Tumut
Snowy
Mountains
Highway
Goobarragandra
Powerline
Road
Yarrangobilly
River
Yarrangobilly
See Broken Cart Trail for route notes to this area
Road
Plain
Long
Long Plain Hut
Rules Point
Kosciuszko
Lick
Hole
Creek
Talbingo Reservoir
(Management vehicles only)
Blue
Creek
Road
Jounama Homestead Ruins
Creek
Yarrangobilly
River
Middle
Creek
Powerline
Hole
Lobbs
Trail
Bar
(Managment vehicles only)
Toll
Trail
(Management vehicles only)
Yarrangobilly Caves
Lobbs Hole
Plain
Creek
Yarrangobilly
River
National
Ravine
Elliott
Maragle State Forest
Sue City
O'Hares Rest Area
Road
Way
Park
Snowy
Eucumbene
Map not to scale
Not all roads shown
Three Mile Dam
Kiandra
Ravine
Tumut No 2 Power Station
Mountains
To Adaminaby
Highway
Map Legend
Trek Route
4WD Tracks
2WD Roads
Walking Tracks
River
Road
Link
Road
Mount Selwyn Alpine Resort
River
Tumut
Road closed in winter
Kings
Cross
Cabramurra

TREK EIGHTEEN

RAVINE - HIDDEN VALLEY

When gold was discovered in the Kiandra region in 1859 the population of surrounding areas swelled with the arrival of many 'hopefuls' in search of their fortune. At this time the major route to Kiandra passed through an area known as Lobbs Hole, which before long became a stopover point for travellers venturing to the harsh Kiandra fields.

However, with the onset of the snow and blizzards of winter, many miners chose the sheltered valley of Lobbs Hole as a winter settlement to avoid the extreme weather found higher up the mountains, giving a one time permanency to this now deserted valley .

Copper mining and smelting was also carried out in the Lobbs Hole area from the 1890s to the 1920s. The town's name was changed to Ravine in 1910 when at the time it was well populated with a police station, several boarding houses, shops and a twelve bedroom hotel. However, its boom time was short lived with the demise of this hidden valley coming during the 1920s when the price of copper fell and the mines flooded.

Things to Do and See

As mining was at the forefront of the area's growth there are plenty of old mine ruins to inspect. At Kiandra there is the self guided Kiandra Heritage Trail that will take you on a journey of the town's past. Down in the valley at Ravine there are mullock heaps, mine shafts and ruins of the old copper mining equipment scattered beside the Yarrangobilly River. The ruins of the Washington Hotel, built in 1909 and made from rammed earth are also still visible.

Both Three Mile Dam and the Yarrangobilly River are popular trout fishing spots. You can also walk the cross-country ski trails that lead from Three Mile Dam.

In summer enjoy a swim in one of the many holes in the Yarrangobilly River at Ravine.

Explore the ruins of Jounama Homestead—once a splendid building and the venue for many social events, dances and fundraising functions during the 1940s and 1950s.

Whilst in the area visit Tumut No. 2 Power Station—an underground power station and part of the Snowy Mountains Hydro Scheme. There are guided tours of the facility. Ph 1800 623 776 for further information.

Another attraction is a visit to Yarrangobilly Caves and Hot Springs, situated just off the Snowy Mountain Highway north of Kiandra. Here you can take a self guided tour through the Glory Cave or join a guided tour through one of the other caves in the system. Also, take a dip in the hot thermal spring in the caves reserve. Phone 02/6454 9597 for details.

fast facts

Three Mile Dam to the Snowy Mountains Highway via Ravine

Trek distance: 42km

Standard: Easy

Fuel and supplies: Adaminaby/ Cabramurra and Talbingo

Trek highlights: Three Mile Dam, Ravine town site, Yarrangobilly River, Jounama Homestead ruins

Track conditions:
NPWS Tumut
Ph 02/6947 7000

Access

Three Mile Dam is the start point for this trek and is accessible via the bitumen Kiandra - Cabramurra Road, 6km west of Kiandra on the Snowy Mountains Highway and 14km east of Cabramurra.

The Trek

Leaving Three Mile Dam our route heads west towards Cabramurra before turning south onto the signposted Lobbs Hole - Ravine Road. This gravel road, which is well maintained, winds its way down to the Yarrangobilly River at Ravine.

Once at Ravine there are numerous tracks leading to old mine sites and riverside camping areas that you might like to explore.

From Ravine the route crosses the Yarrangobilly River to pick up the Lobbs Hole Powerline Road. This track winds its way up to the top of the ridge where you get views over the top end of Talbingo Reservoir. This track is generally in fair condition although some sections are narrow and at times potholed.

Once on top of the ridge the track evens out and after detouring the short distance to visit the ruins of Jounama Homestead is an easy drive to the finish of the trek on the Snowy Mountains Highway.

Standard

This trek is rated as easy. The route traversed throughout this trip generally follows well maintained gravel roads although some sections may become slippery after rain.

The only difficulty that may be encountered is the Yarrangobilly River crossing at Ravine. It is wise to check the depth of the river and look for any possible obstructions before crossing here. During high water this crossing is impassable.

THINGS TO DO AND SEE

Three Mile Dam

Located on the northern side of Mt Selwyn and just off the Cabramurra - Kiandra Road, the picturesque Three Mile Dam is a haven in this section of Kosciuszko National Park. Fringed by snow gums, the dam was originally built in 1882 by Chinese gold miners to provide water for sluicing operations at New Chum Hill near Kiandra.

Apart from the dam's role in the areas early mining operations, it also served as a base camp during the 1950s for the Snowy Mountains Hydro-electric Authority workers.

Nowadays, Three Mile Dam is a popular destination and enjoyed by trout fisherfolk; either angling from the dam's shore or whilst paddling around in a canoe, campers who can find numerous sites around the dam's foreshore, walkers and in winter, cross-country skiers.

The main camping and picnic area has facilities including pit toilets, picnic tables and fireplaces and access is signposted from the Cabramurra - Kiandra Road.

ABOVE: *Three Mile Dam*

ABOVE: *Crumbling ruins of 'The Washington' Hotel at Ravine.*

Camping

There are some delightful spots beside Three Mile Dam and facilities here include tables, fireplaces and pit toilets.

At Ravine there a number of bush camp sites available, however you may need to spend some time following the many tracks until you find that 'perfect' spot. There are no facilities here.

You can also camp at Yarrangobilly Village on the Snowy Mountains Highway. Here you will find excellent grassy spots beside the Yarrangobilly River. Facilities include toilets, fireplaces and tables.

Permits/Restrictions

This trek is not affected by seasonal closures, although the Kiandra - Cabramurra Road is sometimes closed during the winter months due to snow coverage. However, it is not recommended as a winter journey and is best undertaken during the warmer months.

Recommended Maps/Guides

The CMA Tourist Map *The Snowy Mountains* shows this route, as does the CMA *The Snowy Mountains Tourist Atlas.*

Topographic maps for this trek are the *Cabramurra*, *Ravine* and *Yarrangobilly* 1:25 000 series.

Further Information

National Parks and Wildlife Service
7 Adelong Road, Tumut NSW 2720 Ph 02/6947 7000 Fax 02/6947 4170

Snowy Region Visitors Centre
Kosciuszko Road, Jindabyne Ph 02/6450 5600

Tumut Regional Visitor Information Centre
5 Adelong Road, Tumut Ph 02/6947 7025

Brochures - Kosciuszko National Park: *Yarrangobilly Caves*

Trek commences at Three Mile Dam Rest Area on the Kiandra-Cabramurra Road

▼ 0.0 (0.0)
Zero trip meter at SP Three Mile Dam Rest Area on the Kiandra-Cabramurra Road. This is 6km west of Kiandra on the Snowy Mountains Highway and 14km east of Cabramurra. Proceed in a westerly direction towards Cabramurra.

▲ *41.8 (2.5)*
SP Three Mile Dam Rest Area on left. Good camping here. Road SO leads 6km to Kiandra on Snowy Mountains Highway.
GPS S:35 53.494 E:148 26.891
UTM Zone 55 0630705E 6027109N

▼ 2.5 (2.5)
Road junction. TR onto gravel. SP Ravine 15. This is SP Lobbs Hole Ravine Road.

▲ *39.3 (7.5)*
Road junction with bitumen. This is the Kiandra-Cabramurra Road. TR for Cabramurra 12km. Notes TL.
GPS S:35 53.127 E:148 25.778
UTM Zone 55 0629042E 6027809N

▼ 10.0 (7.5)
Track junction. TR. Track on left is a SMA road.

▲ *31.8 (7.4)*
Track junction. TL uphill. Track on right is a SMA road.

▼ 17.4 (7.4)
Track junction. TL. Track SO leads to old mining sites and ruins. Camp sites beside the river with good swimming holes.

▲ *24.4 (0.1)*
Track junction. TR heading uphill. Track on left to old mining area.
GPS S:35 47.470 E:148 23.908
UTM Zone 55 0626374E 6038310N

▼ 17.5 (0.1)
Track junction. TL. Track on right to camp sites.

▲ *24.3 (0.9)*
Track junction. TR. Track on left to camp sites.

▼ 18.4 (0.9)
Minor tracks on right lead to ruins of the Washington Hotel - built 1909 by mine owner Julius Forsstrom. The walls are made of pise (rammed earth). Track on left leads short distance to small camp site. Notes CSA on main track.

▲ *23.4 (0.2)*
Ruins of the Washington Hotel on left. CSA.
GPS S:35 47.141 E:148 23.597
UTM Zone 55 0625916E 6038927N

▼ 18.5 (0.1)
KL and cross Yarrangobilly River. Track SO leads to camp site. *NB:* When crossing river ruins of a bridge can be seen downstream.

▲ *23.2 (1.9)*
KL and cross Yarrangobilly River. Over river KR. Track on left to camp site.
GPS S:35 47.102 E:148 23.571
UTM Zone 55 0625877E 6038998N

▼ 20.5 (2.0)
Track on left. KR uphill.

▲ *21.3 (0.4)*
Track on right. KL downhill.

▼ 20.9 (0.4)
Track junction. KR. Keeping power pylon on left.

▲ *20.9 (1.5)*
Track junction. TL.

▼ 22.4 (1.5)
Tollbar Trail on right. SP Management Trail – Authorised Vehicles Only. KL.

▲ *19.4 (5.0)*
Tollbar Trail on left. CSA.

▼ 27.4 (5.0)
Track on left. CSA.

▲ *14.4 (9.4)*
Track on right. KL.

▼ 36.8 (9.4)
SP Blue Ck Fire Trail on left, this is a management only trail. CSA.

▲ *5.0 (0.2)*
SP Blue Ck Fire Trail on right, management only trail. CSA.

▼ 37.0 (0.2)
SP Blue Ck Fire Trail on right. Notes CSA.
▲ *4.8 (3.0)*
SP Blue Ck Fire Trail on left. VR.
GPS S:35 41.948 E:148 25 479
UTM Zone 55 0628886E 6048481N

Jounama Homestead Ruins Detour

Turn into SP Blue Ck Fire Trail.

▼ (1.0)
CSA. SP Yans Crossing Fire Trail. Track on right SP Blue Ck Fire Trail.

▼ (0.3)
SP Jounama Homestead Ruins.
GPS S:35 42.258 E:148 26 013
UTM Zone 55 0629686E 6047901N

▼ 40.0 (3.0)
Site of old homestead on right. CSA.
▲ *1.8 (1.8)*
Site of old homestead on left. CSA.

▼ 41.8 (1.8)
Junction with bitumen road. This is the Snowy Mountains Highway. TL for Talbingo. TR for Yarrangobilly 5km and Cooma 123km.
▲ *0.0 (0.0)*
Zero trip meter at junction of Snowy Mountains Highway with SP Lobbs Hole Ravine Road. Proceed through fence into Kosciuszko National Park. This is 5km north of Yarrangobilly and 20km south of Talbingo.
GPS S:35 39.547 E:148 25.096
UTM Zone 55 0628374E 6052932N

ABOVE: *This disused mine shaft at Ravine is a reminder of the areas once prosperous past.*

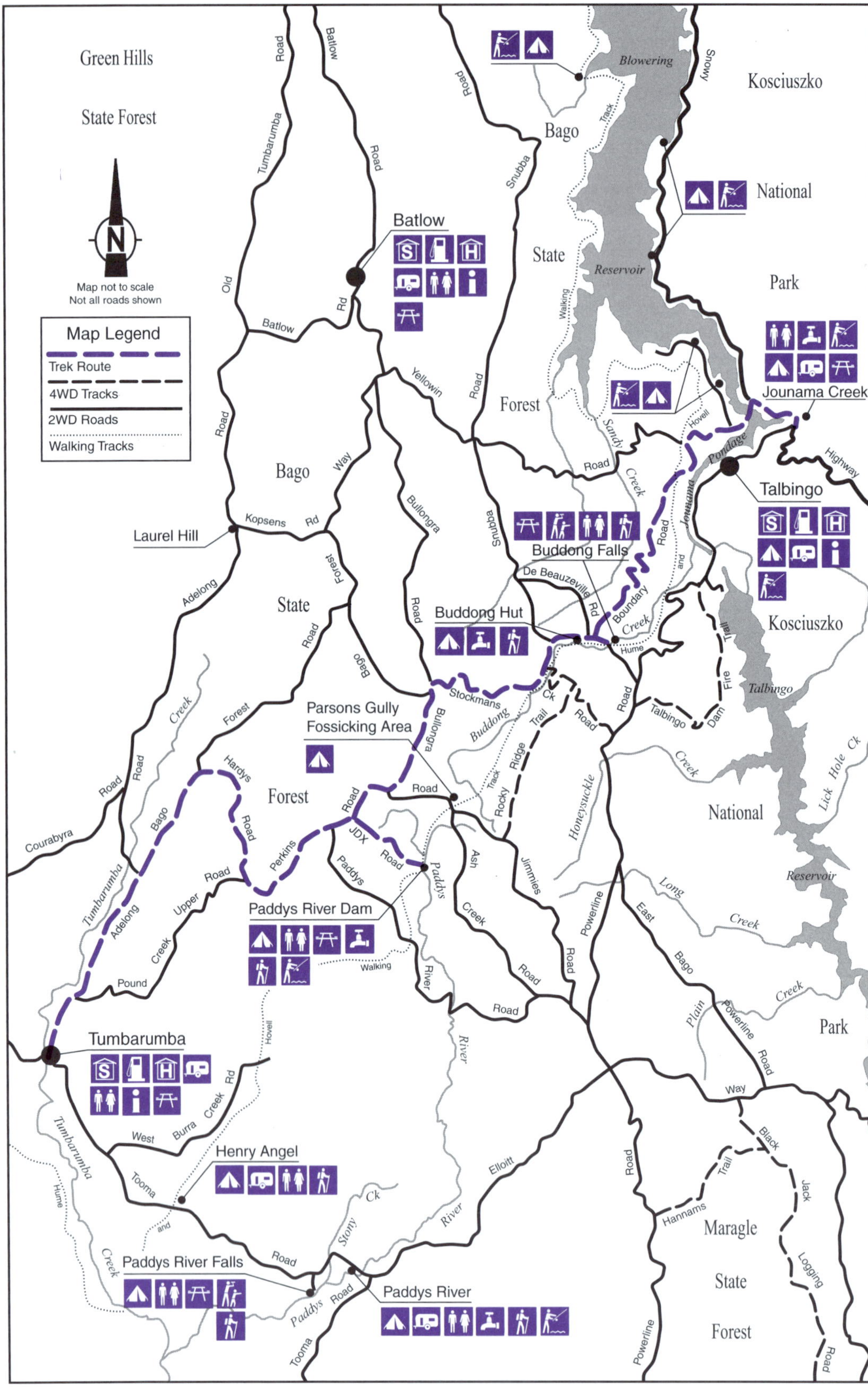
Green Hills
State Forest
N
Map not to scale
Not all roads shown
Map Legend
Trek Route
4WD Tracks
2WD Roads
Walking Tracks
Batlow
Laurel Hill
Bago
State
Forest
Kosciuszko
National
Park
Blowering
Reservoir
Jounama Creek
Talbingo
Buddong Falls
Buddong Hut
Parsons Gully
Fossicking Area
Paddys River Dam
Tumbarumba
Henry Angel
Paddys River Falls
Paddys River
Maragle
State
Forest
Talbingo
Reservoir
Batlow Road
Tumbarumba Road
Old Road
Batlow Rd
Snubba Road
Yellowin Road
Bago Way
Kopsens Rd
Adelong
Forest Road
Bullongra Road
Snubba
De Beauzeville Rd
Jounama Road
Hovell and Boundary Creek
Pondage
Highway
Hume
Stockmans
Buddong Ck
Rocky Ridge Track Trail
Road
Bago Forest Road
Hardys Road
Perkins Road
JDX Road
Paddys River
Ash Creek Road
Jimmies Road
Honeysuckle
Powerline Road
East Bago Plain Powerline Road
Talbingo Dam Fire Trail
Creek
Lick Hole Ck
Long Creek
Courabyra Road
Bago Road
Tumbarumba
Adelong Upper Creek Road
Pound Creek
Walking
Hovell
West Burra Creek Rd
Tooma Road
Hume and Hovell
Tumbarumba Creek
Elliott River Way
Stony Ck
Paddys Road
Tooma
Hannams Trail
Black Jack Logging Road
Powerline
Way

TREK NINETEEN

BEST OF BAGO

THE EXPLORERS HAMILTON Hume and William Hovell were the first Europeans to visit this area back in 1824-25 during their epic expedition in which they pioneered an overland route from Sydney to Port Phillip Bay. The almost impenetrable barrier of the Snowy Mountains kept forcing the explorers to the west on their southbound journey, causing them frustration as they battled their way through valleys and swamps. In early November 1824 the party camped in the vicinity of where the town of Tumbarumba now stands, Hume saying of the magnificent forests as being 'moderately thick but of the very best quality'.

Today, almost 160 years since these courageous adventurers stamped their mark on this area, you too can follow in their footsteps taking in the delightful snow gum woodlands, towering brown barrel forests, gurgling mountain streams and the chance to sight some brumbies in full steam.

Things to Do and See

There is plenty of evidence of times past scattered throughout these forests. Large cleared sites where sawmills once stood now hide rusting equipment and ruins of buildings. There are also man-made dams for gold sluicing and streams where prospectors from all nations once panned for gold and current day fossickers still try their luck.

Buddong Hut, nestled in a small clearing just off Buddong Road is a legacy of stream flow monitoring and was built in the early 1920s to provide accommodation for staff taking the readings on Buddong Creek. The hut was restored in 1986 as part of the Hume and Hovell Walking Track and now provides shelter for intrepid walkers who venture through this area.

fast facts

Tumbarumba to Talbingo via Paddys River Dam and Buddong Falls

Trek distance: 66km

Standard: Easy (Dry weather only)

Fuel and supplies: Tumbarumba and Talbingo

Trek highlights: Paddys River Dam, Buddong Hut, Buddong Falls, Blowering Dam and Jounama Pondage

Track conditions:
State Forests Tumbarumba
Ph 02/6948 2400

State Forests Tumut
Ph 02/6947 3911

At Buddong Falls there is a benched walking track to the viewing area over the upper falls. The walk is a little over a kilometre return but is well worth the effort. You can also continue on the track for a couple of hundred metres to view the larger lower falls. Like most waterfalls the best time to view them is after rain, however Buddong Falls seems to almost always have a reasonable flow of water cascading over the mountainside.

Access

There is signposted access to Tumbarumba via the Elliott Way from the Snowy Mountains Highway at Kiandra and from Tumut via Batlow.

The Trek

Leaving Tumbarumba head out of town towards Batlow where our route picks up the Bago Forest Drive, taking you into the heart of Bago State Forest. Once in the forest turn into the signposted Hardy's Road which after a time becomes Perkins Road. Keep on the main track (Perkins Road) passing a number of tracks running off to both the left and right before the road again becomes Hardy's Road which is followed until its junction with JDX Road.

After taking the short detour along JDX Road to explore or camp at Paddys River Dam, backtrack to Hardy's Road and continue onto a major track junction with Bullongra Road which is then followed, passing Bago Forest Way until the turn to Stockman's Creek Road is reached. This part of the forest is a good brumby spotting area.

Stockman's Creek Road takes you through a number of logging coupes before our route turns into an unnamed track that leads past Buddong Hut then out to De Beauzeville Road, and a short distance latter, after passing Boundary Road arrives at Buddong Falls.

After taking the walking track through the picnic area to view the falls backtrack to the Boundary Road junction and turn into Boundary Road which drops off the mountain down to Jounama Pondage. From this track there are glimpses over Talbingo Reservoir and Tumut No. 3 Power Station, both part of the Snowy Mountains Hydro-electric Scheme.

Once across the dam wall of Jounama Pondage it's only a short run to the end of the trek on the Snowy Mountains Highway near the town of Talbingo.

Standard

This trek is given an easy rating. In the dry it is easy going, however in the wet this would be a different story with most of the tracks becoming very greasy. JDX Road to Paddys River Dam is a dry weather only route.

HISTORY

Brumbies

'Brumby' is the term given to wild horses that roam parts of the High Country and is believed to have originated from James Brumby, a farrier and soldier with the New South Wales Corps. The story goes that when Brumby moved to Tasmania in 1804 he left a small number of horses behind in New South Wales. When people asked who owned the horses, the reply was "they're Brumby's".

Horses have played an important part in Australia's history with the first horses arriving here in 1788. Due to the long sea voyage and arduous conditions only the fittest and strongest survived. These horses were used for farm work, transport and by explorers. It wasn't until about 1810 that thoroughbreds were imported from England when horse racing began in the new colony.

Brumbies are rarely consistent in size or colour and were originally a mix of breeds including draught and thoroughbred horses and domestic mares that escaped and joined feral herds. Horses that escaped due to lack of fencing and those that where abandoned for machinery also joined mobs and became feral.

The resourcefulness of these wild horses is evident during dry weather when they will paw at sandy creek beds until water is available

ABOVE: *There are glimpses over Jounama Pondage from Boundary Road.*

Camping

There is good camping available at Paddys River Dam. This High Country haven, set amongst snow gum and black sallee forest was constructed in 1936 by Eurabbie Power Company when it dammed Paddys River to guarantee a reliable water supply to the powerhouse at Tumbarumba. Facilities here are limited to a picnic table, fireplaces and pit toilet.

There is a small camping area at Buddong Hut as well as a host of sites located on both the western shore (state forest) and eastern shore (national park) of Blowering Dam. Many of these sites have good facilities.

A number of possible bush camp sites are also detailed in the route notes.

Near Talbingo at the conclusion of the trek is Jounama Creek Camping Area which is a pleasant grassed area beside the creek.

Permits/Restrictions

Generally this trek is free of restrictions, however at times heavy snow during winter may make some of the roads and tracks impassable for short periods. During dry, hot summers there is a solid fuel fire ban in Bago State Forest.

Recommended Maps/Guides

The best maps for this trek are the CMA Tourist Map *The Snowy Mountains* and the CMA *The Snowy Mountains Tourist Atlas*.

Topographic maps for this trek are the *Courabyra*, *Batlow* and *Talbingo* 1:25 000 series.

Further Information

State Forests of New South Wales
Winton St, Tumbarumba NSW 2653 Ph 02/6948 2400 Fax 02/6948 2773

State Forests of New South Wales
76 Capper St, Tumut NSW 2720 Ph 02/6947 3911 Fax 02/6947 2865

National Parks and Wildlife Service
7 Adelong Road, Tumut NSW 2720 Ph 02/6947 7000 Fax 02/6947 4170

ROUTE NOTES

Trek commences in the town of Tumbarumba.

▼ 0.0 (0.0)
Zero trip meter on SP The Parade in Tumbarumba at intersection with the Wagga Wagga Road (SP Albury Street). PSA through town centre in northerly direction towards Batlow/Tumut. This junction is opposite the Union Hotel.

▲ *24.6 (7.8)*
Tumbarumba. Wagga Wagga Rd on right. Union Hotel on left.

GPS S:35 46.605 E:148 00.588
UTM Zone 55 0591264E 6040344N

▼ 7.8 (7.8)
Road junction. TR. SP Bago Forest Rd.

▲ *16.8 (4.7)*
Road junction. This is the Tumbarumba-Tumut Road. TL.

GPS S:35 43.015 E:148 02.889
UTM Zone 55 0594807E 6046942N

▼ 12.5 (4.7)
Grid. Enter SP Bago State Forest Sanctury. CSA to road junction. At junction TR SP Hardys Rd. Road on left SP Shedley's Rd.

▲ *12.1 (0.9)*
Road junction. TL and cross grid exiting Bago State Forest. Road SO SP Shedley's Rd.

GPS S:35 40.893 E:148 04.526
UTM Zone 55 0597313E 6050837N

▼ 13.4 (0.9)
Tracks on left. CSA.

▲ *11.2 (0.1)*
Tracks on right. CSA.

▼ 13.5 (0.1)
Track on right leads to site of old sawmill. Notes CSA.

▲ *11.1 (0.6)*
Track on left. CSA.

▼ 14.1 (0.6)
Track on left. KR.

▲ *10.5 (0.3)*
Track on right. CSA.

▼ 14.4 (0.3)
Track on left. CSA. SP Perkins Rd. Dry Weather Only.

▲ *10.2 (2.6)*
Track on right. CSA.

▼ 17.0 (2.6)
Minor track on right. CSA.

▲ *7.6 (0.6)*
Minor track on left. CSA.

▼ 17.6 (0.6)
Track junction. CSA. Track on left SP Scotchmans Creek Road.

▲ *7.0 (0.6)*
SP Scotchmans Creek Road on right. CSA.

▼ 18.2 (0.6)
Track on right. KL uphill. SP Bannons Rd.

▲ *6.4 (0.6)*
SP Bannons Rd on left. CSA.

▼ 18.8 (0.6)
Track on right. CSA. SP Hardys Rd.

▲ *5.8 (1.0)*
Y junction. KR.

GPS S:35 43.183 E:148 05.679
UTM Zone 55 0598984E 6046739N

▼ 19.8 (1.0)
Track junction. KL. Track on right SP Lookout Logging Rd.

▲ *4.8 (1.1)*
SP Lookout Logging Rd on left. KR.

▼ 20.9 (1.1)
Track junction. CSA. Track on right SP Steam Winch Road.

▲ *3.7 (0.7)*
SP Steam Winch Road on left. CSA.

▼ 21.6 (0.7)
Track junction. CSA. Track on right SP East Burra Ck Fire Rd.

▲ *3.0 (0.9)*
SP East Burra Ck Fire Rd on left. KR.

▼ 22.5 (0.9)
Sign on left. CSA. SP Hardys Rd.

▲ *2.1 (0.5)*
Sign on right. CSA. SP Perkins Rd.

▼ 23.0 (0.5)
Minor track on left. CSA.

▲ *1.6 (0.3)*
Minor track on right. CSA.

▼ 23.3 (0.3)
Track junction. CSA. Track on left SP Toppins Rd.
▲ *1.3 (0.4)*
SP Toppins Rd on right. KL.

▼ 23.7 (0.4)
Track junction. CSA. Track on right SP Paddy's River Rd.
▲ *0.9 (0.4)*
SP Paddy's River Rd on left. CSA.

▼ 24.1 (0.4)
Track junction. CSA. Track on left SP Quartsville Rd.
▲ *0.5 (0.5)*
SP Quartsville Rd on right. CSA.

▼ 24.6 (0.5)
Track junction. TR. SP JDX Rd. SP Paddy's River Dam.
▲ *0.0 (0.0)*
JDX Road junction. Zero trip meter and TL.
GPS S:35 41.840 E:148 08.409
UTM Zone 55 0603151E 6049023N

▼ 26.1 (1.5)
Track junction. KL. SP Paddy's River Dam.
▲ *21.8 (0.3)*
Paddys River Dam and camping area. Return to JDX Road junction at 17.9km and zero trip meter.

▼ 27.0 (0.9)
Creek crossing.
▲ *21.5 (0.2)*
Tracks on left to camp sites. KR.

▼ 28.0 (1.0)
SP Paddy's River Flora Reserve. CSA.
▲ *21.3 (1.0)*
SP Paddys River Flora Reserve. CSA.

▼ 28.2 (0.2)
Tracks on left to camp sites. KR.
▲ *20.3 (0.9)*
Creek crossing.

▼ 28.5 (0.3)
Paddy's River Dam and camping area.
GPS S:35 42.906 E:148 10.040
UTM Zone 55 0605590E 6047022N
Return to JDX Road junction at 24.6km and zero trip meter.

ABOVE: *Remains of an old sawmill in Bago State Forest.*

▲ *19.4 (1.5)*
Track junction. KL. SP Paddy's River Dam.

▼ 0.0 (0.0)
JDX Road junction. Zero trip meter and TR.
▲ *17.9 (1.6)*
Track junction. TL. SP JDX Road. SP Paddy's River Dam.

▼ 1.6 (1.6)
Road junction. TR. Track on left SP Back Creek Rd.
▲ *16.3 (0.5)*
Road junction. TL. SP Hardys Rd. SP Paddy's River Dam. Road SO SP Back Creek Rd.

▼ 2.1 (0.5)
Road junction. TL. SP Batlow. This is Bullongra Road. Road on right leads 2.5km to Parsons Gully fossicking area.
▲ *15.8 (1.9)*
Road junction. TR. SP Hardys Rd. SP Paddy's River Dam.
GPS S:35 41.380 E:148 09.235
UTM Zone 55 0604410E 6049859N

▼ 4.0 (1.9)
Road junction. CSA. Track on left SP Shortcut Road.
▲ *13.9 (1.6)*
SP Shortcut Road on right. CSA.

▼ 5.6 (1.6)
Track junction. CSA. Track on right SP Fishing Track.
▲ *12.3 (0.3)*
SP Fishing Track on left. CSA.

▼ 5.9 (0.3)
Track junction. KR. SP Bullongra Road. Road on left SP Hydes Old Road. SP Batlow. SP Bago Forest Way.
▲ *12.0 (0.4)*
Track junction. CSA. SP Bullongra Road. SP Paddy's River Dam. Road on right SP Batlow.
GPS S:35 39.561 E:148 10.364
UTM Zone 55 0606146E 6053201N

▼ 6.3 (0.4)
Possible bush camp site on left. Old sawmill site on right. Notes CSA.
▲ *11.6 (0.1)*
Old sawmill site on left. Possible bush camp site on right. Notes CSA.

▼ 6.4 (0.1)
Track junction. TR. SP Stockmans Ck Rd.
▲ *11.5 (0.5)*
Track junction. TL. This is Bullongra Road.

▼ 6.9 (0.5)
Track on left. CSA.
▲ *11.0 (0.1)*
Track on right. CSA.

▼ 7.0 (0.1)
Track on left. CSA.
▲ *10.9 (0.7)*
Track on right. CSA.

▼ 7.7 (0.7)
Track junction. TR.
▲ *10.2 (0.8)*
Track junction. KL.

▼ 8.5 (0.8)
Track on right. KL.
▲ *9.4 (1.7)*
Track on left. CSA.

▼ 10.2 (1.7)
Track on left. CSA.
▲ *7.7 (2.8)*
Track on right. CSA.

▼ 13.0 (2.8)
Track junction. TL.

OPPOSITE: *Upper Buddong Falls.*

▲ *4.9 (1.4)*
Track junction. TR. SP Stockmans Rd.
GPS S:35 39.365 E:148 12.811
UTM Zone 55 0609847E 6053517N

▼ 14.4 (1.4)
Track junction. CSA. Tracks on left SP Buddong Road.
▲ *3.5 (0.2)*
Tracks on right SP Buddong Road. CSA.

▼ 14.6 (0.2)
Tracks on right lead short distance to Buddong Hut. Notes CSA.
▲ *3.3 (2.7)*
Tracks on left lead to Buddong Hut. Notes CSA.
GPS S:35 38.596 E:148 13.158
UTM Zone 55 0610391E 6054935N

▼ 17.3 (2.7)
Track junction. TR. SP Buddong Falls.
▲ *0.6 (0.2)*
Track junction. TL. SP Buddong Road.
GPS S:35 38.361 E:148 14.466
UTM Zone 55 0612367E 6055339N

▼ 17.5 (0.2)
Track junction. CSA. SP Buddong Falls. Road on left SP Boundary Rd.
▲ *0.4 (0.4)*
Track junction. CSA. SP Batlow. SP Boundary Rd on right.

▼ 17.9 (0.4)
Buddong Falls. Picnic area and walk to scenic falls. Zero trip meter at falls car park.
▲ *0.0 (0.0)*
Buddong Falls car park. Return way you came.
GPS S:35 38.570 E:148 14.743
UTM Zone 55 0612782E 6054954N

▼ 0.0 (0.0)
Buddong Falls car park. Return way you came.
▲ *15.8 (0.4)*
Buddong Falls. Picnic area and walk to scenic falls. Zero trip meter at falls car park.

▼ 0.4 (0.4)
Track junction. TR. SP Boundary Rd.
▲ *15.4 (6.5)*
Track junction. TL. SP Buddong Falls.

ABOVE: *Camp site at Paddy's River Dam.*

▼ 6.9 (6.5)
Track on left. KR downhill.

▲ *8.9 (0.9)*
Track on right. CSA.

▼ 7.8 (0.9)
Track on left. CSA.

▲ *8.0 (1.4)*
Track on right. CSA.

▼ 9.2 (1.4)
Track on right to possible bush camp site beside dam. Notes CSA.

▲ *6.6 (3.5)*
Track on left to possible bush camp site. CSA.

▼ 12.7 (3.5)
Track junction. TR. This is Yellowin Rd.

▲ *3.1 (0.4)*
Track junction. TL onto lower track.

▼ 13.1 (0.4)
Track junction. TR and cross Jounama Dam Wall. Track on left leads to SP Jounama Camping Area 2.5km.

▲ *2.7 (1.1)*
Track junction. TL. This is Yellowin Road. Track SO SP Jounama Camping Area 2.5km.
GPS S:35 33.931 E:148 18.312
UTM Zone 55 0618282E 6063457N

▼ 14.2 (1.1)
Road junction. This is the Snowy Mountains Highway. TL for Tumut. Notes TR.

▲ *1.6 (1.6)*
Road junction. TL and cross Jounama Dam Wall. SP 1 Jounama Dam. SP 27 Batlow.

▼ 15.8 (1.6)
Intersection of Snowy Mountains Highway and SP Murray Jackson Drive on right. Leads to SP 3 Talbingo. SP Jounama Creek Camping Area on left.

▲ *0.0 (0.0)*
Zero trip meter at junction of Snowy Mountains Highway and SP Murray Jackson Drive to Talbingo. Proceed in a northerly direction on the Snowy Mountains Highway towards SP Tumut.
GPS S:35 34.061 E:148 19.565
UTM Zone 55 0620169E 6063191N

Grab a Map
and see the
best spots in
New South Wales..
The Snowy Mountains Tourist Atlas
MOUNT KOSCIUSKO
TUMUT
The Sydney Map Shop
Lands Building
23 Bridge Street Sydney 2000
Phone: 9228 6315 Fax: 9221 5980
OR
The Bathurst Map Shop
Panorama Avenue Bathurst 2795
Phone: 6332 8200 Fax: 6331 8095
www.lpi.nsw.gov.au
lpi nsw
Land and Property Information

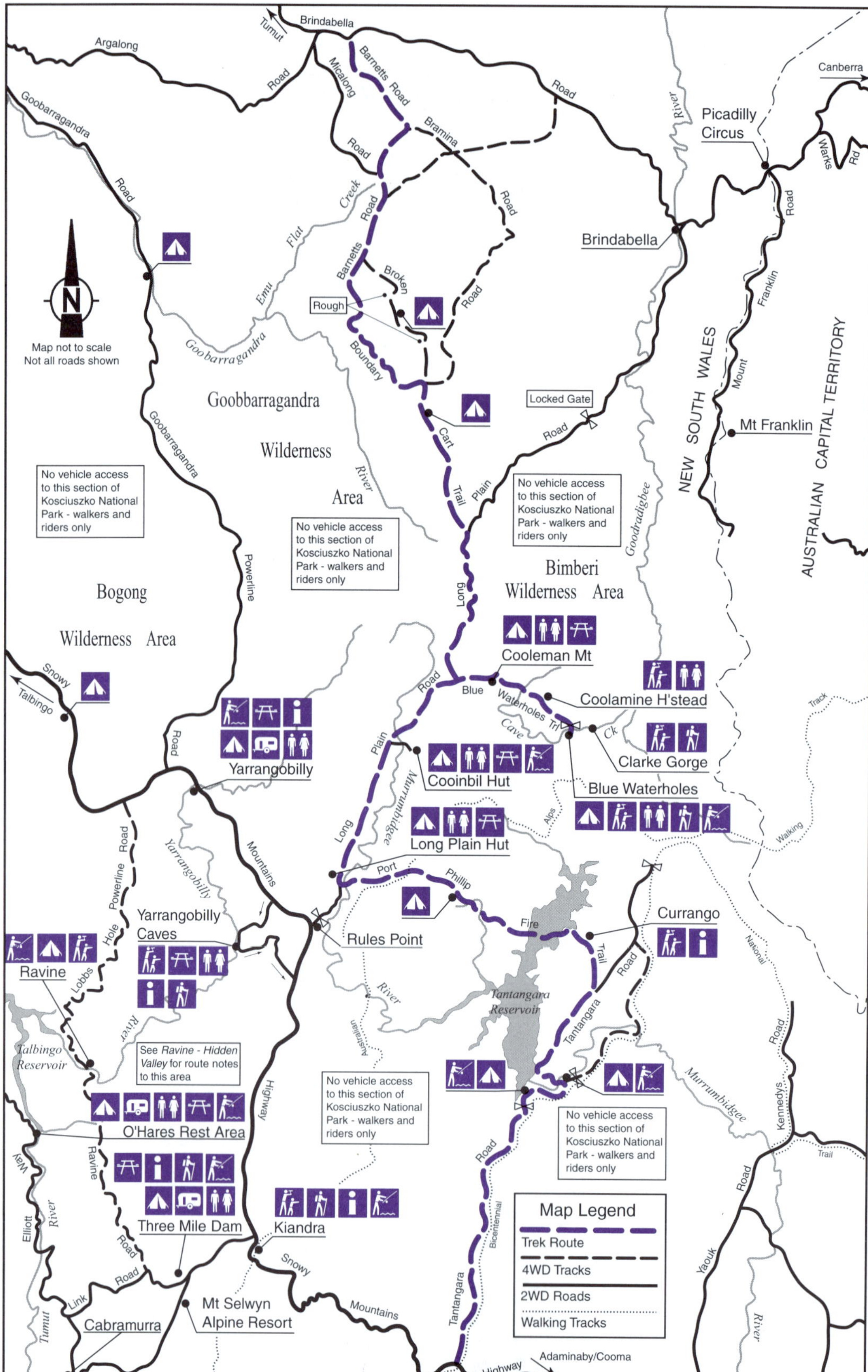

Brindabella
Tumut
Argalong
Road
Goobarragandra
Road
Micalong
Road
Barnetts Road
Bramina
Road
Road
Canberra
Picadilly Circus
River
Warks Rd
Road
Brindabella
Emu Flat Creek
Barnetts
Broken
Road
Rough
Boundary
Goobarragandra
Map not to scale
Not all roads shown
Franklin
Goobbarragandra Wilderness Area
Locked Gate
Road
Cart Trail
Plain
Mount
Mt Franklin
NEW SOUTH WALES
AUSTRALIAN CAPITAL TERRITORY
Goobarragandra
River
No vehicle access to this section of Kosciuszko National Park - walkers and riders only
No vehicle access to this section of Kosciuszko National Park - walkers and riders only
No vehicle access to this section of Kosciuszko National Park - walkers and riders only
Goodradigbee
Powerline
Bogong Wilderness Area
Long
Bimberi Wilderness Area
Cooleman Mt
Snowy
Talbingo
Road
Blue Waterholes Trl
Coolamine H'stead
Cave Ck
Clarke Gorge
Track
Yarrangobilly
Plain
Cooinbil Hut
Murrumbidgee
Blue Waterholes
Road
Long Plain Hut
Alps
Walking
Powerline Road
Yarrangobilly
Mountains
Long
Port Phillip
Fire
Trail
Currango
Yarrangobilly Caves
Lobbs Hole
Rules Point
Ravine
River
National
Road
Tantangara Reservoir
Tantangara
Talbingo Reservoir
River
Australian
See Ravine - Hidden Valley for route notes to this area
Highway
No vehicle access to this section of Kosciuszko National Park - walkers and riders only
Murrumbidgee
O'Hares Rest Area
Road
No vehicle access to this section of Kosciuszko National Park - walkers and riders only
Kennedys
Road
Way
Ravine
Bicentennial
Trail
River
Elliott
Road
Three Mile Dam
Kiandra
Map Legend
Trek Route
4WD Tracks
2WD Roads
Walking Tracks
Road
Road
Snowy
Yaouk
Link
Mt Selwyn Alpine Resort
Mountains
Tantangara
River
Tumut
Cabramurra
Highway
Adaminaby/Cooma

TREK TWENTY

BROKEN CART TRAIL

GRAZIERS FIRST OPENED up the northern area of the New South Wales Alps, which is now part of Kosciuszko National Park, in the 1830s when livestock from the lower slopes and plains were driven up to the snow plains for the summer months. Part of the attraction to graziers to this northern area of the High Country was the large expanse of roughly 700 square kilometres of treeless plains.

Even with the adverse winter weather conditions, some of these grazing leases, such as Currango and Coolamine, were occupied for twelve months of the year. This saw the construction of more substantial homesteads, unlike the cattlemen's huts built by the seasonal graziers. Coolamine Homestead, which is visited on this trek, saw habitation from the 1880s through to the 1940s.

Things to Do and See

Tantangara Dam, which is part of the massive Snowy Mountains Scheme, is the focal point of the initial stage of this trek. It is a popular trout fishing destination, as are most of the streams in the area.

A number of the original graziers huts and homesteads still remain and a few are visited on this trek, including Long Plain Hut, Cooinbil Hut and Coolamine Homestead. The homestead complex at Currango and Coolamine have both been carefully restored and it is worth spending some time looking them over.

At Blue Waterholes you can explore the limestone caves and visit Clarke Gorge. See the *Blue Waterholes* fact box on page 185 for details.

fast facts

Providence Portal to the Tumut - Brindabella Road via Tantangara Dam and Blue Waterholes

Trek distance: 120km

Standard: Easy (Dry weather only)

Fuel and supplies: Adaminaby/Talbingo and Tumut/Canberra Suburbs

Trek highlights: Tantangara Dam, Currango Homestead, Long Plain and various huts, Coolamine Homestead, Blue Waterholes

Track conditions:
NPWS Tumut
Ph 02/6947 7000

State Forests Tumut
Ph 02/6947 3911

Access

The trek commences on the all weather Snowy Mountains Highway at the signposted turn to Tantangara Dam (Tantangara Road), 18km south of Kiandra near Providence Portal.

The Trek

This trek takes you on an interesting run through the northern section of Kosciuszko National Park. From the Snowy Mountains Highway near Providence Portal the route notes travel past Tantangara Dam, which is part of the Snowy Mountains Hydro-electric Scheme and onto Currango Homestead where you pick up the Port Phillip Fire Trail.

Port Phillip Fire Trail runs across the top end of Tantangara Dam and at times may be closed when the water level of the dam is high. It is best to check with the NPWS before your trip, especially in spring after the snow melt.

Port Phillip Fire Trail joins with Long Plain Road, which then crosses Long Plain to Coolamine Mountain and Blue Waterholes. There are short detours to Long Plain Hut and Cooinbil Hut from Long Plain Road.

At the junction of Long Plain Road and Blue Waterholes Trail follow Blue Waterholes Trail, passing Cooleman Mountain Camping Area before arriving at Coolamine Homestead. It's only a short walk to the homestead complex and is worth a look over, giving an insight into life of the High Country pioneers.

Continuing on Blue Waterholes Trail it is only a short distance to the end of the road at Blue Waterholes Picnic and Camping Area. There are many interesting natural features in the Blue Waterholes area and it is well worth a few hours of exploration (see *Blue Waterholes* fact box on page 185).

From Blue Waterholes our route backtracks to the junction with Long Plain Road which is then followed until it meets with Broken Cart Trail. Turn into Broken Cart Trail, passing some bush camp sites until it exits Kosciuszko National Park into state forest at its junction with Boundary Road. Our route then traverses Boundary Road and Barnetts Road before concluding on the Tumut - Brindabella Road.

Standard

This route is rated as easy. Port Phillip Fire Trail is impassable with high water levels in Tantangara Dam and Broken Cart Trail is recommended as a dry weather only trail.

Camping

There are established camp sites with facilities near Long Plain Hut, Cooinbil Hut and Cooleman Mountain. There are also camp sites with limited facilities down near Blue Waterholes.

A number of bush camp sites on Broken Cart Trail and in the state forest area are detailed in the route notes. There are no facilities at these.

Accommodation is also available in a number of cottages at Currango Homestead. Ph 02/6454 2388 for details.

Permits/Restrictions

Tantangara Road, Port Phillip Fire Trail, Long Plain Road and Broken Cart Trail all have seasonal closures placed on them during winter. These closures normally apply from June through to October.

Recommended Maps/Guides

The CMA Tourist Map *The Snowy Mountains* details this route, as does the CMA *The Snowy Mountains Tourist Atlas*.

Topographic maps for this trek are the *Rules Point*, *Peppercorn*, *Brindabella* and *Bobbys Plains* 1:25 000 series maps.

Further Information

National Parks and Wildlife Service
7 Adelong Road, Tumut NSW 2720 Ph 02/6947 7000 Fax 02/6947 4170

State Forests of New South Wales
76 Capper St, Tumut NSW 2720 Ph 02/6947 3911 Fax 02/6947 2865

Tumut Regional Visitor Information Centre
5 Adelong Road, Tumut Ph 02/6947 7025

Snowy Region Visitors Centre
Kosciuszko Road, Jindabyne Ph 02/6450 5600

Blue Waterholes

Blue Waterholes are part of a limestone, or karst, system and are the most accessible permanent water supply on Coolemine Plain. The area is so named after the blue green waters tinted by the calcium and magnesium salts from the limestone. Caves and sinkholes are formed when rainwater seeps through the earth's surface dissolving the limestone with these features being common to this area.

Exploring the Blue Waterholes Area

A number of walking trails of varying length leave from the picnic area at the end of Blue Waterholes Trail.

The *Jennings Walk,* which takes in some of the best features of this karst area commemorates the late Dr Joseph N Jennings who spent 30 years studying Blue Waterholes. He was an active member of the Canberra speleological society which initiated and funded these walks. Limestone features along the way include dry valley, disappearing streams and dolines.

The *Clarke Gorge Walk* follows an unmarked track (which crosses Cave Creek downstream from the picnic area) for around 1½km to provide spectacular views of this gorge along Cave Creek. It is also possible to follow Cave Creek downstream to its junction with the Goodradigbee River.

Day walks in the area can be made to the Goodrabidgee River, Harrisons Hut, Bill Jones Hut and Harris Waterhole—a sinkhole on a tributary of Cave Creek.

ABOVE: *Entrance to Murray Cave on the Jennings Walk*

The Caves

The Coolaman Caves tell us about changes in climate, vegetation and animal life throughout time. New methods for dating sediments and bones and recording past temperatures have helped unfold the story that has been preserved for eons. However, there's still much to learn. Temperatures inside caves are generally warmer than the outside in winter and cooler in summer. This stable cave environment helps to preserve sediments, bones and fossils.

For tens of thousands of years animals have fallen into caves, lived, died and eaten their prey in them. Bones have helped identify many extinct species and ancestors of living animals. Some cave deposits of south-east Australia have found to be 65 million years old.

ABOVE: *Cave Creek*

Caves to Visit

Five caves in the Blue Waterholes Area are open to the public. These are Blue Waterholes Cave, Coolaman One and Two, Barbers and Murray Caves, with Coolaman One and Murray Caves recommended for inexperienced cavers. Each caver should always carry a good torch or flashlight and wear solid, non-slip shoes.

NPWS permission is required to visit other caves in the area.

ROUTE NOTES

Zero trip meter at intersection of Snowy Mountains Highway and SP Tantangara Road.

▼ 0.0 (0.0)
Junction of Snowy Mountains Highway and SP Tantangara Road. Turn into Tantangara Road. SP Tantangara Dam 18.
▲ *60.0 (0.1)*
Junction with bitumen. This is the Snowy Mountains Highway. TL for Adaminaby and Cooma. TR for Kiandra and Tumut.
GPS S:35 55.702 E:148 36.831
UTM Zone 55 0645588E 6022791N

▼ 0.1 (0.1)
Track on left. CSA.
▲ *59.9 (0.7)*
Track on right. CSA.

▼ 0.8 (0.7)
Track on left. CSA.
▲ *59.2 (6.1)*
Track on right. CSA.

▼ 6.9 (6.1)
Track junction. CSA. Track on left SP Wares Yards Horse Camp.
▲ *53.1 (0.6)*
SP Wares Yards Horse Camp on right. CSA.

▼ 7.5 (0.6)
Track junction. CSA. Track on left SP Nungar Creek Fire Trail.
▲ *52.5 (5.7)*
SP Nungar Creek Fire Trail on right. CSA.

▼ 13.2 (5.7)
Track junction. CSA. Track on left SP Tantangara Dam Fire Trail.
▲ *46.8 (2.8)*
SP Tantangara Dam Fire Trail on right. CSA.

▼ 16.0 (2.8)
Track on right. CSA.
▲ *44.0 (0.2)*
Track on left. CSA.

▼ 16.2 (0.2)
Y junction. KR. SP Tantangara Dam. Track on left to camp sites beside dam.
▲ *43.8 (0.6)*
Track on right. CSA.

▼ 16.8 (0.6)
Track on left. CSA.
▲ *43.2 (0.6)*
Track on right. KL.

▼ 17.4 (0.6)
Tantangara Dam Wall. CSA.
▲ *42.6 (0.6)*
Tantangara Dam Wall. CSA.
GPS S:35 47.782 E:148 39.805
UTM Zone 55 0650312E 6037358N

▼ 18.0 (0.6)
Winter Barrier.
▲ *42.0 (0.7)*
Winter Barrier.

▼ 18.7 (0.7)
Bridge over Murrumbidgee River. Over bridge KR SP Pockets Saddle Road.
▲ *41.3 (0.2)*
Bridge.

▼ 18.9 (0.2)
Track on right leads to possible bush camp sites. KL.
▲ *41.1 (8.2)*
Track on left. CSA.

▼ 27.1 (8.2)
Track junction. TL. SP Port Phillip Fire Trail. SP Blue Water Hole. Dry Weather Only. Road SO SP Track Terminates in eight kilometres.
▲ *32.9 (1.3)*
Track junction. TR. SP Pockets Saddle Road.
GPS S:35 44.955 E:148 41.948
UTM Zone 55 0653629E 6042533N

▼ 28.4 (1.3)
Track on left. CSA.
▲ *31.6 (1.0)*
Track on right. CSA.

▼ 29.4 (1.0)
Y junction. VL. SP Port Phillip Fire Trail. Road SO SP Currango leads 300m to Currango Historic Site.
▲ *30.6 (0.5)*
Track junction. TR. SP Port Phillip Fire Trail.

▼ 29.9 (0.5)
Track junction. TL.
▲ *30.1 (0.4)*
Track junction. TR. SP Port Phillip Fire Trail. Road SO leads short distance to Currango Historic Site.

▼ 30.2 (0.3)
Track on right to historic steam engine. Notes CSA.
▲ *29.7 (2.7)*
Track on left to historic steam engine. CSA.

▼ 33.0 (2.8)
Bridge across upper reaches of Tantangara Dam. This is the Murrumbidgee River.
▲ *27.0 (1.9)*
Bridge across upper reaches of Tantangara Dam.
GPS S:35 43.399 E:148 39.931
UTM Zone 55 0650638E 6045460N

▼ 34.9 (1.9)
Track on left. CSA.
▲ *25.1 (6.5)*
Track on right. KL.

▼ 41.4 (6.5)
SP Ghost Gully Horse Camp on left. CSA.
▲ *18.6 (0.1)*
SP Ghost Gully Horse Camp on right. CSA.

▼ 41.5 (0.1)
Track junction. CSA. Track on right SP Mosquito Creek Fire Trail.
▲ *18.5 (4.1)*
SP Mosquito Creek Fire Trail on left. CSA.

▼ 45.6 (4.1)
Bridge. Track on left over bridge to possible bush camp site. Notes CSA.
▲ *14.4 (0.4)*
Track on right to possible bush camp site. Notes CSA over bridge.

▼ 46.0 (0.4)
T intersection. This is Long Plain Road on Long Plain. TR. SP Coolamine Homestead. SP Blue Water Holes. Immediately after turning track on left SP Long Plain Hut Road leads 1km to Long Plain Hut and camping area. Notes CSA on Long Plain Road.

ABOVE: *Cave at Blue Waterholes.*

▲ *14.0 (9.1)*
Track on right SP Long Plain Hut Road leads 1km to hut and camping area. Notes CSA to next junction and TL. SP Port Phillip Fire Trail.
GPS S:35 42.029 E:148 32.811
UTM Zone 55 0639946E 6048168N

▼ 55.1 (9.1)
Cross the Murrumbidgee River.
▲ *4.9 (0.9)*
Cross the Murrumbidgee River.

▼ 56.0 (0.9)
Track junction. CSA. Track on right SP Cooinbil Rd leads 1.1km to Cooinbil Hut and camping area.
▲ *4.0 (4.0)*
SP Cooinbil Rd on left to hut and camping area. Notes CSA.

▼ 60.0 (4.0)
Track junction. TR. SP Coolamine Homestead. SP Blue Water Holes. Zero trip meter here.
▲ *0.0 (0.0)*
Junction with Long Plain Road at 44.1km. Zero trip meter and TL.
GPS S:35 36.024 E:148 36.894
UTM Zone 55 0646285E 6059172N

Blue Waterholes Route Notes

Junction on Long Plain Road. Turn into track SP Coolamine Homestead. SP Blue Water Holes.

▼ (2.6)
SP Cooleman Mountain Camping Area. CSA.

▼ (2.2)
Creek crossing.

▼ (0.7)
Coolamine Homestead on left. CSA. SP Blue Water Holes.
GPS S:35 36.577 E:148 39.772
UTM Zone 55 0650605E 6058076N

▼ (2.8)
Blue Waterholes. Scenic area, camping area and walks. Zero trip meter here and return to junction with Long Plain Road.
GPS S:35 37.452 E:148 41.043
UTM Zone 55 0652502E 6056425N

▼ 0.0 (0.0)
Track junction with Long Plain Road at 60.0km. Zero trip meter and TR.
▲ *44.1 (0.8)*
Track junction. TL. SP Coolamine Homestead. SP Blue Water Holes. Zero trip meter here.

▼ 0.8 (0.8)
Track junction. CSA. Track on left SP Peppercorn Fire Trail. Track on right SP McLeods Spur Fire Trail. *NB:* These are both management only trails.
▲ *43.3 (6.5)*
Track junction. CSA. SP McLeods Spur Fire Trail on left and SP Peppercorn Fire Trail on right. NB: *These are both management only trails.*

▼ 7.3 (6.5)
Track on right. CSA.
▲ *36.8 (1.7)*
Track on left. CSA.

▼ 9.0 (1.7)
Track on right. CSA.
▲ *35.1 (0.7)*
Track on left. CSA.

▼ 9.7 (0.7)
Track junction. TL. SP Broken Cart Fire Trail. Road SO to locked gate.
▲ *34.4 (7.5)*
Track junction. TR. This is Long Plain Road.
GPS S:35 31.836 E:148 37.410
UTM Zone 55 0647190E 6066900N

▼ 17.2 (7.5)
Creek crossing. Possible camping in this vicinity.
▲ *26.9 (0.1)*
Creek crossing.

▼ 17.3 (0.1)
Creek crossing. This is Broken Cart Creek. Directly over creek track on left SP Fients Fire Trail. Notes CSA.
▲ *26.8 (2.1)*
SP Fients Fire Trail on right CSA over Broken Cart Creek. SP Broken Cart Fire Trail.
GPS S:35 28.543 E:148 35.755
UTM Zone 55 0644789E 6073023N

▼ 19.4 (2.1)
Cross roads. TL. This is SP Boundary Road.
▲ *24.7 (7.4)*
Cross roads. TR. SP Broken Cart Fire Trail and enter SP Kosciuszko National Park.
GPS S:35 27 563 E:148 35.914
UTM Zone 55 0645058E 6074837N

▼ 26.8 (7.4)
Bridge over Dubbo Creek.
▲ *17.3 (1.5)*
Bridge over Dubbo Creek.

▼ 28.3 (1.5)
Track junction. TR. This is Barnetts Road.
▲ *15.8 (1.4)*
Track junction. TL. SP Boundary Rd.
GPS S:35 24.693 E:148 33.152
UTM Zone 55 0640969E 6080209N

▼ 29.7 (1.4)
Track on right. CSA.
▲ *14.4 (3.5)*
Track on left. CSA.

▼ 33.2 (3.5)
Cross roads. CSA. SP Barnetts Rd. Track on right SP Powerline Rd.
▲ *10.9 (1.1)*
Cross roads. CSA. SP Barnetts Rd. Track on left SP Powerline Rd.

ABOVE: *Newspapers lining the interior walls of Coolemine Homestead date back to the 1920s.*

▼ 34.3 (1.1)
Track on right. CSA.

▲ *9.8 (0.4)*
Track on left. CSA.

▼ 34.7 (0.4)
Road junction. CSA. SP Barnetts Rd. Road on left SP Micalong Rd. SP Tumut 55km.

▲ *9.4 (3.0)*
Road junction. CSA. SP Barnetts Rd. Road on right SP Micalong Rd.

▼ 37.7 (3.0)
Road junction. TL. SP Barnetts Rd. Road on right SP Bramina Rd.

▲ *6.4 (2.1)*
Road junction. TR. SP Barnetts Rd. Road SO SP Bramina Rd.
GPS S:35 20.295 E:148 35.292
UTM Zone 55 0644333E 6088287N

▼ 39.8 (2.1)
Road junction. CSA through pine forest. Road on right SP Little Oaks Ck Rd.

▲ *4.3 (2.1)*
SP Little Oaks Ck Rd on left. CSA.

▼ 41.9 (2.1)
Road junction. CSA. Road on left SP Gass Link Rd.

▲ *2.2 (0.6)*
SP Gass Link Rd on right. CSA.

▼ 42.5 (0.6)
Road junction. CSA. Road on left SP Gass Creek Rd.

▲ *1.6 (1.6)*
SP Gass Creek Rd on right. CSA.

▼ 44.1 (1.6)
T intersection. This is Brindabella Road. TL for SP 46km Tumut. TR for SP Canberra 77km.

▲ *0.0 (0.0)*
Zero trip meter on Brindabella Road at junction with SP Barnetts Road and SP No 4WD Access Broken Cart Trail Closed June-Oct. Turn into Barnetts Road and PSA.
GPS S:35 17.645 E:148 33.156
UTM Zone 55 0641177E 6093234N

FURTHER READING

The following books will provide additional information on individual aspects of the High Country. It is by no means a complete collection, however the titles that are recommended are a worthwhile addition to your home and travelling library.

A number of these titles are widely available at specialist map shops and at various retailers throughout the High Country. The Octagon Bookshop in Day St, Omeo has one of the best book collections we have come across covering the High Country. Phone 03/5159 1411 for details.

Some of these books may be out of print. Check out your local library or second hand bookshop.

- ***Australian Alps Walking Track – Walhalla to Canberra,*** by John Siseman. Pindari Publications, 1998
- ***Names on the Victorian Alps,*** by Peter Gardner. Ngarak Press, 1991
- ***Names On The Great Alpine Road – between Wangaratta and Omeo,*** by Peter Gardner. Ngarak Press,
- ***Names On The Great Alpine Road – between Omeo and Bairnsdale,*** by Peter Gardner. Ngarak Press,
- ***The Great Alpine Road, Victoria from Harrietville to Omeo, a tourist guide,*** by Fiona Magnussen. 2000.
- ***Huts Of The High Country***, by Klaus Hueneke. Tabletop Press. (Recommended)
- ***People of the Australian High Country,*** by Klaus Hueneke. Tabletop Press. (Recommended)
- ***The History of Wonnangatta Station,*** by Wallace Malcolm Mortimer. WM Mortimer, 1997.
- ***Wonnangatta Station – The Next Twenty Years,*** by Wallace Malcolm Mortimer. WM Mortimer, 1995.
- ***The Wonnangatta Mystery,*** by Keith Leydon and Michael Ray. Warrior Press, 2000. (Recommended)
- ***Ghost Towns of the High Country,*** by Luke Steenhuis. ABC Maps. (Provides an insight into the many gold towns that once existed in the High Country — Highly Recommended)
- ***Ghost Towns of the Mountain Goldfields,*** by Luke Steenhuis. ABC Maps. (Recommended)
- ***The Dogs Grave – An account of droving days in early Gippsland,*** by Flora Johns with O S Green. Stratford and District Historical Society, 1992.
- ***Kosciuszko National Park,*** NSW National Parks and Wildlife Service, 1998.
- ***Australian Alps, Kosciuszko, Alpine and Namadgi National Parks,*** by Deirdre Slattery. UNSW Press, 1998. (Recommended)
- ***Best Bushwalks in Kosciusko National Park,*** by Harry Hill. Kangaroo Press, 1996.
- ***Wild Guide – plants and animals of the Australian Alps,*** by Barbara Cameron-Smith. Envirobook in association with the Australian Alps Liaison Committee, 1999. (An excellent field guide to the plants, animals and climates of the Alps — Highly Recommended)
- ***Ghosts and Gold In The Victorian High Country,*** the story of mining & settlement in Victoria's Historic Alpine Areas, by Rob Christee. High Country Publishing, 1999.
- ***Wildflowers of the Snow Country, a field guide to the Australian Alps,*** by Ian Fraser & Margaret McJannett. Vertego Press, 1998.
- ***The Hume & Hovell Walking Track Guidebook,*** by Harry Hill. Crawford House Press Pty Ltd, 1993.
- ***Cattlemen & Huts of the High Plains,*** by Harry Stephenson. Penguin Books Australia Ltd, 1988.
- ***Victoria's Alpine National Park – A bushwalker's guide,*** by John Siseman. Macstyle Media, 1997.
- ***Explore the Australian Alps – touring guide to the Australian Alps National Parks.*** New Holland Publishers, 1998. (Recommended)
- ***Snowy – the Making of Modern Australia – celebrating 50 years of the Snowy Mountain Hydro Electric Scheme,*** by Brad Collis

USEFUL CONTACTS

Map/Guidebook Retailers

Victoria

Mapland
372 Little Bourke St, Melbourne, 3000
Ph 03/9670 4383 Fax 03/9670 7779
Web: www.mapland.com.au

Melbourne Map Centre
738-740 Waverley Rd, Chadstone 3148
Ph 03/9569 5472 Fax 03/9569 8000

259 High St, Kew, 3101
Ph 03/9853 3526 Fax 03/9853 4888

187-189 Thomas St, Dandenong, 3175
Ph 03/9708 5744 Fax03/9708 5966
Web: www.melbmap.com.au

Mapworks
184 Keilor Rd, Essendon North, 3041
Ph 03/9379 7533 Fax 039379 7532
Web: www.mapworks.com.au

Information Victoria
356 Collins St, Melbourne, 3000
Ph 1300 366 356

New South Wales

Boiling Billy Publications (Mail order)
Ph/Fax 02/6493 8311
Web: www.boilingbilly.com.au
4WD and camping guides and maps

The Sydney Map Shop
Lands Dept Building
23 Bridge St, Sydney, 2000
Ph 02/9228 6315 Fax 02/9221 5980
Web: www.lpi.nsw.gov.au

Planet Maps
452 Princes Hwy, Rockdale, 2216
Ph 02/9567 2256 Fax 02/9567 9900
Web: www.planetmaps.com.au

Map Centre Parramatta
440 Church St, North Parramatta, 2151
Ph/Fax 02/9890 2080
Email: mapcentre@bigpond.com.au

Map World
371 Pitt St, Sydney, 2000
Ph 02/9261 3601 Fax 02/9261 2640

Cnr Willoughby Rd & Albany St,
Crows Nest, 2065
Ph 02/9966 5770 Fax 02/9966 5775

Queensland

World Wide Maps and Guides
Ground Floor, 187 George St,
Brisbane, 4001
Ph 07/3221 4330 Fax 07/3211 3684
Web: www.worldwidemaps.com.au

4WD Accessory Retailers

New South Wales & ACT

4WD Megastores
Ph 02/9622 1000 for your nearest stockist.
Email: 4wdhouse@dot.net.au
Web: www.4wdwarehouse.com.au

ARB 4WD Accessories
Ph 02/9821 3633 for your nearest retailer.
Web: www.arb.com.au

Traction 4
3 McLachlan Ave, Artarmon, 2064
Ph 02/9438 4404 Fax 02/9906 4417

Monaro Off Road
25 Stephens Rd, Queanbeyan, 2620
Ph 02/62976006 Fax 02/92970896

Victoria

ARB 4WD Accessories
Ph 03/9761 6622 for your nearest retailer.
Web: www.arb.com.au

Piranha Off Road Products
Factory 4, 383 Dorset Rd, Boronia, 3155
Ph 03/9762 1200 Fax 03/9762 1400
Web: www.piranahaoffroad.com.au

Queensland

4WD Megastores
Ph 02/9622 1000 for your nearest stockist.

4WD Tyres

Cooper Tires
Freecall 1800 050 060 for your
nearest retailer
Web: www.coopertires.com.au

4WD Driver Training (NSW)

Great Divide Tours
Ph 02/9913 1395 for details
Web: www.greatdividetours.com.au

Global Positioning Systems

Garmin (GME Electrophone)
Phone 02/9844 6666 for your
nearest retailer
Web: www.gme.net.au

Maptrax (Digital Maps)
Ph 07/5526 4992 for details
Web: www.maptrax.com.au

GPS OZ (GPS Accessories)
Web: www.gpsoz.com.au

Country Fire Authority (VIC)

High Country Fire Restrictions

CFA Head Office - Burwood
Ph 03/9262 8444
www.cfa.vic.gov.au

Region 10 - Sale
Ph 03/5144 2933

Region 11 - Bairnsdale
Ph 03/5152 3048

Region 23 - Wangaratta
Ph 03/5721 4122

Region 24 - Wodonga
Ph 02/6056 3022

National Parks General Info

Victoria

Parks Victoria
Ph 131 963
Web: www.parkweb.vic.gov.au

Dept Natural Resources and Environment
Ph 136 186
Web: www.nre.vic.gov.au

New South Wales

NSW National Parks and Wildlife Service
Ph 1300 361 967 or (outside NSW
Ph 02/9253 4600)
Web: www.npws.nsw.gov.au

State Forests of NSW Information Centre
Ph 1300 655 687 or 02/9871 3377
Web: www.forest.nsw.gov.au

Seasonal Track Closures

Victoria

Parks Victoria
Ph 131 963
Web: www.parkweb.vic.gov.au

Treadlightly Victoria
Web: www.treadvic.org.au

New South Wales

NPWS Snowy Region Visitors Centre
Ph 02/6450 5600